CONTACT!

For Richard,
James and Edd

CONTACT!

A Victor Tanker Captain's Experiences in the RAF Before, During and After the Falklands Conflict

BOB TUXFORD

Grub Street • London

Published by
Grub Street
4 Rainham Close
London SW11 6SS

A CIP record for this title is available from the British Library

ISBN-13: 9-781-910690-22-2

Printed and bound by Finidr, Czech Republic

CONTENTS

FOREWORD

Rowland White – Author of *Vulcan 607*

I first wrote to Bob Tuxford back around 2003. At the time, my approach was laced with a certain amount of anxiety. I wanted to write a book about Black Buck 1, the long-range Vulcan bombing raid that opened Britain's account in the campaign to retake the Falkland Islands. There were a handful of people without whom I wasn't sure I could contemplate embarking on the project. One was Marshal of the Royal Air Force Sir Michael Beetham, who had been Chief of the Air Staff during the Falklands War. His blessing, I felt, would underpin the whole exercise. Next, for obvious reasons, was Martin Withers, the captain of the attacking bomber, Vulcan XM607. Alongside Sir Michael and Martin on my short list of names was Bob Tuxford, a Victor tanker captain. From the outset I knew that I wanted the RAF's Victor force and, in particular, the contribution made by Bob and his crew, to be at the heart of the book.

Without the Victor tankers there could have been no Vulcan attack on Stanley airfield. Without the Victors, replacement Harriers could not have been flown to the South Atlantic. Without the Victors, Hercules transports could not have resupplied the Task Force in theatre. Nor could Nimrod maritime patrol aircraft have flown long endurance missions lasting over eighteen hours. The Victors were the foundation upon which the RAF effort was built. Bob Tuxford was flying the 'long slot' Victor that, against the odds, kept Vulcan 607's mission on track. In doing so, Bob and his crew demonstrated extraordinary airmanship, determination and, above all, bravery. Bob's Air Force Cross was well earned that night in 1982.

In agreeing to talk to me Bob also kept my mission to write a book about the Black Buck raid on track, but it turned out that my real reward was in properly getting to know him and his wonderful wife Eileen. My visits to their home for further interviews always promised a warm welcome and excellent company. I looked forward to them.

Through those conversations, I knew that Bob had enjoyed an exceptionally interesting, varied and accomplished career in the RAF. I'd had no idea that he was considering writing about it until he phoned out of the blue to suggest I keep an eye out for the post. The next morning, a self-published edition of the book you're holding now arrived; one, I think, of just twenty-five copies Bob had printed. I dived in and I didn't emerge for hours.

Contact! was chock full of great flying stories. From evocative tales of tanker trails through Masirah and Gan in the Victor K1 to the far east to an exchange tour with the USAF in the late seventies, and from the extraordinary challenge and intensity of the Falklands War to the world renowned Empire Test Pilots' School followed by the introduction of the RAF's Tristar tanker, Bob's book was catnip for anyone like me with an interest in Cold War aviation history. It didn't seem fair that only twenty-five of Bob's friends and family should have the chance to read it and I urged him to try to get published commercially, knowing full well that he should have no anxiety at all about either its quality or potential appeal to readers.

Speaking at an Old Cranwellians dinner at RAF College Cranwell after my own book, *Vulcan 607*, was published, I urged those who were there to share their stories. Their Cold War experiences, I suggested, were as important and fascinating as those of their WWII forebears. I don't think Bob was there that night, but *Contact!* perfectly supports my contention. It's a fantastic read with, at its heart, a brand new perspective on that epic night in 1982 when Bob and his crew ensured that, with Black Buck 1, the RAF once again wrote its name into history.

RW
2016

AUTHOR'S NOTE

It has been said that there is a book in all of us. A few years ago, I would have contested this view. However, since retiring, I have been approached by a number of people on more than a few occasions to write chapters for their books. As I sit in my study and look at the shelves around me and across the hall, I can see seven books written by friends and colleagues from the world of aviation that contain accounts of my own flying experiences, all penned by my own hand.

My father, who was some twenty years senior to my mother, served in both World Wars. He was of a generation that spoke little of his experiences. A particularly accomplished rider at the age of fifteen, he joined the Territorials and served with the 1st/1st North Midland Field Ambulance. Because of his equine skills, he was selected to assist with the commandeering of horses and mules for pulling wagons as the impending hostilities in Europe accelerated. During the Great War, at seventeen years of age, he saw action all over the war zone in Northern France. In the Royal Army Service Corps, he witnessed at first hand the horrific injuries of his comrades and the indescribable suffering across the war-torn battlefields of the Somme. In 1918, he was assigned to the General's Staff as a despatch rider between the lines. During the Second World War, he was directly involved in the early radar direction-finding operations of the Royal Observer Corps, and achieved the rank of wing commander. Looking over the plotting tables in the fighter control room, my father witnessed the terrible punishment that Coventry endured at the hands of the German bombing offensive.

I knew little of my father's service record for many years, apart from a few facts gleaned from family photographs showing his not-inconsiderable riding skills. It was only on visits home during his latter years that I managed to elicit any first-hand recollections of those dark days. Eventually, after some persuasion from my mother, he began to realise that his children were hungry to learn more. His subsequent anecdotal accounts are littered with the most remarkable detail: locations and names of comrades that could not have passed his lips for over half a century. So engrossed did he become in completing this personal perspective of his service life, that he became quite agitated when he thought he might not finish it. The night before he passed away, and in a frail state, he put pen to paper for one last time in an effort to conclude a unique and fascinating personal record.

Moving on a generation, my son Richard and his cousins James and Edd have always taken an interest in my flying career. However, I was surprised to receive an unexpected telephone call around four years ago. Fortified by several pints of beer, Richard and James conveyed to me in slurred tones their combined view that I should write down my flying memories. I was taken aback by the spontaneity of their genuine if inebriated request, and inwardly pleasantly surprised. Reflecting on how much I value my own father's missives, how could I not respond to their touching appeal? Accordingly, and over the last three or four years, I started collating a few highlights from my early squadron tours. About a month before Richard's birthday on 30 December 2014, my wife Eileen came up with the idea of completing the project. With barely two weeks before the Christmas recess, I turned into a hermit at my desk, and set about completing the task. With over fifty years of flying experience, it seemed apposite to limit the scope of the book to my Royal Air Force flying in the vain hope of making the tight deadline. There was little time for proofreading as I presented the rushed manuscript titled 'A Paid Hobby' to a local printer. I am pleased to say I was able to give Richard a copy of the paperback on his 42nd birthday.

The 'hobby' of course refers to flying. Everyone nowadays has access to and is familiar with flying in the world of civil aviation. When I toyed with the idea of becoming an RAF pilot, the piloting profession was regarded as one of the most respected and admired. I did consider and still regard the pilot's vocation as special and privileged. I certainly never tried to take things for granted, and always applied myself to the job in hand with a personal diligence that has stayed with me throughout my career. It is important to me however to mention one particular routine that always went along with my going to work. Eileen was always meticulous in seeing me off in the morning (or last thing at night) before I left the house. She might not necessarily have known that I would be flying that particular day. Irrespectively, I always went to work with a clear head free from any worries at home; I was always appreciative of this, although I might not have openly shown it at the time. I do believe because she had grown up in the RAF environment with her own father an RAF pilot, she understood the value and importance of this act. So many times I have flown with young pilots who have clearly not had their minds on the job, and whose preoccupations clouded their judgement and performance on the day. We tried never to separate with unfinished business or personal dispute in the air, and I was always waved off from the doorstep. This routine was a most important premise to the start of my day in the 'office', and it continued to the end of my flying career. For that I am eternally grateful. Nevertheless, some of the flying incidents related here might come as a complete surprise to Eileen, as I usually chose to protect her from those more eventful and sometimes alarming occurrences. Those less-considerate colleagues who could not wait to spill the beans often scuppered my good intentions. To quote Tom Hanks in *The Green Mile*, I always worked on the adage, 'what happens on the Mile, stays on the Mile'.

What follows is a collection of reminiscences from the time of my earliest interests in aviation. It traces initially my career as a military pilot involved in the particular world of air-to-air refuelling – a role which would feature predominantly throughout my RAF career. After serving tours in both Royal Air Force and United States Air Force refuelling squadrons, I qualified as a flying instructor. Teaching student pilots to fly brought particular rewards and personal job satisfaction. An unexpected return to the Tanker Force in the early 1980s lead to my subsequent involvement in the South Atlantic operations brought on by the Argentine invasion of the Falkland Islands. In the decaying years of the British Empire, this unique campaign perhaps marked the last great ambitious flexing of the muscles of the combined three armed forces. In my case, it opened up the possibility of my attending the RAF's test pilot school. I was most fortunate to conclude my military career as a qualified test pilot, involved with the trials flying of virtually all the RAF's large aircraft. These were interesting times in the aftermath of the Falklands War, and we are unlikely to see such a tri-service campaign again in the light of progressive cuts from ongoing strategic defence reviews.

I chose to leave the RAF, not out of disenchantment, but out of a feeling that I would never achieve such intense job satisfaction again. The thought of being 'grounded' gave me the incentive to embark upon a new career path as a commercial airline pilot. In that way, I could at least ensure that my office would still be above the clouds, where the sun always shines. My hope is that the reader will enjoy some of the unique privileges, thrills and spills that I have been so fortunate to embrace. There is no doubt that my time as a military pilot was enriched during the Cold War era, when the constraints of political correctness and health and safety were yet to smother personal achievement and ambition. I have been incredibly fortunate throughout the last five decades to have been able to pursue and satisfy a lifetime's ambition in the air.

I always knew that writing a book would come at a price. I have never found it easy to put pen to paper, and it usually takes me three or four goes to shape the words and sentences into something that hopefully reads well and even entertains in places. Even then, I have relied heavily on my wife Eileen to proofread my efforts and offer the much-needed constructive criticism. The process resulted in my absence for hours at a time, often day after day, as I immersed myself in the project. Accordingly, I owe Eileen a profuse apology for ignoring her on so many occasions over the last year, but more importantly, offer her my heartfelt thanks and love for her invaluable assistance and encouragement.

PROLOGUE

My Guardian Angel

By 23 October 1982, I had just completed my third detachment during the Falklands War on Ascension Island at Wideawake Auxilliary Airfield. Island fever usually struck after five or six weeks on that remote staging post, and on this occasion, I was more than ready to return to Blighty. I was flying as No. 2 in a pair of Victor tankers. Up ahead was my leader Flt Lt Pete Heath, who was returning after his first spell on the island. Hours earlier, I had refuelled from one of my colleagues to enable the non-stop transit home to RAF Marham, the home of the Tanker Force. Around 400 nm from the south-west approaches, I was cruising at an altitude of 40,000 ft, and holding a loose formation three or four miles astern of my leader and off to one side by a mile or so.

Wideawake I was not after seven hours in the air. At that altitude, the powerful Rolls-Royce Conways seemed to utter little more than a gentle whine in the earphones of my bone dome. I remember looking back into the dimly lit cockpit. The syncopated heavy breathing of my rear crew seemed to blend in perfectly with the drone of the Victor's engines. The fact that the formation leader had the responsibility for keeping our flight on track absolved my two navigators from continuously monitoring our precise position. Hence the reason that both their heads were slumped on the navs' table. To their right-hand side, the aircraft's many independent systems were all displayed at the air electronic officer's station.

The AEO's primary role was to keep an eye on the critical electrics and hydraulics, which were paramount in keeping the Victor in the sky. With all systems behaving themselves perfectly, he was also in a state of semi-consciousness. My co-pilot alongside was clearly taking a snooze, and was away with the fairies. I was aware that I was the only one awake. During these long transits, I had become accustomed to loosening off the lap straps and shoulder straps of my Martin Baker ejection seat. In this way at least, I could shuffle around on the hard seat pan under my backside to restore some circulation to my lower regions. This was not particularly wise whilst strapped to a bang seat, because one would always wish to be able to pull the handle without hesitation should the need arise in the event of an unforeseen emergency.

Just at that moment, I became strangely unsettled, and a feeling of anxiety ran through my body. There was no particular reason for this, given the totally relaxed state of affairs. Although I was at odds with the inexplicable sense of unease, I systematically roused myself and set about tightening all my seat straps. I had no reason whatsoever to disturb my slumbering crew, and so I remained silent. Firmly strapped in once more, I gripped the spectacle of the control column with my right hand, and deliberately placed my left hand over the four throttles. Before I could come up with any logical explanation for my increased state of awareness, or dare I say anticipation, all hell broke loose and the aircraft flew wildly out of control. The nose pitched up quite violently, accompanied by a rapid yawing and rolling motion to the left in a way that a fighter might make an evasive manoeuvre. The difference was that this was a seventy-tonne aircraft that was neither designed nor stressed for such an occurrence.

Incredulously, as if pre-warned with a sense of foreboding, I was strangely ready for the unexpected manoeuvre. As the rudder kicked sideways, I distinctly felt the separation of the airflow as it tumbled off the rear edge of the rudder – characterised by a noticeable tramping motion felt through the rudder pedals. This was something quite alarming, as I had never experienced it in the Victor before. Lesser airframes subjected to such a violent side force have resulted in the complete structural failure and separation of the vertical fin. Within a couple of seconds, the angle of bank had increased to the point where the aircraft was literally standing on its left wing tip. It was at this stage that my crew, almost in unison, spluttered startled expletives along the lines of "what the f***'s going on?" Poised on the controls throughout, I gingerly returned the aircraft to level flight whilst trying not to compound the possibility of structural damage suffered by my overstressed airframe. As some degree of normality returned, my AEO in the rear took stock of things, and reported all hydraulics and electrics were normal. My co-pilot was now eyes wide open and watching me with trepidation. I continued to fly the aircraft manually – the autopilot having tripped out at the onset of the divergence.

My immediate concern was for the integrity of the rear end of the aircraft. The massive tailplane of the Victor was mounted atop the tall vertical stabiliser, or fin. In the development days of the Handley Page Victor, this had proven to be a concern following the loss of more than one development aircraft. Subsequently, the mounting points were strengthened, and the height of the fin reduced by about 18 inches. Throughout the five years of my flying the Mk 1 Victor in the early 1970s, and more recently the Mk 2, I had no reason to doubt the structural integrity of that fine aircraft. However, I had never before experienced the 'fin stalling' or separation of the airflow across the vertical stabiliser.

I called Pete to advise him of my predicament, and asked him to make a turn back and formate on my port side and to the rear at a safe distance. He rejoined me within a few minutes, inspected my airframe, and gave me the thumbs up that all looked OK superficially. I asked him to shadow me so that he could keep an eye on things. Still an hour's flight time to the nearest RAF diversion at St Mawgan in Cornwall, I decided to commence a very gentle descent towards the south-west of England. We discussed the option of landing as soon as possible, although it seemed that the aircraft was functioning perfectly normally by that time. Could it have been just a one-off disturbance caused by a patch of rough air? At that altitude, it was unlikely that we might have encountered the wake from say a passing airliner, as none was reported in the area, let alone cruising at such a high altitude. I was certain that at no time was it possible that I flew through the wake of the Victor ahead of me. There were no unusual cloud or meteorological signs that would indicate the presence of severe clear air turbulence, which might have caused the unwarranted upset. In hindsight after forty years of flying, I can say that I have never encountered such a condition that would account for the exceptional out-of-control situation that we witnessed that day.

The air traffic control authorities were now well aware of our predicament after I had put out a Mayday call on the appropriate frequency. Once we were within R/T reception of our own air defence radar coverage, I established two-way comms and updated our intention to continue towards RAF St Mawgan for the time being. I recall that it was a Saturday afternoon, and the south-western approaches were unusually quiet. Once the airfield was in sight, we had flown for approximately 45 minutes without any untoward activity since the unusual occurrence. As I leveled at an altitude of 10,000 feet, I decided to continue at a safe airspeed toward our base in Norfolk. We were offered a beeline course across the whole expanse of southern England to Marham. Not wishing to change the aircraft's configuration apart from having to lower the gear of course, I elected to perform an unusual flapless landing, which I'm pleased to say was uneventful.

How was it that I had sensed something was amiss just prior to the unexpected in-flight event? I have never believed in the supernatural, or things that go bump in the night. Someone however was certainly looking out for me that day. So I do believe that we all have a guardian angel, and mine certainly earned his or her wings that day!

Chapter One

First Solo

No 1401 Air Training Corps (Alfreton & Ripley) Squadron December 1963 to September 1967

My interest in aviation can be traced back to my earliest years. I was making model aeroplanes long before I was aware of an interest in flying. From the age of about ten, I developed a keen interest in aero modelling. Much of my spare time was spent chasing my hand-launched gliders down the slopes of the fields across the road from our house in Derbyshire. Fine tuning the aerodynamics to achieve the longest glide and repairing the inevitable crash damage was all part of the game. I never tired of the reward and enjoyment of a perfectly executed flight and graceful landing. Control-line powered models followed where the main aim was to chop off the trailing streamer of my opponent's model, while standing shoulder-to-shoulder at the centre of the combat circle. The princely sum of 10 shillings and 6 pence (about 55p) per week earned from my paper round did not enable me to take my hobby to the next level of remote control modelling.

One of my father's treasured books in which I had started to take an avid interest was a rather beaten-up copy of *Britain's Wonderful Air Force*. Its pages were illustrated with exploded views of Spitfires, Mosquitoes and Lancasters: icons of the Second World War. I thrived on the accounts of the tactics employed by the RAF's fighters and bombers, and must have read the whole book from front to back a dozen times. In those days during the early 1960s, the size of the RAF was staggering compared with that of today. The Royal Air Force's prowess and presence was felt across the globe. The book nurtured a life-long passion in the service, and generated a longing to fly.

My first flight came when I was about twelve during one of our perennial holidays to Skegness in Lincolnshire. Encouraged by my older sister Diana, who seemed well aware of my growing fascination in aeroplanes, I climbed aboard an Auster and took to the skies with rather more enthusiasm than fear. Not satisfied with straight and level flight, I was soon asking the pilot to manoeuvre a little more vigorously. Diana's face was a picture as I encouraged the pilot to demonstrate a stall. Needless to say, my thirst was whetted, and my sights were set firmly from that day on becoming a pilot.

I joined No 1401 (Alfreton & Ripley) Air Training Corps Squadron on 12 December 1963 when I was fourteen. During my four years with the ATC, there was never a single month when I failed to attend at least one of the weekly training parades. Before long, I was making day visits to nearby stations. The first of these was to RAF Newton near Nottingham. My memories are of a windswept airfield, only spasmodic flying activity, and iconic Nissen huts heated by wood-burning stoves. I could easily have been discouraged from joining the RAF at this first encounter. However, something about the prospect of getting airborne in a Chipmunk trainer at some stage during the day was sufficient incentive to keep me hanging on. I recall little of those flights, except that my first wish was always to take control just as soon as possible. We shared our excitement after landing with the enthusiasm of fighter pilots in the Battle of Britain! Other experience flights were undertaken at RAF Lindholme and RAF Strubby in the Varsity twin-engine advanced trainer, and at RAF Swinderby in gliders. Needless to say, I never missed the opportunity of attending these flying experience days.

Promotion through corporal to sergeant followed reasonably swiftly, and still only sixteen years old, I was selected for the two-week long gliding course at the No 2 Gliding Centre Swinderby. After a brief period of ground instruction covering the principles of flight, meteorology and so on, I was repeatedly hurtled into the dull overcast skies of Nottinghamshire. My steed was the Slingsby T-31 high-wing glider. The tandem-seat arrangement with the instructor seated behind meant that an archaic Gosport tube was fitted between the cockpits to enable the instructor to bark commands to his student in the front seat. The less than graceful gliding characteristics of this aeroplane gave rise to its nickname: 'The Barge'. Fortuitously, a week later when training continued, I got to fly the superior Sedbergh Mk III in which instruction was made easier with the side-by-side seating arrangement.

Launch was by a cable, drawn in by a powerful winch situated at the far end of the grass airfield. The cable was attached under the nose of the glider by a quick-release shackle. A

Stood next to a Sedbergh Mk III glider RAF Spittalgate – February 1966.

launch height of about 800 ft above ground level (agl) was normal, before the nose had to be lowered and a toggle pulled to release the cable. Immediately, the aircraft would rebound upwards free of the tensioned wire. This had to be followed by a prompt nose-down correction in order to achieve a correct attitude to get the best gliding range. In the cold damp February days on that bleak featureless airfield, there was no opportunity for thermal soaring to extend the flight's duration. The basics of effects of controls were demonstrated and practised on the crosswind and downwind legs. Given the short-duration circuits, there was barely enough time for the instructor to teach all aspects of the approach to, recognition of, and recovery from the stall. Nevertheless, I quickly grasped the salient features of the stall and was able to demonstrate that knowledge to him. The correct height and speed on finals turn was drilled into me as I was instructed to achieve the correct landing point along the grass strip. The ultimate aim was to accomplish three solos after the pre-requisite instruction. After a couple of dozen dual flights, I gingerly took to the air on my first solo on 3 February 1966. An exterior confidence soon gave way to an inner anxiety once the reality sank in of not having my mentor in the adjacent seat. Under the watchful eye of the instructor on the ground, there were to be no heroics on these tentative solos; just a classic circuit pattern and safe return to the landing strip without giving him a heart attack! My three solos totalled about ten minutes in duration and they were over in the blink of an eye. At the end of the fortnight, I was presented with my 'B' Proficiency Flying Badge – my first 'wings'.

The pinnacle of my earliest flying experiences in the ATC came with the award of a flying scholarship in August 1966. At the time, this was a much sought-after course that involved thirty hours of powered flying instruction with the aim of qualifying for the award of the private pilot's licence. My training lasted over a month, and I was based at Castle Donnington near Derby at the Midlands School of Flying. The chief flying instructor was a rather aged and modest character by the name of Frank Spencer, the namesake of the celebrated television sitcom actor whose life was a permanent string of accident-prone encounters. I was unaware at the time that Frank was a widely respected pilot, whose illustrious career was well documented in aviation circles. I was somewhat humbled when I read his obituary, which spread across a full page in ***Flight International*** magazine, many years after he had sent me solo.

Two other ATC cadets, one of whom I was to train alongside at Cranwell the following year, joined me on the scholarship. We were placed in a lovely bed and breakfast pub in the quiet village of Belton near the airport. More importantly, the landlady had a sixteen-year-old daughter. The fledgling flyers were soon in competition for the affections of our new quarry. To help with the administration of the flying school at the airport, Frank had a secretary whose attributes also stirred our imagination (and our loins). This blond bombshell had a voluptuous figure, and she was very aware of the effect she had on the student pilots. As she was tasked with picking us up from the pub each morning, the prospect of getting out of bed to make those initial early training sessions was made considerably easier. Our ground studies were compressed into the first couple of weeks in order to take the necessary Civil Aviation Authority exams, a pre-requisite to the subsequent solo flying and issue of a licence. An introduction to the de Havilland Chipmunk T Mk 10 followed. The Chipmunk was the RAF's basic trainer, and although it had been in service for some years, it was still regarded as an ideal preliminary platform with which to assess the flying ability and potential of the service's future pilots. Not particularly demanding to fly, as a 'tail dragger' however, it required respect – particularly during take-off and landing.

Those early dual-instruction lessons were demanding. The not-inconsiderable din from the 150-horse power Gipsy Major engine made concentrating on Frank's dulcet tones difficult to say the least. Repeating the flying exercise whilst maintaining the required airspeed, heading and altitude started to bring home just how hard the task ahead was. All the time, one had to keep an awareness of the position of the aircraft, particularly when rejoining the circuit. Often there could be three or four other trainers in the air, each vying for space in the circuit. East Midlands at the time was also an up-and-coming busy airport; trying to stamp its presence on the international travel scene. Lumbering Argonauts, four-engine monsters by my standard, slotted in with venerable DC-3s and Handley Page Heralds as they competed for departure and arrival. Lower down the pecking order, we would often have to hold off while they were given priority for take-off and landing.

Sat on the canopy rail, Frank Spencer leaning on the wing – August 1966.

Piece by piece the bits of the jigsaw fell into place. Navigation was assisted considerably by the presence of the nearby power station cooling towers, and my knowledge of the local area grew day by day. I'm not sure what the local farmers thought of the frequent dummy approaches made down to tree-top height as we would practise forced landings with regular monotony. Basic aircraft handling skills mastered (to a degree), the next part of the syllabus was circuits and bumps. Under Frank's expert guidance, I flew circuit after circuit until he was satisfied that I was ready to solo. After I had accumulated the grand total of 8 hours and 25 minutes dual instruction under my belt, a brave Frank Spencer climbed out of the rear cockpit, secured his now vacant seat harness, and invited me to fly the 'Chippy' on my first powered-flight solo. There seemed to be a lot more at stake than when I had launched in the Sedbergh glider on my own a few months earlier. I remember trying to relax on the downwind leg, and take in the reality of the occasion for posterity on that fifteen-minute first solo. However, if truth were known, I was coiled like a compressed spring with the expectation of an inevitable engine failure or other such emergency. The experience was over before I had chance to enjoy it.

A brief consolidation dual session followed my first solo sortie after which I was able to sign for the aircraft as captain in my own right. This done, I completed the walk-around external check and boarded my aircraft with a swagger. My ground crewman in front of the propeller called for "switches OFF", at which point he pulled the prop through a couple of turns. With "switches ON", a further swing of the prop caused the engine to splutter into life. I waved the chocks away, and gave the Gipsy Major's throttle a nudge of power to taxi towards the take-off point. I recall this moment as being truly poignant, as I was about to take to the skies for the whole sortie from start to finish without Frank's reassuring presence. After power checks, I called for clearance to take off.

With the engine at full chat and climbing through about 100 feet or so, my perfect day was about to be rudely interrupted. The starboard engine cowling, which was hinged along its top edge, suddenly flew upwards directly in front of my line of sight and flapped precariously in the prop wash. It threatened to smash straight through the front windshield. Virtually paralysed with fear, instinct somehow took over. I snatched the throttle and mixture lever closed and pointed the aircraft back towards terra firma. Fortunately, enough of Castle Donnington's runway remained ahead of me to attempt a forced landing without having to stray into the adjacent field. The perimeter fence was unnervingly close however, and there were a whole bunch of approach lights on poles dead ahead.

I don't think I had either the presence of mind or capacity to utter a distress call to ATC. Unknown to me, a vigilant controller in the tower on seeing my predicament had already hit the crash alarm. Fortuitously, I somehow managed to put the aircraft down without too much trouble, and miraculously avoided all the ground obstacles in the over-run area. The perimeter hedge was looming rapidly, but in the soft earth, I pulled her up about 5 yards from the boundary. In very strange territory, I collected my wits, and I sensibly cut the mag switches to stop the engine. A beefy fireman clad in full fire-fighting gear appeared at the side of the cockpit by the time I had stopped the aircraft. In a familiar broad Derbyshire accent, he reassuringly said words to the effect of "are you all right lad?" Before I had chance to utter a response, he took one look at the offending cowling, and without recourse, secured it with the snap connecters. I was thinking this was enough excitement for one day.

On return to the flight line, the cowling was briefly checked for damage by my trusty ground crew and declared OK. Still seated in the cockpit, my ever-calm instructor approached my open canopy and suggested casually that the best thing was to get straight back into the air. I can't say that I followed the logic of this move, but I was not in a position to argue. So it was that with heart still racing, I set off once again to prove to Frank, and more importantly to myself, that I had what it took to do the job. The second flight was without drama, and I arrived back at East Midlands Airport almost an hour later with the aircraft still in one piece.

Around the time of my flying scholarship, the Ministry of Aviation (now named the CAA) extended the flight time requirement for the issue of a private pilot's licence to thirty-five hours. The thirty flying hours that the Ministry of Defence had allocated and financed for my flying scholarship was insufficient for the grant of the licence therefore. With typical generosity, Frank Spencer suggested I return to perform a few ground handling duties, which would be rewarded with the extra five hours of flight time gratis. I was fortunate that my father was able to find the time to drop me off at Castle Donnington over the next few weekends. Under the initial supervision of our flying school ground personnel, I was soon swinging props, and even changing plugs on the Gipsy Majors. I completed my thirty-five hours in due course, and was able to pin my flying scholarship 'wings' above my glider pilot's wings. As a seventeen year old at school, I could fly an aircraft, but could still not drive a car.

During my second year in the sixth form, along with my A level colleagues, I half-heartedly started thinking about my university options. The primary requirement was that any such university must have a university air squadron to satisfy my ever-increasing wish to fly. My prime interest by that stage however was focused on joining the Royal Air Force. Although my flying experiences at RAF Newton were always exciting and rewarding, the summer camps at RAF Leuchars in 1964 and RAF Binbrook in 1965 broadened my outlook considerably. One of Fighter Command's front-line stations, Leuchars was home to the striking delta-shaped Gloster Javelin. The sight and sound of these majestic fighters breaking into the circuit in diamond-four formations was sensational. The other aircraft that always caused us to look skyward, was the superb Lightning interceptor. This aircraft was at the very cutting edge of design and technology. It was another purely British product from the English Electric Company. Britain led the world in aircraft and engine development in that decade, and the Lightning was by far the most superior fighter/interceptor of its kind. Capable of flying at twice the speed of sound, this aircraft raised the bar for offensive aircraft in the new jet age. Little did I know that I would get to fly alongside the impressive Lightning interceptors within a few years, in the field of air-to-air refuelling flying Victor tankers. Even more significantly, I would eventually fly the outstanding Lightning at Boscombe Down seventeen years later in the autumn of its service life. Back at school however, such a prospect was merely a pipe dream.

One of our most senior masters at Swanwick Hall Grammar School was Mr Northing. Always bedecked in his long black gown, Mr Northing as head of the English department was an austere man who commanded great respect. English was not my best subject, and I scraped a pass in Grammar with the narrowest of margins. Literature on the other hand, and especially the likes of Shakespeare, was totally beyond my comprehension. I failed that subject in spectacular fashion. Despite my weakness in our national language however, an interest in flying and the RAF in particular somehow resulted in a special relationship with Mr Northing. I am afraid to say, however, that I could not avoid joining in the giggling during his English lessons. His right leg would inexplicably and without warning start tracking erratically under the desk, apparently of its own accord. It transpired that he had spent part of the Second World War in the RAF's elite Pathfinder Force as a Lancaster air gunner. Bomber Command lost more than 55,000 casualties during the bomber offensive of Germany. Mr Northing had survived that ordeal, but not without being badly wounded. His leg still harboured the shrapnel from those heroic operations, and the shattered nerves still triggered the involuntary leg spasms that caused such great hilarity amongst his ignorant students. Mr Northing's personal interest in my aspirations seemed to outweigh my deficiencies in English, and a genuine affection grew between the two of us. At a school reunion twenty-five years later, long after he had passed away, I was bitterly disappointed in not getting the opportunity to share my achievements in the service with one of my earliest heroes.

In order to gain entry into the RAF as a pilot, I was looking at around five O levels (succeeded by GCSEs). I managed six at the first go, failing not surprisingly at another language, French. Retaking French was a must however because of my infatuation with the 19-year-old French student teacher who was spending a couple of years attached to Swanwick Hall. In fact, it took me two more goes (fortuitously) to scrape the all-important grade six pass. The target then was to achieve two passes at A level to qualify for entry to the RAF College at Cranwell. During my first year in the sixth form, I had applied for a scholarship to Cranwell. This involved a set of interviews and physical ability assessments during January 1966 at the Aircrew Selection Centre, RAF Biggin Hill.

The name of Biggin Hill was synonymous with the Battle of Britain, and a Spitfire gate guardian stood proudly at the camp entrance. Entering those famous gates was an awe-inspiring experience for this grammar school lad. The business of attending interviews was virgin territory for me, and I felt very under-confident against the prevalence of public school boys against whom I seemed to be competing. Practical assessments consisted of scenarios, which comprised of teams getting from one side of a hangar to the other across various imaginary rivers and obstacles. Armed only with lashings of rope, planks, poles and car tyres, and under the leadership of an appointed chief, we set off under the watchful eyes of our invigilators. When it came to my turn as team leader, I remember getting as far as the final gorge, with my team balanced precariously on a beam slung under an A-frame of poles – rapidly running out of ideas. We never did cross that river.

Before the final one-on-one interviews, having swapped notes with my competitors, I added to my slender list of hobbies the subject of 'reading'. I have never been an avid reader, and the books that I had read at that stage of my life could probably be counted on the fingers of one hand. My inquisitor latched onto this fact, and promptly asked me which was the last book that I had read. Grasping at straws, I went for *The Dambusters*, an account of the famous raids on the dams in the Ruhr Valley. My mind then froze as I was asked to recall Guy Gibson's name as the celebrated leader of that most famous of Bomber Command's epic missions. I guess they had seen this repeatedly from hopeful blaggers trying to pull the wool over their eyes.

No one was more surprised than I was when an official letter from the Ministry of Defence dropped on the doorstep some weeks later announcing that I had been accepted for a cadetship at the RAF College. This was the premier RAF training establishment from where supposedly all future marshals of the Royal Air Force were groomed. I can only speculate that my record in the ATC, and in particular the succesful completion of gliding and flying scholarship courses gave me an edge against the others. Certainly I had the enthusiasm and all the necessary aspirations to join the RAF, but an award of a cadetship at Cranwell was beyond my greatest expectation.

Only one last ambition remained during my tenure with ATC. Each year, the International Air Cadet Exchange (IACE) programme gave about thirty or so cadets the opportunity to travel the world through exchange visits with other air forces. Particularly sought after were the North American venues. In July 1967, I was very fortunate to be offered a place on the scheme, and more significantly, I landed the very popular and sought-after Canadian option. Despite my uncontained excitement at such a prospect, and thinking that I would more than likely be able to travel to North America in the future, I surprised myself by swapping Canada with Turkey as a destination. I had never even been onto the continent at that stage of my life, let alone fly across the Atlantic. However, I saw the chance of visiting this fascinating country as a far more exciting prospect. We were kitted out with Khaki No 1 dress uniforms for the hot climate, and Union Jack badges were sewn onto our shoulders to distinguish our individual national identity. In my case, I was also proud to wear my recently awarded flying scholarship wings and my gliding badge.

Along with two other British cadets, we embarked on the journey of a lifetime. Flying from RAF Brize Norton, the epicentre of the RAF's Transport Command, our graceful Comet airliner took us through RCAF Zweibrücken to the USAF base at Rhein Main in Germany. Joining other IACE cadets, we then boarded a much less glamorous twin-engine piston aircraft, a Convair 44 of the Turkish air force. The images as we winged our way across Europe were emblazoned in my memory forever; the majestic snow-capped Alps set against clear cloudless skies, and isolated rocky islands fringed by azure blue water scattered haphazardly around a shimmering Mediterranean Sea.

Our arrival into the beautiful city of Izmir confirmed to me that I had made a wise choice in Turkey as a destination. Brilliant blue skies and a heat that I could not have imagined burned a lasting impression in my mind. Courtesy of the Turkish air force once more, we were shepherded into an old Dakota the next morning to fly to Ankara the capital. We were escorted around the spectacular Ataturk's Mausoleum, a tribute to the founder and first president of modern Turkey, Mustafa Kemel Atatürk.

Over the next two days, we explored the ancient bazaars and mosques of this fascinating city. During our stay in a multi-storey hotel, we (the three Brits) were resting in our room situated on the fifteenth or sixteenth floor. Without warning, and inexplicably, the whole room started moving to and fro. Startlingly, the wardrobe doors began thrashing between wide open and fully closed. We looked in amazement and some amusement at the third cadet as he rather bizarrely appeared from the bathroom screaming in terror with his trousers crumpled around his ankles. Suddenly, the sheer horror of the occasion struck us with the realisation that we were witnessing an earthquake of some magnitude.

After what seemed like an eternity, the slamming wardrobe doors stopped, and the swaying ceased. Although our modern hotel was undamaged, there was quite extensive damage throughout the city with a number of fallen minarets and collapsed buildings. Little did I know that the international press jumped on the headlining story, and news flashes were sent worldwide. On hearing the news in England, my father in his inimitable style, immediately called the Foreign Office, and was connected to the British Embassy in Ankara to seek assurance of our safety. Despite the limitations of international telecommunications in the sixties, in no time at all, I was able to reassure him personally by telephone that we were safe and well.

After four days in the capital, our trusty C-47 took us westbound to the ancient city of Eskişehir. At the military officers' mess, we attended a formal lunch, attired in our best dress uniforms. At the Inonu gliding camp, I took my first ride in a performance glider, a Polish Bocian. Unlike the laboured winch launches at Spitalgate over a year earlier, the continuous-loop system merely launched us to around 500 feet. The immediate proximity of mountains on the edge of the airfield provided instant ridge lift. Within minutes, we were soaring up to 3,000 feet or so and I spent the next half hour performing effortless aerobatics over the spectacular mountainous terrain. A second treat followed in the form of a powered flight with an instructor aboard a Piper Pawnee trainer at another local air force base.

Not having travelled abroad previously, I could never have anticipated the antiquated pace of rural life in what was referred to as modern Turkey. I recorded pictures of a local farmer driving a pair of harnessed oxen pulling a wooden sledge over freshly harvested wheat, a simple method of threshing. Along the roadside, there were water holes located to provide basic irrigation for the fields. These wells were characterised by a shaduf, a simple manual device for hauling up water from below ground. Dating back to the times of the Pharaohs, these contraptions consisted of a long pole supported on a fulcrum. The pole was weighted at the short end, usually by a large rock, and counterbalanced at the other by a bucket at the end of a rope. By raising the rope next to the weight, the bucket could be lowered into the well to fill with water. As the rope was released the bucketful of water would be lifted by the counterbalance above ground level to the edge of the irrigation channel. I can only speculate that characterless pumping stations have long since replaced many of these icons of ancient civilisation in modern Turkey.

Our next port of call was Istanbul, or as the Romans christened it, Constantinople. Situated at the mouth of the ever-busy Bosphorus Straits, this supremely important city sat at the confluence of current day Asia and Europe. I marvelled at the beauty of the Byzantine church, completed in 537 AD, known now as Hagia Sophia. Occupying a high point on Istanbul's skyline, it was recognised as the largest church in the world for over one thousand years. More recently in the 17th century, the Blue Mosque stood nearby. Characterised unusually by six slender minarets (rather than the customary four), it got its name from the exquisite 20,000 blue tiles inside the dome.

Also on our itinerary was the bustling Grand Bazaar where rugs and a myriad of merchandise and bric-a-brac were crammed into the 3,000-shop complex. We were given free rein to explore at our will the maze of alleyways and savour the smells of scents and spices, which bombarded our nostrils. Back in Izmir a few days later, we visited one of the ancient Seven Wonders of the World, the ruins at Ephesus. My recollections and photographs of this historic sight were of absolute unspoilt splendour. We strolled as a group, unhindered by other visitors, as opposed to the thousands of tourists who almost certainly overrun the place today. Nearby, we visited the modest house of the Virgin Mary, which is widely recognised as the last resting place of the Blessed Virgin, Mother of Jesus Christ. Nearly fifty years on, as I look at my simple snaps taken at the time, I feel privileged that I was able to visit this holy site before it was added to and developed for the sake of modern tourism. The return flight staged through Rome Ciampino Airport. Two decades later, I would become very familiar with this destination as an airline pilot during my time with Monarch Airlines. Our dutiful Comet then whisked us back via Germany to RAF Benson, after a three-week enlightening visit to a remarkable country.

Barely a month later, I hauled my suitcase onto a train bound for Sleaford in Lincolnshire. My destination was the RAF College at Cranwell. The prospect of my becoming a pilot in Her Majesty's Royal Air Force was about to become a reality.

Chapter Two

'The Towers'

Royal Air Force College Cranwell
October 1967 to March 1970

The main gates at the RAF College Cranwell.

At the tender age of eighteen, leaving home and reporting to the Royal Air Force College at Cranwell in Lincolnshire was a daunting prospect. The towering wrought iron gates and imposing fences seemed to separate the college cadets from the outside world a little too emphatically. Mounted on sturdy brick pillars, each gate was adorned with the familiar embossed RAF crest. Below the Imperial Crown, the eagle (irreverently referred to as the 'shite hawk' for the rest of my career) with outstretched wings is superimposed on a circlet bearing the inscription 'PER ARDUA AD ASTRA'. The literal translation 'through hardship to the stars' would be fully appreciated and understood by the time our stay at Cranwell was complete.

Through the gates, the gravel drive bifurcated around the central circle of grass known rather confusingly as 'The Orange'. Placing a foot on this hallowed ground was on penalty of death. The turf was cut with precision, and the symmetry of the surrounding flowerbeds and shrubs was spectacular. One of the very few occasions I can recall being allowed to walk on the grass was on the occasion of a Lords Taverners cricket match played against Old Cranwellians. That is apart from the time we staked out one of our rather more irritating colleagues dressed only in his birthday suit with croquet hoops.

The two drives met after describing a full circle around the Orange, and swelled to form the parade square where graduation parades had taken place in the presence of kings, queens, prime ministers and top brass from all the world's armed forces. Facing the main gates and aligned tangentially with the far edge of the Orange beyond the parade ground was College Hall itself. The imposing Palladian design was characterised by carved stone pillars, and a striking bell tower, with clock faces reflecting the four points of the compass. Lateral wings connected by single storey corridors topped by smaller towers, housed the four squadrons of senior cadets. This impressive structure was affectionally known as 'The Towers'.

The main building was entered through heavily embossed doors supported by intricately carved stone surrounds, again surmounted by decorative heraldic displays. Inside, one was met with an expansive and breath-taking atrium. A richly decorated carpet known as 'The Queen's Carpet' (yet another surface that had to be circumnavigated) was concentrically located beneath a rotunda. Portraits of Her Majesty Queen Elizabeth II our commander-in-chief and Prince Philip hung as guardians of this wonderfully evocative entrance hall. Corridors leading off in either direction gave access to the public rooms, dining room, ante-room, bars and other reception rooms. In the upper level, the library contained a unique collection of volumes, which served the enquiring minds of student pilots, navigators and engineers alike. A number of fascinating manuscripts were also housed in this marvellous sanctuary, from all ages and military conflicts. Despite being the junior service, a fact drilled into us often by our cousins dressed in navy blue and khaki brown, the RAF had distinguished itself during its relatively short existence, and there was much testament to this effect in the College Hall library. It was dedicated to a former Cranwell graduate, T. E. Lawrence, known universally as Lawrence of Arabia.

The splendour and comforts of such a hall of residence were not within our immediate grasp however. In fact, occupation of the main building was limited to a brief investiture where we were encouraged to 'sign on the dotted line'. Few of us realised the implication of this short ceremony at the time. Apart from swearing our allegiance to the Queen, we unwittingly pledged the next twenty years of our lives to the RAF. We were then herded like raw recruits to our accommodation block that was to be home for the next six months. Barking non-commissioned officers soon put us in our place, and we quickly adjusted to being the lowest form of life. Officer status was obviously something that would have to be earned. Despite being officer cadets, the white bands prominently displayed around our SD (Service Dress) hats forecast to all and sundry that we were merely airmen. The term of address used by our drill sergeants was in the form of 'Mister' Tuxford, but the tone in which it was articulated left one in no doubt as to which one of us was really superior to the other.

Ninety-seven was the number of our flight cadet entry, and little did we know that our ranks would be depleted by about a quarter before our graduation two-and-a-half years later. We would spend much of the first term of five with few privileges and certainly no runs home. Our billets were in fact barrack blocks, which slept around eight to ten cadets. They were aligned in rows rather like POW huts, and were known as the South Brick Lines. Each of us had our clearly defined bed space, with a single small footlocker and wardrobe. The communal bathroom at the end of the block was spartan to say the least, and any individual modesty was soon forfeited. Adjacent to the huts was the inevitable parade square, with which we would become very familiar from day one. I found myself thrown together with a mixed bunch, but our common predicament meant that strong bonds were forged in fairly short order.

Among the pilot cadets in my billet was the stocky Welshman Sid Rees, who seemed to know something about everything. Phil Haigh on the other hand was a quietly confident character who seemed very streetwise, and impressed me as a potentially useful partner in crime. Paul West was a very private person who tended to keep himself to himself, but was nevertheless a friend that I took to. A short while later, Paul was the only one of our team who had wheels to give us the independence to explore the distant lights of Nottingham. Many months later, his immaculately maintained Morris Minor (with split screen) faithfully carried us to and from the female colleges and university campuses of the big city in our quest to escape from captivity. The fifth member who made up our inner circle of friends was Andrew Lambert. Andy had been assessed as not having the necessary aptitude for pilot training, and so was pursuing a career as a navigator. A product of Wellington College, he was well drilled in service matters, and I was somewhat in awe of this intelligent character. He spoke with the only refined accent amongst us, and displayed the usual tell-tale qualities of a public school education. His Achilles heel was an aversion to physical education and any form of arduous adventure training. Andrew's way of making life as easy as possible was to bribe us with money. He was always concerned that his rich mummy was spending the family fortune on frequent cruises. Compared to the rest of us, he seemed to have a limitless supply of cash to keep us in extra pocket money as we undertook menial tasks designed to protect him from any form of physical hardship.

A feature of life while confined to the South Brick Lines was the ever-present threat of a raid mounted by the senior cadets. Known as 'crowing', these unwelcome intrusions into our private lives came without warning and usually in the dead of night. I well remember before the first month was over, standing to attention in my shreddies (service issue knee-length pants) in front of our hut. Bare foot on the snow-covered ground in the depth of winter, I shivered uncontrollably in a state of fear and trepidation. 'Ninety-three' was the number of our senior entry intake. Leading the banter of insults and derogatory comments thrust at our quivering bodies was a certain under officer by the name of John Waterfall.

Under officers were the promoted 'prefects' and as such, wielded even more power than the other senior flight cadets. After much prodding and verbal abuse as to the collective uncertainty of our parentage and so on, our bed spaces were torn apart under the guise of snap kit inspections. I had put out my razor blades symmetrically and they gleamed like mirrors in anticipation of the kit inspection. However, after being handled deliberately by our tormentors to ensure that fresh fingerprints would be in evidence, I would have to clean them all over again.

Much can be argued as to the true value of these 'character-building' episodes. A failure to stand your ground and resist with an independent defiance in the face of physical and insulting effrontery could have been seen as lacking in moral fibre. Despite the occasional tears on the part of the less resilient junior cadets, we were united in a common resistance to the onslaught, and managed to come through the crowing without long-term psychological damage. No doubt the touchy-feely health and safety organisations would clamp down on this public school behaviour in the 21st century. Personally, I feel there is something to be said for the fine-tuning and strengthening of one's personal capabilities that comes from such shock treatment. After all, we were being selected for a fighting service, and any weaknesses needed to be identified and rooted out quickly. I was to share a flight deck with John Waterfall as my Monarch Airline captain in Boeing 757s twenty years later. Despite the sometimes distasteful nature of those early encounters, I developed a genuine liking for Johnny. Our friendship and mutual respect continued to flourish over the following years. He was a great mentor not only at Cranwell, but also during my early days as an airline pilot as I adjusted to the very different world of civilian aviation. John's sense of humour was wicked, and although he could offend those of a delicate disposition, I really admired him and we never failed to have wonderful times down the route.

Alongside the South Brick Lines was the junior cadets' mess, which was modelled on a standard officers' mess. We were required to assemble in our mess shortly after our arrival to meet with the representatives of the distinguished military tailor, R.E. City of Sleaford. During the private individual fittings that followed, a very old school tailor measured me rather too attentively for my liking. We were to be outfitted with our first No 1 Service Dress uniform, and the impressive No 5 Mess Kit for dinner nights. What really took the biscuit however was the measurement of my feet to enable our bespoke tailors to hand-make my uniform shoes. This was unfamiliar territory for a grammar school boy from Derbyshire.

Daily square bashing, superb sporting facilities, and a gymnasium with international-length swimming pool meant that we quickly became fit. As a senior cadet, I captained the badminton team and played third string in the tennis team, and achieved college colours in both sports. One of the hardest games of singles tennis I played as a senior cadet was against an old Cranwellian ex-fighter pilot who finished the war with an artificial leg. Although a little sluggish around the court, this former county player had lost none of his racquet skills. Needless to say, I did not need to offer this chap any sympathy at all, and we had a closely contested game.

In company with Sid, Andy and Phil, our common interest in sub-aqua diving took up much of our spare recreational time. Frequent sessions of training in the pool led to the award of a British Sub-Aqua Club certificate (known universally now as a PADI

RAF College Cranwell Tennis Team – 1968 (Top row left).

qualification). Our reward for this came much later over two summer breaks with the opportunity to dive in the Mediterranean. We explored the remote pristine waters off the Pan Handle of Cyprus without restriction for a fortnight. On the second occasion, we did this under the guise of adventure training, receiving a monetary grant to cover the expenses, and planned and executed the whole trip unsupervised. The four of us completed a further diving expedition to Corsica following our graduation. Not only did we manage to get that expedition funded, but we also convinced our masters that the most practicable method of transport would be a self-drive hire car. Needless to say, this afforded us considerable flexibility.

The unplanned stopover in Marseilles prior to the ferry passage to Corsica turned into a drunken bash, followed by the four of us sleeping on the beach. We did manage to locate and dive on a wartime B-17 Flying Fortress which had ditched off the harbour at Bastia. However, after barely half a dozen hours underwater, our equipment was seized for the best part of a week after Phil triumphantly returned to the beach holding a magnificent grouper. Unfortunately, he advertised the fact by holding it aloft on a harpoon from one of our spear fishing guns. The local police took an instant dislike to our casual disregard of the laws relating to spear fishing in the Mediterranean. Only after interjection from the embassy staff did we get our gear back, in time to drive our way back to England having detoured via Italy and the majority of Europe's capital cities. How we survived crossing the Brenner Pass in an old Ford Cortina estate with bald tyres (and no chains), in the middle of the night during March does not bear thinking about. Back at Cranwell, we were required to submit a paper designed to justify the funding for this 'adventure training'. I seem to recall Sid and Andy used their not-inconsiderable literary flair to create a largely fictitious catalogue of our 'accomplished' dive programme. It was truly a work of art, and clearly sufficiently believable as far as our masters were aware.

An unexpected and welcome intrusion into our early training was a brief encounter with the Chipmunk once more. The pilot cadets were put through an additional preliminary flying skills evaluation that was designed to avoid any oversight made during our Biggin Hill assessments. Accordingly, I flew the Chipmunk once more for nine hours at the end of 1967: all dual instruction apart from a brief solo flight. Having accumulated thirty-five hours on type during my flying scholarship, I'm pleased to say that this was a real bonus for me. There were those amongst us however who had not flown 'tail draggers' before, and so they no doubt found this test quite daunting.

Academic training took the form of studies in all subjects to ensure everyone was at a similar level. Whittle Hall stood just outside the college gates, and was named after the brilliant jet engine designer – also a graduate of the college. Tuition in service knowledge included our first encounter with the formidable volumes of air force administration and air force law, both subjects bound in tomes that weighed a ton. Our service training was supplemented by the curious 'Customs of the Services', a small yet famed document penned by a man known as Straddling. This was the part of our education designed to turn us into officers and gentlemen. Many rules would have to be mastered regarding etiquette at the dining table, introductions, responding to invitations and so on. The particular tradition of 'Calling' – that supposedly informal get-together by the wives – was something that hopefully could be put on the back burner for the time being.

On a different level, we were introduced to international studies, which included the wider aspects of global politics, and military studies. Further academic training was accomplished in Trenchard Hall. Marshal of the Royal Air Force Lord Trenchard was regarded as the father of the RAF, and it was largely due to his foresight and stewardship that the RAF was borne out of the Royal Flying Corps in 1918. This massive building was situated on the RAF Cranwell station side of the base, a mile or so down the road towards Sleaford. Its facilities matched those of any of our red brick universities of the day. Trenchard Hall was the learning centre where engineering cadets studied for their three-year degrees. Inevitably, and with the usual irreverence, it was also referred to as 'Sleaford Tech'. Pilot cadets studied all the sciences in its many labs, including aerodynamics, thermodynamics and jet propulsion. There was even a subsonic and supersonic wind tunnel facility where we explored the world of future aircraft development and design.

The general service education and further academic studies undertaken within Whittle and Trenchard Halls were all designed as a precursor to terms four and five. In the case of pilot cadets, this was the part of the syllabus to which the budding aviators really looked forward: the basic flying training course on the Jet Provost. One was never beyond earshot of the noisy Viper engines of the Jet Provost trainers that were always circling overhead. My concentration in the classroom, especially in Trenchard Hall, where some of the windows faced out onto the South Airfield, was perpetually challenged by the rather more attention-seeking action on the flight line. How envious we used to be of our seniors who had already started the flying phase of their training.

Finally, the time came when academic training gave way to the ground school that preceded the actual flying training. Dual instruction flights with my assigned QFI (qualified flying instructor), Jon Hill, started around May 1969. Jon was a former Hunter ground-attack pilot, who had seen action in the Radfan during the Aden Emergency. I was in awe of this sharp operator, and I had the utmost respect for him. Another QFI however by the name of Tony Cunnane was destined to send me off on my first jet solo.

To ease the congestion of Cranwell's many JPs in the visual circuit, the satellite airfield of RAF Barkston Heath was used frequently. Situated about five miles away as the crow flies, Barkston took the balance of 'circuit bashing' aircraft as the students practised their take-off and landing skills. A few hours into the course, I flew across to the relief landing ground with Tony to consolidate my circuit training. After a couple of patterns during which time I had managed to demonstrate that I was ready for solo, Tony was convinced to let me go it alone in Barkston's circuit.

Having secured the straps of the unoccupied ejection seat and fitted an apron to keep them in place, my instructor stepped onto the foothold on top of the engine intake, and vacated the cockpit, exiting over the back of the starboard wing. As he waved me off with some calm words of encouragement, I cranked the canopy forward and taxied to the take-off point. Before I knew it, the wheels were off the ground and I raised the undercarriage. I checked to see that the three green lights on the undercarriage indicator had extinguished to confirm normal gear retraction. Instead, I was mortified to see three red lights burning brightly. (Unknown to me, the undercarriage had jammed halfway up with the legs cocked at about 45 degrees to the horizontal.) Without thinking, I instinctively pressed the down button to extend the undercarriage in the hope that it would return to a safe condition. After a successful extension with three greens illuminated, I was thankfully reassured. So far, so good.

However, rather than accept the status quo and put the aircraft back on the ground, I began to wonder if my eagle-eyed instructor back on the tarmac had witnessed my predicament. Perhaps I had not fully pressed the up button? Thinking like the tyro student pilot that I was, I firmly and deliberately pressed the up button once more, only to be presented with the same unsafe gear indications of three red lights. I jabbed the down button a second time, and fortunately, I was rewarded with three greens. All this had taken barely half a minute, and the aircraft was still climbing on the runway heading. With my wheels safely down and locked, I started to think more clearly. As no engineering facilities existed at Barkston Heath, and sensing that I should not tempt fate any further, I decided to return to my home base leaving the undercarriage lowered. I called the tower and informed air traffic control that I had a gear retraction problem, and was returning to Cranwell (with instructions to inform my QFI). I left my slightly bemused and exasperated instructor standing helplessly on the tarmac as I disappeared over the horizon with his ride. With no real harm done, I was later fined the customary couple of beers, and told to learn from the experience. To put it all in perspective – it could have ended somewhat differently had the undercarriage stayed in a semi-retracted state.

The next discipline was to pass the instrument flying phase, so that we could safely negotiate cloud and poor visibility that would otherwise prevent us from departing and arriving in less than ideal weather conditions. An introduction to night flying followed shortly afterwards. We were tasked with flying solo around a triangular track over 200 miles at medium altitude, confirming our position obtained from radio bearings and so on. I remember vividly the night that I was planned to fly this exercise. The sky was gin clear, and the visibility was unlimited across the whole of southern England. Heading south-east from Cranwell, my route took me around the dazzling lights of Cambridge, west towards the massive conurbation of Coventry and Birmingham, before turning back onto a north-easterly heading and the final leg home. At night, I soon learned that distinct city lights many miles away always appeared much closer than expected. As I sauntered around the navigation route at an altitude of 15,000 feet, I was thrilled to see the illuminated built-up areas bathed in sodium lighting. I remember feeling rather pleased with myself at my great personal achievement to date as I controlled my jet trainer through the calm black sky that night. After landing, having spent the better part of forty-five minutes aloft, I was enthusiastic to share the sheer enjoyment of my successful sortie with my counterparts. There was some concern however at the operations desk about an overdue fellow student, who was running significantly behind on his expected time of arrival. Eventually, this particular student pilot landed almost thirty minutes late. More worrying for the instructors was that he was virtually out of gas. Unaware of his navigational and timing errors, the student had missed the first turning point by a considerable margin, and had misidentified London for Cambridge! He had then continued undaunted around his extended triangular route and virtually circumnavigated the whole of the southern counties before staggering back to Cranwell. His enthusiastic comment on swaggering into ops was, "Isn't Cambridge massive?"

The next phase of our basic flying training would include those 'applied flying' disciplines of aerobatics, low-level navigation and formation flying. Another highlight at this juncture was my conversion onto the JP 4, which had around 2,500 lbs of thrust as opposed to the Mk 3's 1,750 lbs. This was a significant step-up in terms of performance, especially during aerobatics and low level. Aerobatics enabled the student to improve his handling skills, and instil and develop the confidence that would enable him to utilize the whole of the aircraft's performance envelope. This was paramount in order to master the basic principles of air-to-air combat. I can't say that my aerobatic skills during this phase were particularly refined. Indeed Jon might have preferred to use the term agricultural. However, I loved the freedom of tearing around the sky with carefree abandon. The fact that my sequences would not place me in the running for the coveted aerobatics prize awarded to the most skilful cadet did not deter me. Interestingly, ten years later, I would find myself teaching those same manoeuvres to my students at Church Fenton. The satisfaction of witnessing 'Bloggs' (the name given to all student pilots) see the penny drop and execute a classic stall turn for example was priceless.

Low-level flying was a multi-tasking role whereby the student would have to demonstrate his ability to fly the aircraft at high speed in close proximity to the ground, whilst navigating along a pre-determined course. This was about the time that I first realised that two hands were not enough in the JP. Jon expected me to maintain a target speed using my left hand on the throttle, whilst balancing a map between thumb and finger to keep track of the navigation. My right hand would grip the control stick (often far too tightly) and hack the stopwatch to monitor the timing. Keeping the jet at 250 feet agl whilst whizzing through the glorious Peak District of my home county Derbyshire, or darting around the Yorkshire Dales, was a great adrenalin rush. This part of the course was perhaps the most demanding for me, albeit the most exhilarating. On the other hand I seemed to take to the formation-flying phase with relative ease however, and found it perhaps the most enjoyable.

The exercise sorties demanded intense concentration and hand/eye coordination. The thrill of controlling the aircraft to a precise position within a formation always set my heart racing, mainly because my wingtip was in such close proximity to my leader's aircraft. In most operational scenarios, whether it involved flying fighter, bomber or tanker aircraft, the ability to fly in close formation was a necessary pre-requisite for most squadron pilots. Interestingly, I was to spend a major part of my subsequent career flying Victor tanker aircraft in close proximity to others in the role of air-to-air refuelling. Of all the applied flying disciplines, I found this part of the course the most satisfying and rewarding, despite being scrutinised by the ever-present critical instructor seated alongside.

Towards the end of the fourth term in 1969, as part of my general training, I was selected to take part in a standard-bearer party. The occasion was the reformation of 43 (Fighter) Squadron at RAF Leuchars in Scotland. The 'Fighting Cocks', a squadron that dated back to 1917 when part of the Royal Flying Corps, were taking delivery of the RAF's latest acquisition, the Phantom FG1. The four Cranwell cadets in the colour party were

Solo formation in JP 4 Code '94' – 12 November 1969.

tasked with handing over the squadron standard which had been laid up at the RAF College. We were ferried up to Leuchars in one of our resident Varsities from the far side of the airfield. After arrival, the parade formed up on the apron in front of 43 Squadron's buildings, and we proudly returned the standard for their safekeeping. Following the usual march past by station and squadron personnel, we all retired to their impressive brand-new crew room on the side of the adjacent hangar.

Several local dignitaries were in attendance, as were a number of former squadron commanders. As the party got under way, the fresh Scottish breeze outside took on gale force dimensions. Before long, the resident ground crew informed us that our Varsity was starting to skip around the tarmac in the now ferocious winds. Assisted by squadron airmen, we tethered our aircraft to suitable lashing points on the apron, and headed back to the warm snug of the crew room. The new boss of the reformed Fighting Cocks, and leading very much from the front, was a character who was clearly held in great esteem by his pilots. Not only did he sport a noticeable suntan, but his good looks and athletic frame were concealed in something which I thought did not exist – a tailored flight suit. I seem to recall that he was affectionally known as 'Mad Tan Martin'.

In the general melee of noise and banter, I have the hazy memory of an air commodore, walking stick in one hand supporting his unsteady frame, and tankard in the other, announce that it was far too stuffy. Only an ex-squadron boss could get away with what happened next. With a lunge at one of the newly installed double-glazed windows, he used his artificial leg to smash a hole straight through the pristine glass. The storm force winds on the outside had an immediate air conditioning effect, and almost without noticing, the squadron jocks and their guests returned to their refreshments. Before the night was out, needless to say, the remaining windows were similarly despatched by an assortment of boots and shooting sticks! In fact one former squadron commander received the first battle damage in the shape of a serious leg wound in the process of the glazing modifications. Such high jinks on one of the RAF's front-line squadrons left us Cranwell cadets mesmerized and totally in awe of these shenanigans, and I could not wait for the day I that I might be a part of that elite club.

One last treat was in store for the 97 Entry flight cadets. Each year, the odd-numbered intakes got to participate in an exchange visit to the United States Air Force Academy in Colorado. The campus is located in the fabulous surroundings of Colorado Springs, high in the Rockies. The rows of Corvette Stingrays, E-Type Jaguars and Porsches owned by our American counterparts left us speechless when compared with the rusting Morris Minors, Ford Anglias and Minis owned by the minority of Cranwell cadets. However, the hierarchy within the student cadre left a lot to be desired, with the way that first year students in particular were treated. We were also somewhat ambivalent when informed of their 'honor code', and not entirely convinced of its true worth and effectiveness.

Facilities at the base were quite exceptional, and the tennis and basketball courts extended as far as the eye could see. I soon met my match in the squash courts when we put up a team against their best and got slaughtered. Playing at 8,000 feet above mean sea level when not acclimatised did nothing for our perceived fitness. On a recreational day off, along with Andy, Sid and Phil, I saddled my sturdy pony, and we trekked along the trail of Pikes Peak, the highest peak at over 14,000 ft in the southern front range of the

Rocky Mountains. In the rarefied atmosphere and under a cloudless sky, we burnt badly as we soaked up the fantastic mountain scenery.

Despite the apparent advantages of a superior location and immaculate facilities, our American hosts seemed equally impressed when they came to our college. Their envy became very apparent when they realised that at two-and-a-half years, our course was not only considerably shorter, but also it included 150 hours of basic flying tuition on the Jet Provost trainer. They had to wait almost five years to get to the same point in their flying training.

I received my flying badge at a special 'Wings' ceremony on 27 February 1970. The final days at Cranwell were a time of great celebration. Following on from our student dining-in nights, we were all encouraged to bring a guest to a wonderful boys' luncheon in the College Hall mess. My father was on great form, and he enjoyed the pomp and ceremony immensely. The day clearly triggered fond memories of his former military career. I remember his obvious pride and the relaxed aura he exuded that day in the great dining hall. He was not a man to show his feelings openly, but that day was a notable exception. I was very honoured to show him around College Hall that day, and share that special father-and-son moment at such a memorable occasion.

Cranwell's graduation parades were magnificent celebrations. Each of the five cadet entries paraded in their respective squadrons, with the senior graduating entry centre stage of course. We mustered on the parade ground in front of the Orange for one last time. An immaculately timed fly-past of thirty or so JPs formed up in the shape of the entry number 97. The formation seemed to fill half the Lincolnshire sky as it flew past in salute to the newly commissioned officers. Following the formalities of the day, and as a finale, the graduation ball brought it all to one tumultuous conclusion.

The majority of my family were able to be with me on that wonderful occasion. There is no doubt that it was an immense privilege to have attended the RAF's premier training establishment. We were often cajoled and teased by the other commissioned officers in the RAF about our Cranwell heritage, just like our counterparts from Sandhurst and Dartmouth. We certainly were given the best possible leg-up in our chosen careers. However, I have always suspected there was more than a smidgen of envy in those not lucky enough to have been selected for the RAF's college. In reality, once we left that hallowed place behind and fell in line with the rest of the RAF pilots sporting pristine brevets, any advantage faded quickly. One thing was for sure: there was going to be no free ride through the next phase of our advanced flying training, irrespective of one's previous background.

Chapter Three

Spreading My Wings

No 5 AFTS, RAF Oakington, Cambridge
April to September 1970

Before progressing onto my advanced flying course, I was invited to 'waste' a couple of months. In the early 1970s, there was a rapidly developing backlog in the training system that was to affect me even more so later in the year. The number of pilots waiting for advanced flying courses was far in excess of that number of available places at the training establishments. Following my graduation from the Towers, I needed to find somewhere to bide my time. Preferably, this would entail some flying so as not to let the dust gather on my new wings. RAF Newton came to mind as the station where I had my first experiences of the RAF, and was conveniently close to home. The Chipmunks were still operating there under the guise of the East Midlands University Air Squadron, and so I was able quickly to qualify again on the Chippy. After a brief dual check, I soloed once more and added a handful of hours to my logbook total over the next month. I even ventured across to RAF Barkston Heath for a session of circuit bashing amongst the latest student pilots flying their jets from Cranwell. At the end of winter 1970, Newton was bitterly cold, and the desolate and largely deserted airfield gave it the feel of a forgotten station. It was hard to imagine the scene thirty years earlier, when it was a bustling bomber airfield that supported two Vickers Wellington squadrons.

By contrast, RAF Oakington was a much larger airfield, and had a considerable history by the time I entered its gates in the springtime of 1970. I have distinct recollections of six sunny months in Cambridgeshire as I embarked upon No 5 Advanced Flying Training School (AFTS). Having served also as a bomber base through the latter part of the Second World War, Oakington had become a Training Command station; and home to dozens of the venerable Varsity T Mk 1 multi-engine trainer.

From the same stable as the Wellington, that iconic twin-engine geodetic-framed bomber, the fat squat appearance of the Varsity resulted inevitably in its unflattering pseudonym, the 'Pig'. Ungainly it may have been, but our advanced trainer was a superb multi-crew training aircraft. Moreover, unlike its modern counterparts, it would take punishment all day long from the unskilled students at her controls. The engines were turned over at around 8:30 in the morning as the first crew boarded. Usually, four student-training sorties each of ninety minutes duration were flown during the day, interspersed by half-hour running turn-rounds. At teatime, after nearly eight hours of continuous running, the engines were shut down on dispersal prior to their refuelling and routine maintenance in preparation for the next day. Although there must have been occasional hiccups in the programme, I cannot recall any significant disruptions in the flying rate that summer as a result of aircraft un-serviceability. Certainly, the likes of the Jetstream trainer that followed the Varsity some years later could never offer the rugged and reliable service that was achieved by the Pig.

During ground school, we were introduced to the intricacies of the bewildering fourteen-cylinder Hercules radial engine. This monster sleeve-valve engine delivered just short of 2,000 horsepower, and was a development of the engine that powered many of the RAF's bombers during the war. As we were about to start the flying phase, we met our flying instructors. My tutor, Flying Officer Leo Faulkner was a diminutive character, whose weathered features made him look older than his years. At this point, I too was a flying officer like Leo, having benefitted from accelerated promotion as an ex-Cranwell cadet. He had been commissioned much later in life; the recipient of a branch commission offered to those long-serving airmen. His flying career to date had been spent entirely as a non-commissioned officer, and the ribbons on his uniform bore testament to a wealth of experience, not to mention wartime operations. I felt humbled to fly with such an experienced flier, and privately pleased not to be taught by one of the creamed-off instructors barely three years my senior.

The departure from Oakington's active runway took us around the former bomber airfield of RAF Waterbeach. We were required to maintain a circuit height of 800 feet as we circled before climbing to the north of Cambridgeshire. During my first dual instructional sortie, I was surprised by the way that Leo utilised this wasted five minutes or so in level flight. Shortly after take-off, he gave me control as we approached the circling altitude. After opening the sliding starboard side window, he casually lit a cigar, and proceeded to puff away to his heart's content, completely in contradiction of Queen's Regulations – not to mention safety precautions. As a student pilot with all of a couple of hundred hours under my belt, I was not about to comment on his actions, and pretended not to be perturbed in the least. I would recall this incident with wryness years later after joining Monarch Airlines as a new first officer. Taxiing the Boeing 757 along the mile-long parallel taxiway to runway 08R at London Gatwick, Captain Geoff Tong would fire up a small cigar. The only difference was that in the civil jet airliner, he could not open the side window. It was always a long tearful night to the Canaries and back in the tight confines of that smoky flight deck.

Within a couple of weeks, and having accrued around thirteen hours in the Varsity, I soloed with my partner in crime and fellow Cranwell graduate, Sid Rees. Indeed, many subsequent flights were undertaken with a student colleague acting as co-pilot in the right-hand seat. Much bravado was exhibited on these 'mutual' sorties. After demonstrating suitable confidence and skill in handling the Pig on one engine, every opportunity was taken during the general handling sessions to get one over one's fellow student in the other seat.

Whilst setting up for a stall for instance, the operating pilot acting as captain in the left seat would bank the aircraft to the left and right of track to ensure the airspace around us and below was clear. On straightening out with wings level, the throttles would be closed to flight idle to allow the speed to decay to the point of the stall. As the nose dropped

Varsity T1 multi-engine trainer RAF Oakington – summer 1970.

with the wing fully stalled, the flying pilot would then move the control column forward to unstall the wings and simultaneously apply full power. As the airspeed recovered above the stalling speed, the aircraft could be pulled out of the dive and recovered to level flight. At least that was the theory.

On 16 July 1970 in aircraft WF371, my student captain was also an ex-Cranwellian from my entry. Dave was built like a rugby prop forward. Although his flying skills were without question up to the mark, they were nevertheless lacking in subtlety. As he made his clearing turns prior to a practice stall, I surreptitiously selected off the ignition cutout switch on the overhead panel, which controlled the spark to the magnetos of the left engine. I did this as he was looking out to the left during his clearing turn, so he was very unaware. The airflow even as the engines were throttled back would continue to 'windmill' the rotating propeller masking any indications of an impending engine failure. That is of course until the throttles were advanced.

Dave lowered the nose after the stall, pushed open the throttles with his usual finesse, and of course, the starboard engine responded immediately as all 2,000 horses powered the big radial into life. There was a deadly lack of response however from the port side as there was no spark to ignite the fuel pouring into the fourteen cylinders. As one engine raced towards full power and the other stayed at idle, the aircraft responded like a squealed pig (excuse the pun) and started to roll over on its side. Dave instinctively looked up at the overhead panel, and seeing the ignition switch off, reached up and instinctively flicked it back on before I could stop him.

With its throttle fully forward, and the cylinders full of unburnt fuel, the port engine exploded into life with an almighty 'crack' that reverberated through the airframe. By now, the wings were almost vertical as the Varsity was responding with agility strangely at odds with her normal sedate handling qualities. Using both hands on the 'spectacles', Dave aggressively rolled the wings level to recover a normal attitude, whilst I gently eased back the throttles to reduce boost on the thundering engines. Startled, we stared at each other for a couple of seconds, and then fixed our combined glare on the left engine gauges, looking for any abnormalities. Boost and RPM levels looked normal, oil pressure and cylinder head temperature indicated steady. We must have flown straight and level for several minutes to allow everything to settle. Such was the durability of these sturdy old radials; it seemed that they would take any amount of ill treatment. I guess this was like one of those articles that used to appear in the RAF's Flight Safety magazine *Air Clues* entitled 'I learned about flying from that!'

Following the general handling part of the flying syllabus, our piloting skills were broadened by instruction in navigation, instrument flying in cloud, airways procedures, low-level flying and the inevitable splash of night flying. In the case of the latter discipline, I remember not so much the flying as the sessions in the night-flying bar afterwards. The mess bar was always equipped with a few crates of Newcastle Amber to fuel the thirsty students eager to share their 'war stories' after each session. Further exploratory sorties were undertaken into the kitchens, where fried egg and bacon sandwiches were rustled up with alacrity.

During the navigational exercises, we were introduced to the mind-boggling early nav kit known as Decca. Its principle was based on a phase comparison of signals received from master and slave ground stations. The hyperbolic reproduction of the familiar ¼ million scale maps in its roller map display resulted in distorted presentations of Britain's coastlines and features. Familiar topography became almost unrecognisable. Mounted on the coaming, this baffling piece of kit was a mystery to all of us initially, but with familiarity, we grew to appreciate its eccentricities and compensate for its weird display.

With very few exceptions, we all seemed to progress well though the course. We even survived a particularly memorable navigation test along an airway over eastern England. With half a dozen of us in the back of the Varsity waiting to take our turn, our student captain had to maintain the centre line along the designated airway using navigation beacons only and without the assistance from a navigator in the rear. Inevitably, at some stage, the instructor in the right seat would simulate an engine failure by surreptitiously closing a fuel cock for example. The absolute priority for the student pilot, acting as captain, was to correctly identify the failed engine before demonstrating the feathering procedure.

If the left engine lost power, the aircraft nose would swing to the left, and to keep the aircraft straight it was necessary to boot the right rudder pedal to counter the yaw. As the right leg straightened to apply the rudder force, the left leg remained bent and was relieved of any force. A useful memory aid of 'dead leg – dead engine' was helpful in identifying the failed engine: i.e. in this case, dead (left) leg = dead (left) engine. Our trainee skipper up front on this occasion obviously got his legs and engines confused, and we witnessed for the first time the dreaded 'double hush'. Along with identifying (wrongly) the failed engine, he promptly pulled back the throttle on the 'live' engine, resulting in loss of power on both engines. The aircraft dropped like a stone out of the bottom of the airway, and the deafening noise in the rattling fuselage around us was replaced by an eerie silence. There was considerable sphincter tightening until such time as the ever-alert instructor came to the rescue. If I'm honest, we all performed a double hush at some stage of our training. Indeed, I think it was par for the course, and a necessary experience in humility to learn from that heinous crime.

In between learning our trade, the glorious summer of 1970 was quite memorable for other reasons. My close buddy also from 97 Entry, Graham Timms, played *Bridge over Troubled Water* incessantly until he wore out his 45-rpm vinyl. Another lasting memory is of crowding into a beautiful old Alvis convertible and careering into Cambridge to take on the university students. The car I recall was passed on from course to course. I'm not sure that anyone ever bought the road tax to make it legal. The hood was worse than useless, but this did not matter in the endless sunny days of June and July. Our skills in the punts on the Cam were marginal at best. In spite of our alcohol-fuelled state (or perhaps because of it) we were more than a good match for the university wimps. That is not to say that we did not get a frequent soaking because of the inherent lateral instability of those treacherous boats. Our luck with the girls in the student union was often mixed, despite the fact that I believe the university students felt we RAF types presented a considerable threat. During a subsequent excursion to Cambridge that summer, Graham and I went on a recce one night only to find Joe Cocker performing live in the union. Little did I know how much of a legend in the music industry he would become. I recall on that occasion, my sidekick spotted and identified a stunning brunette, whom he would marry the following year.

Never having been a frustrated fighter pilot, I was starting to feel really at home in the Varsity. With a backside-to-knee length too great for me to fit into the tiny Gnat advanced fighter trainer, my future lay inevitably in the RAF's large aircraft. Experiences with fellow students in our less glamorous steed however had its advantages. I have often thought that being able to share those experiences in the air, and face the banter in the bar afterwards gave us 'heavy' boys a distinct edge.

This would be brought home vividly in later years on numerous occasions after sharing one of the more precarious moments in the air with a crew. Of course, chucking an agile fighter around the skies has an appeal and satisfaction all of its own. We always took the mickey out of our fast jet cousins in the bar, as they couldn't wait to get their hands above the waist to graphically demonstrate their airborne prowess that day. Of course, we have always expected our fighter pilots to be brash, overconfident and aggressive. On the other hand, Oakington was the breeding ground for a different mentality of pilots; pilots who would learn how to work within a team and hold that team together, generate confidence and trust in one's fellow crewmembers, and command respect in the air.

On graduation, we were asked to make a preferred choice of the aircraft type that we would wish to fly following posting. Although there was no guarantee of achieving this wish, I had always been struck by the sheer futuristic look of the Handley Page Victor. One of the RAF's V-Force trio of swept-wing bombers, the Victor Mk 1s in service in the early 1970s had been converted into refuelling tankers. The role was one that appealed to me immensely; one that I calculated would offer a good chance of seeing the world. Fortunately, my masters at Oakington found me suitable for my first choice, and it was soon after that I was given a posting notice to the Victor Operational Conversion Unit (OCU) at RAF Marham.

With too many pilots still chasing too few places within the training system, it would be a further nine months or so before I could start my course. Once more, I was invited to find alternative employment to buy some time. Some students were quick to take up assignments as operations officers on front-line stations to get near to the action. The problem with those positions was that, apart from the occasional ride in the back of a squadron fast jet, you were unlikely to get much hands-on flying. As graduates of basic and advanced flying schools our airborne experience was minimal and restricted to training aircraft only.

My thoughts focused on a holding posting which might at least offer some regular flying. In the event, I chose RAF Manston in Kent. I had the idea that at least there would be a diversity of aircraft in this prominently placed airfield, even if they were only passing through to the continent. Furthermore, I was aware that an airline called Invicta was operating passenger and freight services from the station at the time. Thinking outside the box, I surmised passenger-carrying aircraft must mean air stewardesses? One thing I did know for sure about Manston was that there was an air experience flight, which operated the faithful Chipmunk trainer. I correctly anticipated that as a freshly graduated pilot from advanced flying school, my services might just be useful. A check with my posting officer revealed that the unit, No 1 AEF, would indeed be delighted to take me on for a few months. Accordingly, I packed all my belongings into my minivan, and headed for the far reaches of Thanet.

Chapter Four

Lord of the Manor

No 1 Air Experience Flight, RAF Manston, Kent
October 1970 to June 1971

With the pilot backlog situation imposing delays of anything up to a year for those caught up in it, I resigned myself to a few months of care-free flying at my new base. Contrary to the bustling environment that I expected, Manston occupied a rather quiet corner of the UK. Indeed the total number of officers on the camp could be counted on the fingers of two hands. Most of them were air traffic controllers who manned the air traffic control building that enabled the station to respond to any aircraft in distress needing a safe haven. Furthermore, as a master diversion airfield, Manston provided the facility of runway foaming, which very few airfields throughout the RAF possessed. If an aircraft was unable to lower its landing gear for example, the fire crews would respond at short notice to use their tenders to lay a foam carpet on part of the runway as a fire suppression agent. Manston's quiet times were punctuated by periods of high drama whenever the hooter went off announcing the prospect of an emergency landing.

From time to time, the RAF's premier flying display team the Red Arrows used to drop by for practice sessions. Their Gnat aircraft, resplendent in crimson red livery, were afforded considerably quieter skies in which to practise their displays. The mess always came to life during the visits from those icons of the RAF; lead by non other than the legendary Ray Hannah. Their red Land Rovers, doors emblazoned with gaudy badges, were instantly recognisable by the local female population. They always drew much attention around the hot spots of Margate and Ramsgate.

Sadly, my aspirations concerning Manston's resident civilian airline came to naught, as Invicta Airways had cancelled their passenger-carrying operations just before my arrival. The pool of attractive unattached flight attendants never came to fruition. Along with just two other junior officers, we had the run of the modest officers' mess which perhaps more closely resembled a private country residence. Met by the senior mess steward on my arrival, I was offered the choice of several bedrooms, and selected a particularly spacious room with two bay windows overlooking the attractive front gardens. With so few living-in mess members, I was able to add a few extra items of furniture to make it even more comfortable. I felt like the lord of the manor. Before long, I became the bar officer, with obvious benefits, and later the house member. Together with a small catering staff of serving personnel, I had specific charge over the messing arrangements of the kitchens. With only two or three people to serve in our small dining room through the week, the catering sergeant often took time out to meet in the late afternoon after flying.

He would always let me know if a delivery of particularly tasty looking steaks or other prime cuts of meat had just arrived. I was never to see this level of personal attention in the rest of my career at any of my future messes.

On a cold day early in October 1970, I reported for duty at No 1 AEF. A wheezing and slightly portly man in a well-worn flying suit was the unit's only permanently established pilot. As soon as we settled in his office to discuss my new appointment, he lit a cigarette and started coughing repeatedly. After questioning me about my flying experience, he was delighted to learn I'd logged around fifty hours in the Chipmunk. Without further ado, he reached for the old leather headset hanging over the back of his chair, and beckoned me outside. My new boss was obviously keen to get me into the air so that I could be of use to him immediately. What I did not realise was that my arrival would virtually eliminate the need for him to fly anymore, and he spent the majority of the next eight months tucked away in his snug office. I learned later the reason behind his laboured breathing was in part a result of having flown unpressurised Spitfires at extreme altitude in the photo-reconnaissance role.

Our seventy-five minutes in the air was sufficient for me to take a quick recce around Pegwell Bay, down to Dover, and complete a circuit of the North Foreland. Back in the overhead, I demonstrated a couple of stalls for my new boss, a spin, and rattled through my rather rudimentary aerobatic sequence. The runway at Manston was 9,000 feet long and unusually about 500 feet wide. It had been constructed specifically to accommodate three Lancasters landing abreast after returning desperately short of fuel from bombing missions over Germany. I could have landed the Chippy across the width of that massive landing strip. I did take the opportunity to demonstrate to my observer in the back seat my competence in landing on the unforgiving concrete runway, where the propensity to bounce was much more likely. As a routine however, we normally used the grass strip adjacent to the AEF buildings for convenience. Gasping for breath as he hauled himself over the canopy rail, my boss secured the now vacant rear seat, and invited me to fly off for another session to consolidate.

After a few more flights with the voluntary reservists who made up the complement of the unit's pilots, I took an aircraft across to RAF White Waltham to be checked as competent to fly passengers. Before long, I was carrying cadets from the Air Training Corps (ATC) and Girls Venture Corps (GVC) who were the reason for our existence of course. With running turn-rounds, it was not uncommon to be strapped in the Chipmunk for up to 2½ hours at a time, offering four or five cadets the experience of a lifetime. My own memories of flights as an ATC cadet flooded back in my new role as an AEF pilot. Drawing on that experience, I always offered my excited passengers the chance to fly the aircraft at every opportunity.

The flying throughout that winter and the spring of 1971 was largely uneventful with one significant exception. At the end of a detail, I had been cleared by the controller to re-join the circuit from the north, and was informed that there were no conflictions from other air traffic. The Red Arrows had been in town again, and they were about to make a departure to return to their base. Air traffic had cleared them to go, and they commenced their take-offs in quick succession with the intention of joining up in formation when

Chipmunk T10 flown at RAF Manston: 1970–1971.

airborne for the transit home.

Normally after lift-off, aircraft departing to the east would execute a right-hand turn to the south of Manston. However, just as I had come onto the tower frequency, the Reds requested a climbing left-hand turn to the north. The controller, having forgotten that I was approaching the northern edge of the airfield, approved this. Within seconds, I found myself surrounded on all sides by a gaggle of Gnats at full chat concentrating only on chasing their leader. I pushed hard on the stick and threw the Chipmunk into a dive to evade the conflicting targets. Amazingly, I managed by pure luck to avoid them all, and pulled out only after I saw the last red blur flash by. The unsuspecting cadet in the back seat never knew the danger we had been in, and I chose not to enlighten him.

The air traffic controller by now had realised his mistake in turning the Red Arrows towards the same patch of sky into which I had been cleared. I learned later that this novice controller had been sent to Manston to gain experience in what was supposedly a relatively benign air traffic environment. Had I submitted an incident report, it could well have finished his career. In the event, when I saw him later in the bar, he could not apologise enough and spent the whole evening begging my forgiveness. Thinking this was a salutary lesson, and a grave error that he was unlikely to repeat again, I accepted his profuse apologies, along with the next three or four beers which he insisted on buying of course.

Another air traffic controller posted into Manston at that time was a pilot and his family by the name of McLean. Remustered into the ground duties branch, Mac had flown Wellingtons in Bomber Command right at the end of the Second World War, and subsequently a variety of transport aircraft also. The majority of his flying had been achieved on the Valetta – an earlier tail-wheel version of the Varsity. In the Middle East, his obvious flying abilities had been recognised on his unit and he had been designated the squadron VIP staff pilot. Accorded to few, this accolade meant he was often tasked with escorting officers of air rank all over the region. I met Mac for the first time one evening in the mess, just after I had returned from the squash courts. As luck would have it, he had brought his daughter Eileen over to the mess to use the phone so that she could talk with her boyfriend (not only was this pre-mobile phones, but also their quarter did not even have a landline telephone either). Clearly, the sight of my athletic physique and muscular legs had an immediate effect on her, and we are still together after forty-five years. My time was then shared between Mac and Joan's quarter on the far side of the airfield, and the officers' mess. Joan was a marvellous cook, and the temptation to double up on meals over the next few months was irresistible; this did little for my waistline of course.

It was not long before I took the opportunity of flying Eileen in the back seat of my Chipmunk. Thinly disguised as a GVC cadet, I fear she was fooling no one attired in my flying overall made for someone who was almost a foot taller than her. Once airborne, I deliberately flew the aircraft around Pegwell Bay in a northerly direction. This track would mean crossing the extended centreline of Manston's main runway, for which I would need ATC approval. Knowing that Mac would be on duty in the tower, I prompted Eileen to make the R/T call with a request to cross the final approach path. Somewhat surprised to hear the different falsetto voice, but obviously aware of what was happening, Mac duly answered with the approval to cross the centreline, adding that he thought my straps were perhaps a little too tight.

Prior to reporting to Marham for my OCU, I was temporarily posted once more, this time to RAF Manby in Lincolnshire. With the loss of continuity caused by the backlog, it was imperative that all pilots in the training machine picked up where they left off with at least some degree of flying currency. Although I had been fortunate in maintaining currency at Manston, I would nevertheless be required to undertake the flying-refresher course like everyone else. The School of Refresher Flying sported a varied fleet of aircraft including Jet Provost, Varsity and the relatively new Dominie navigator trainer. To get away from the confliction of small jets, much of the flying on the familiar Varsity was undertaken at the delightful satellite base of RAF Strubby, about seven miles to the south east of Manby.

Memories flood back of another fine summer of glorious weather. I can visualise driving through the leafy country lanes in my recently acquired MGB, with the hood permanently down. I clearly recall four of us piling into the 'Bee' and darting over to Strubby known affectionally as 'East Lincs Airlines'. We had all graduated from Oakington previously, so the return to the Pig, particularly for those of us who had kept flying, was a breeze. The atmosphere generated by our instructors was particularly informal, and it was mandatory to enjoy this 'no-pressure' course.

My flight instructor for the first three flights was a character called Dennis Turner, with whom I would have the pleasure of flying years later in Monarch Airlines. This phase of flying culminated with a jolly, which involved a night stop away. In my case, I chose somewhere as far away as possible – RAF Kinloss in Scotland. The main exercise was for the student to stay sober enough to fly the instructor home the next day after an over-exuberant night in the bar. A very casual final handling test was completed a few days later in order to tick all the boxes, and off we went to our respective conversion courses. The only bugbear was that the clutch in my MG finally gave up the ghost, perhaps after the trauma of repeatedly ferrying all those students to Strubby and back. I nursed my ailing sports car into the nearest garage in Louth and hoped that I would be back on the road in time to make the start of my next training course. In the event, the repair was done impressively quickly, and before long, my steed was serviceable once more, and I headed around the Wash to Norfolk. How I afforded the repair bill still escapes me to this day.

Chapter Five

El Adem with Grass

Co-pilot – 214 Squadron, RAF Marham
November 1971 to January 1974

RAF Marham was the home of the Tanker Force. Marham's old timers still referred to the place somewhat irreverently as 'El Adem with grass'. The pseudonym made no attempt to disguise the less than complimentary comparison between Marham's flat unremarkable terrain with that of the barren featureless landscape of the Libyan desert. Although I had never been there, RAF El Adem was apparently regarded as the arsehole of the RAF, and a posting there was nothing short of a prison sentence. Far away from the searing heat of the North African continent, Marham's summers could be pleasant, although its winters were usually bitterly cold and raw.

Three squadrons and a training unit equipped with the Handley Page Victor made Marham one of the largest and busiest bases in the RAF. Converted from the V-bomber marque and designated the Victor K Mk 1, the 'K' denoted the tanker variant. The bomb bays of the former bomber had been modified to carry two large bomb bay tanks that enhanced the fuel capacity of the tanker by about 30,000 lbs. All the internal fuel could be fed either to the engines or offloaded to our receiver aircraft via three refuelling hoses. The largest of these was contained within a hose drum unit (HDU) – referred to verbally as the 'hoodoo' – located in the lower aft fuselage. The other two refuelling hoses were concealed within pods, one mounted under each wing.

The so-called three-point tanker was able to transfer fuel to all probe-equipped fighters in the RAF's inventory. Each of the three squadrons had a hack – essentially a spare aircraft – that was used for crew training and currency. The hacks were usually aircraft that had been converted to an interim fit standard, and were equipped with two under-wing hose units only. These variants were referred to as two-point tankers. They still had the bomb bays of the original bomber, and so could still be operated in the bombing role. No. 232 OCU had a handful of two-point tankers that were used for conversion training.

On arrival at the OCU, we were immediately formed into two student crews. My designated skipper was Flt Lt Ian Brunton, navigator plotter Flt Lt Peter Martin-Smith, and air electronics officer (AEO) Sqn Ldr Tony Coles. A fifth crewmember (the nav radar) would complete the crew after posting to our assigned squadron. My first sortie in the Victor was made on the sixth seat, a rear crew type seat mounted centrally in the cockpit behind the pilots' ejection seats. The feature of this seating arrangement in the Victor, which placed all crew just about within arms reach of each other, was preferred to that in the Vulcan. In the 'tin triangle', the three rear crewmembers sat below the level of the pilots and significantly further to the rear of a split-level cockpit.

From my position on the central crew seat, although it was hard and uncomfortable, I had a particularly good view up front. Significantly, I could look down onto the complicated fuel tray that would become my principal domain. Hinged at its front end at the base of the central instrument panel, it could be swung down in between the two ejection seats. On it was mounted a myriad of fuel pumps and valves to enable control and distribution of fuel. Transfer cocks and switches enabled the transfer of fuel from the tanks to the wing pods and HDU.

Our pilot instructor was Flt Lt Keith Handscombe, one of Marham's longest-serving officers. In 1973, he was to be the only survivor of a tragic accident resulting from a collision between a Buccaneer receiver aircraft and his Victor tanker. Today's flight however was a general handling detail designed to make the new student crewmembers comfortable in their new surroundings. Ian was already at home in the aircraft having just completed a co-pilot's tour on 214 Squadron across the peri track. I would get the chance to sit in the right-hand co-pilot's seat on the next couple of trips before being let loose with Ian on our crew solo on my fourth flight. Following completion of the other syllabus items including navigation exercises, circuit work, practice diversions and simulated drills, we graduated from the OCU and reported to the far side of the airfield where my new squadron's aircraft were dispersed.

As a novice co-pilot on 214 Squadron, I was initially only qualified to fly the two-point Victor. This meant yet another conversion onto the three-point Victor K1 variant, and instruction covering the wider aspects of air-to-air refuelling (AAR). On my second sortie on 20 December 1972, whilst seated alongside Ian, we refuelled Lightnings and Phantoms

214 Squadron Victor K1 XA938 refuelling a pair of F-4 Phantoms. (© Crown)

on one of the many designated refuelling towlines. These were long oval tracks, usually situated off and parallel to the UK coastline. On these tracks, we were able to keep our air defence fighters topped-up as they protected the United Kingdom airspace.

The military radar units situated around Britain's shores assisted in joining the two together by vectoring the fighters and tanker towards a common rendezvous point. The Victor's nav team would then take control of the 'chicks', and direct them onto the 'mother hen' until visual contact was established. Once in close proximity, the tanker would take responsibility for the navigation of the formation whilst liaising with the radar controller using one radio, and exercise tactical control over the receiver(s) during AAR on a second radio. Both pilots learned quickly to juggle both channels simultaneously, with one pilot monitoring the radar unit whilst the other looked after the chicks. The receivers could then be sequenced behind the respective wing hoses, and cleared sequentially for contact so that they could receive the allocated fuel.

We also flew navigational exercises in company with our fighters, where they would be brought into contact at designated refuelling brackets to top up with fuel. These accompanied cross-countries were pre-requisite training exercises prior to the strategic overseas deployments of our fighter squadrons. There was much to learn about the command and control of a formation of tankers and receivers, crossing wide oceans, where fighters whose endurance without in-flight refuelling was limited. Once cleared to refuel all our different fighter types, we were offered a 'lone ranger' to RAF Akrotiri in Cyprus, the first of many excursions to this fascinating base.

Akrotiri lone ranger in Victor K1 XH667 – 24 January 1972.

As the hub of the RAF's Near East Air Force, Akrotiri was a massive airfield, and was one of the RAF's key forward operating bases overseas. Situated at the eastern end of the Mediterranean, it was (and still is) ideally located to serve the UK's interests all over southern Europe and the Near East. Akrotiri's squadrons included Lightnings for air defence, Vulcan bombers, Canberras in photorecce and bombing roles and an array of helicopter types. In the 1970s, her massive ramps teamed with transiting aircraft also, which included tactical and strategic transports such as Andover, Argosy, Hastings and Hercules. Serving our primary routes to the Far East meant that one would always see our long-range Transport Command passenger jets passing through, in the form of Britannias and the VC10s of 'The Shiny Fleet'. The VC10 pilots considered themselves akin to airline pilots, and so superior to those of us at the sharp end. The 'Hooray Henrys' even flew in their blue suits (uniforms) rather than the working flying overalls that the rest of us wore. Such a disparate collection of aircrew in the officers' mess bar resulted in a fabulous melting pot of characters and diverse behaviour. The banter was always highly entertaining, insults were traded irreverently, and some of the ensuing games were quite physical if not directly combative!

Four very enjoyable days in the Levant ensued, as I was to witness for the first time the great job satisfaction of working as part of an independent crew, whilst deployed a couple of thousand miles from home. Frequent runs ashore were made to the local hot spots from the sovereign base area. The journey to Limassol in the local taxi, always seemingly driven by retired kamikaze pilots, was an education in itself. The first restaurant that Ian took us to was owned by a Greek Cypriot called Niazzi. The attraction undoubtedly was the free and unlimited supply of Kokinelli, a Cypriot red wine of uncertain provenance. Despite the fact that tanker crews would drink vast quantities of the dreaded Kokinelli, getting extremely noisy in the process, Niazzi seemed to dote on our patronage. No doubt the profit he made from the tanker crews was the key to the fact that he started a very successful restaurant business in London some years later.

After a wonderful and incredibly long meal of kebabs with the never-ending courses that made up the menu, I was introduced to the delights of Heros Square. This was situated in a dark corner of Limassol, accessible only through a labyrinth of streets barely wider than our battered taxi. Small cafes, bars and a couple of clubs surrounded this unremarkable quadrangle. Badly potholed roads radiated from its four sides into the maze of dimly lit back streets surrounded by decrepit houses made of crumbling stone. Seated at rickety tables scattered around the square by day, conversing elders would pass the time whilst smoking strong cigarettes and drinking Turkish coffee. By contrast, this microcosm of Limassol burst into life at night.

I was quickly introduced to the delights of one particular club, the 'Green Rock' on our first run ashore. This venue was a magnet for tanker crews for some reason. I never understood why, as the quality of the acts was dire. Maybe that was indeed the draw. Perhaps we should have taken more notice of the hastily prepared sign propped up against the makeshift stage. Scrawled on a ripped piece of cardboard were the words: ***'please do not mock the artistes'***. This was often difficult to observe, especially when occasionally the artiste was a scabby old donkey accompanied by a local tart that was well past her sell-by date. I'll leave the rest to your imagination. The alcohol-fuelled 'tanker trash' – as we were affectionally known – always treated the atrocious acts to howls of derision and uncontrollable laughter. The Green Rock was also a popular watering hole for United Nations forces stationed around the island, instantly recognised by their striking light blue berets. The local scantily clad girls offering over-priced bottles of cheap champagne always targeted these well-healed troops. The taxi ride back to Akrotiri always seemed to take less time than the outbound journey, despite the fact that the car's speed was slowed by the extra drag from rear doors being opened wide every time someone shouted "airbrakes". This rarely seemed to faze the manic drivers although occasionally, they did threaten to leave us abandoned by the salt lake unless our antics ceased.

Prior to our departure from the island, the rear hatch of our tanker would often bulk out with boxes of oranges, dozens of amphora purchased from the local potteries, wicker laundry baskets, and demijohns of Kokinelli. The old Mk 1 Victor with its underrated Bristol Siddeley Sapphire turbojets and her fuel tanks full to the gunnels for the long trip home really struggled to get airborne. My first visit to the Near East Air Force and Akrotiri – one of the RAF's most influential bases around the world – was an unequivocal success. The British Sovereign Base Area in particular, and the fascinating island of Cyprus in general became one of my favourite destinations, and I never tired of visiting and transiting through that springboard to the Middle and Far East.

'Two-One-Four' as we always referred to our squadron number, comprised a tapestry of characters in the early 1970s. Our daily routine revolved around the crew room, which always had a variety of interesting occupants. Those crews planned on the daily flying programme would generally rest at home until required to report for duty at operations. The remainder would gravitate to the crew room. Some were given tasks around the squadron such as the planners who managed the flying programme. The remaining individuals were allocated the inevitable so-called secondary duties; for example appointments to the mess committee (as I had experienced at Manston).

Apart from these supplementary duties, there was invariably a certain amount of free time when not flying. This down time was filled, as it always had been in the RAF, by card and board games like Ludo. I suspect that these rituals are not so prevalent in the modern-day Typhoon and Tornado crew rooms. Although I was aware of a thriving poker school, I do not remember seeing money in evidence or changing hands, as this was discouraged. A short bald navigator by the name of Bert Jukes apparently was the holder of a certain black book, which was the master ledger that contained the details of debts owed by individuals across the whole station. I was introduced to card games with names that I can barely remember, but Clag does ring a bell. The arch master of these games was a huge cauliflower-eared navigator by the name of Paul Cross, or 'Crossie'. This rugby-playing monolith had the mind of a professor and a wit as sharp as an ice pick. He had a particular penchant for tagging nicknames to everyone on the squadron, and that included the senior officers. For example, our two flight commanders were known by nicknames that Crossie had resurrected from dubious characters associated with the underworld. He was fascinated and intrigued by prominent criminals like the notorious Hanratty who was executed for the heinous A6 murder in 1962. Along with the conspiracy theories that still surround the assassination of JFK to this day, Crossie would frequently eulogise his own theories in the crew room. Much of what he had to say had to be treated with a pinch of salt. He was not averse to telling a story with himself becoming the central character of a plot based on a storyline that someone else had related – on one occasion from one of my own experiences. Irrespective, he had a knack for remembering detail, and re-inventing stories with humorous artistry. Crossie's tales generated great amusement.

In complete contrast, and never far from Crossie's side was a jovial nav radar called Fred Stokes. Fred and Crossie were like peas in a pod, and apart from their differing statures, could have been brothers. Indeed, the only reason that Crossie never got hitched was that once Fred had married my wife's sister Janet, Eileen had no other sisters for him to marry. We all enjoyed a drink in those days, and it sometimes got us into trouble. Back in Heros Square after a particularly entertaining session at our favourite watering hole, Fred was attempting to coerce one of the local taxi drivers into taking us back to base. Fred, inebriated of course, approached the driver and said something along the lines of: "Officers of the Crown, take us to Akrotiri or I will kick your car". The Cypriot responded in a fairly believable and deliberate tone: "You keeka my carr, and I keel you". Needless to say we did not employ his services that night. Although we always knew we were the best squadron at Marham, 214 was crowned the 'Top Tanker Squadron' that year, and I remember fondly the visit to RAF Waddington to receive the trophy.

Other stalwarts on the squadron were more difficult to get to know. Our esteemed AEO leader Sqn Ldr Peck wore the brevet of a 'WOp/AG'. Greg, inevitably as he was known, had earned his wings as a wireless operator/air gunner in the Second World War flying Lancasters. Even in the early 1970s, the number of serving crewmembers entitled to wear

214 Top Tanker Squadron award at RAF Wallington. Crossie bottom right next to me. (© Crown)

this coveted badge were becoming few and far between. On 214, we simply referred to him as the 'World AEO Leader'. At that early stage of my career, I was in awe of people like Greg. Somewhat hesitantly, I dared to approach Greg Peck on first meeting him in the crew room. He was an impressive character with a shock of silver hair, which gave him the air of a very distinguished man. I held out my hand and had barely opened my mouth when I was abruptly put in my place. In a rather disparaging manner, Greg informed me in no uncertain terms that he would let me know when the time was right for me to approach him. Over the following months, I like to think we did become good friends.

No 214's commanding officer had a personal assistant who was rather like a toned-down Captain Mainwaring of *Dad's Army*. His notices that were pinned to the squadron notice board were literary masterpieces. When inviting applications for courses for example, his flair for the written word usually took the form of 'Officers desirous of attending the xxx course'. The boss' PA beavered about the squadron, and he was the source of great amusement for comics like Crossie and Fred.

In the days when the IRA' s activities had spread to mainland Great Britain, everyone had to be aware of suspicious packages. One fateful day, an unattended briefcase was noticed in a corridor inside the squadron. The word went around for everyone to evacuate the building immediately. The boss called to his assistant to gather his belongings from his office and assemble outside in short order. Rushing around like the proverbial blue a***d fly, his faithful PA dithered about and eventually joined the rest of the squadron personnel in front of the hangar. The RAF snowdrops arrived on the scene, and after checking that no one was missing any bags, removed the offending suspicious device to an open grassy area away from the offices. Then, they promptly blew it up with a small explosive charge. The case flew into the air, and shredded paper rained down like confetti at a wedding. Perusing the scene afterwards, the boss scuffed a few bits of paper aside with his foot when he noticed part of the squadron letterhead on one corner of a singed piece of paper. Turning to his worried-looking PA, he asked where his briefcase was...

RAF Marham provided the AAR support for our fighter squadrons in the defence of the UK, and our aircraft were always on standby. On a 24-hour basis, our tankers could be called on to support Operation Dragonfly. This was the code name for a possible intrusion of the UK airspace, usually by Soviet long-range bombers crawling their way through the Iceland/Faroes gap to the north of Scotland. Our peacetime role was in actuality a war role therefore in those heady days of the Cold War. Our task was to scramble and support the quick reaction alert (QRA) fighters similarly held on standby at places like RAF Leuchars. On 9 February 1972, I was crewed up with my former instructor from Cranwell, Sqn Ldr Tony Cunnane, and my favourite nav team Fred and Crossie. Earlier in the day, we had flown a brief sortie as part of a tactical evaluation (Taceval) exercise which had required us to position to and land at RAF Leuchars. We were required to maintain a state of readiness, when, for the second time that day, we were scrambled on Operation Dragonfly. Our Lightning interceptors, poised in their QRA hangars, were the first to respond. Within a couple of minutes, they were already charging down the runway in full reheat by the time we had donned our flying suits. Directed at supersonic speed towards the unidentified aircraft, the Lightnings would continually demonstrate their ability to intercept the intruders.

Tu-95 Bear intercepted over the Iceland/Faroes gap. (© Crown)

Just minutes later, we raced to our waiting tanker and with ground crews already on the scene, fired up the engines simultaneously using the combustor quick-starting facility. Before long, our cold-soaked aircraft was climbing into the murky Scottish night in pursuit of our quarry. The military radar controllers were calculating the likely rendezvous area where our thirsty chicks would require fuel after guzzling six or seven thousand pounds of avtur in that supersonic encounter. By the time we were on station, we had the first returning Lightning behind one of the wing hoses and were filling his depleted tanks to full. If there was only one 'bogie' (i.e. intruder), one fighter would normally remain and shadow the contact whilst escorting the threat aircraft away from the United Kingdom airspace. On this occasion, the presence of a pair of Lightnings armed with 'hot' air-to-air missiles was sufficient for the intruder to turn tail and return northbound. As the second chick returned for fuel, we filled him to full before clearing them to depart. We were released from task shortly afterwards by our military radar unit, but directed to recover into RAF Leuchars once more in case of further action.

In need of some well-earned crew rest, we retired to the quiet mess and stocked up with a case of beers from the night-flying bar. Right on cue, Crossie produced a pack of cards and we settled back into the comfortable leather armchairs in the ante-room. A couple of hours later as I reached forward, to lay a card on the low coffee table, I winced from a sudden stomach pain. Within minutes, the pain became unbearable, and despite the late hour, we commandeered a station vehicle to visit the only surgery that we could locate.

After driving into the sleepy village of Leuchars, we arrived at the door of a grizzly old Scottish doctor, not at all pleased by our nocturnal intrusion at some ungodly hour. In less than a minute, he announced in an unrecognisable dialect that I was suffering from colic. Thinking this was something that only babies and animals got, I was thankful that it was not a suspected appendicitis. I was driven back to the mess suitably equipped with a supply of pills to eradicate the offending side effects, and we sensibly retired to our beds.

During overseas deployments, the refuelling plan would often call for a number of tankers to accompany the fighters. Assembling the tankers at a rendezvous after climbing would be costly in terms of time and fuel burnt. To avoid the problem, where all tankers depart from the same base, we would plan to take off at close intervals on what was referred to as a 'snake climb'. With aircraft rolling at thirty-second intervals in a tail chase, each jet in turn would climb at a faster airspeed, in order to close up on the preceding one, thus eliminating lost time and fuel penalties that would otherwise be the case during complicated join-up procedures. As a bonus, the outbound track would be tailored to ensure that the most expeditious route was taken towards the first refuelling bracket. The whole process ensured that the maximum amount of fuel was available amongst the tankers to dispense to the receivers along the deployment route. My snake climb training with Captain Ian Brunton followed in early March. Receiver training, which was the qualification whereby one tanker practised the art of taking fuel from another followed a short while later. During mutual refuelling, Ian would fly the aircraft in close formation, whilst the Victor in front (the tanker) would prepare for refuelling by trailing its centre hose. When ready, the aircraft astern planning to take on fuel (the receiver) would position behind the tanker's trailed hose. Once the nav radar acting as the refuelling operator in the offloading tanker was ready, he would indicate to the receiver pilot by operating in sequence the coloured signal lights mounted on the HDU fairing. This meant that the fuel transfers could be achieved without recourse to radio transmissions. A small power application was more than sufficient to create an overtaking speed of no more than a normal walking pace. As the receiver's hose drew near, the idea was to place the probe into the tanker's basket using small control inputs. Once in contact, the nav radar would complete the fuel pump selections to offload the required fuel into the receiver's tanks. During the fuel transfer, it fell to the co-pilot to monitor all the instruments and systems inside the cockpit. In particular, I was responsible for directing the fuel into the respective fuel tanks whilst carefully monitoring the aircraft's centre of gravity. Equally, the co-pilot needed to keep a close eye on the engine parameters whilst the captain was making continuous power adjustments to maintain his position in contact.

Having been checked as a receiver qualified crew, we were once more let loose down the route on our first trail. Each movement of fighter aircraft or 'trail' was given a codeword: 'Panther' trail as a member of the cat family was the pseudonym for the accompaniment of Jaguars; 'Flash' trails referred to our Lightnings; 'Ghost' trails – Phantoms, 'Pirate' trails – Buccaneers, 'Hawk' trails – Harriers and so on. A Ghost trail followed on 5 April 1972 when we were tasked with deploying Phantoms to the island base of RAF Masirah, off the south-east coastline of Oman. Six days later, we were part of a Flash trail ferrying Lightnings over France on the first leg of their deployment to the Far East. More operational trails were flown during the following busy months, with a further Hawk trail on 30 July 1972 tanking Harriers to Akrotiri. In early September, I got my first taste of Goose Bay in Labrador, another one of the RAF's staging posts serving our interests in North America. On this occasion, we accompanied Harriers on one of the infrequent Hawk trails. With the onset of deep winter approaching, 'The Goose' could be a forbidding place. In its defence however, the small RAF detachment personnel there were always welcoming, the beer plentiful, and the steaks very big.

During the latter part of September 1972, I was flying on most days, and sometimes twice a day in the major exercise Strong Express. This was an inter-service affair with joint maritime taskings provided through participating Royal Naval vessels around the UK coastline. I flew nine missions over an intensive eight-day period, mostly during ungodly hours at night or in the early hours of the morning. The demands placed on our ground crews were unbelievably challenging, and all air and ground crews were tested to their limits. Inevitably, a great toll was taken on the airframes, and not surprisingly, we often carried unserviceabilities such as generator failures to get the job done. On my last sortie, I was flying the squadron hack XH667, the two-pointer equipped with wing hoses only. Not for the first time, I had to land with the port wing hose at full trail, its winding gear completely dead after the demands of many consecutive refuellings.

Around the same time, my crew was detached to the Indian Ocean to refuel Phantoms from the island base of Gan. The underpowered Victor Mk 1 always struggled to get airborne from the 7,500-foot strip in the hot humid conditions. In an effort to maximise the runway available, our technique was to turn onto the end of the strip as tight as we could. (At Gan, there was no parallel taxiway, and so a 180-degree turn had to be made at the threshold.) Once lined up, we would hold the jet on the brakes while the engines were run up to full power, and then release the brakes to start the take-off run from a standing start. On that particular occasion, we incurred the wrath of Gan's airfield services. We had unwittingly blown over several approach lights mounted on poles sunk into the shallow water just off the end of the runway. This was not the only time that a Victor tanker visiting this remote staging base would inflict damage to the approach lighting system.

Two weeks later, I set off in my MGB for the weekend down the well-worn route around the old North Circular (pre-M25) from Marham to Kent for the last time. In October 1972, Eileen and I were married in the quaint village church at Manston next to the airfield. Needless to say, Fred, Crossie and a bunch of reprobates from the squadron duly blessed us with their presence. Eileen's parents Joan and Mac provided an excellent celebration in their spacious married quarter.

Soon after, we were fortunate to move into an available quarter of our own on the married patch at Marham. We were especially delighted that the house had one of the few telephones already installed, an exception to the rule in those days. At least I would be totally self reliant as far as contactability was concerned, and be able to call home at will. The only drawback, of course, was that our house became the central notification point for calling out other crewmembers around us. Following a call-out, as I was jumping into a flying suit, Eileen used to dutifully raise the alarm for the others in our locality. On one occasion, she went next door in the freezing cold, wearing my greatcoat. What she did not expect to see was our neighbour who answered the door wearing only his wife's negligee.

Shortly afterwards, we were planned under Ghost trail F24 to refuel Phantoms to the Far East. Eileen has always referred to this three-week detachment as *my* honeymoon. The first stage to Akrotiri, very familiar to me by now, was uneventful. The following leg to Masirah Island off the Omani coast went without a hitch also. With little to sing the praises of this desolate island in the Arabian Sea, I shall always remember the succulent crawfish tails set out for lunch in the mess. Our primitive crew quarters built of corrugated iron were basic to say the least, and the air conditioning was memorable by its absence. The third leg entailed crossing the Arabian Sea from Masirah to Gan Island. No 43 Squadron's boss and his navigator flying a lone Phantom in company with our three tankers took this superb in-flight photograph over a flat calm Arabian sea.

Three Victor K1s en route Masirah to Gan – 27 October 1972. (© Crown)

My crew ended up staying on Gan for over a week because of aircraft problems that resulted in changes to the refuelling plan. At this stage of my career, everything was a new experience. Gan Island was the jewel in the RAF's crown as far as I was concerned. The southernmost island was one of a dozen, which made up the Addu Atoll. It was situated some 400 miles south of Male, the capital of the Maldives. Blisteringly beautiful white sandy beaches surrounded the base, which was bisected by the single runway. The RAF unit at Gan gave employment opportunities to a few indigenous Maldivian locals, and other workers were drafted in from the likes of Ceylon (now Sri Lanka) and Pakistan. My earliest memories of Gan Island are of islanders rowing in perfect harmony in their long canoes from the adjacent islands as they came to and from work. Due to its isolation as an RAF base, postings there were for nine months only, and these often fell to the likes of Marham's co-pilots who failed to get captaincies after their first tours. Fortunately, I managed to avoid this. Nevertheless, a few days there at the pleasure of Her Majesty's government on this idyllic paradise island was not to be sniffed at.

When we were not flying, snorkelling in the crystal clear water was one of the few pastimes on offer. As I was quite an experienced scuba diver by this stage, I was eager to take my skipper Ian Brunton and nav Pete Martin-Smith on our first crew snorkelling experience. We stepped part way across the crumbling remains of the causeway, which linked our beach near the mess to the neighbouring island. Floating on the current between the islands into the interior of the atoll, we snorkelled our way towards the underwater reef some twenty to thirty yards from shore. We then turned to parallel the beach before swimming into shore. I had never seen such a variety of beautiful tropical fish before. Stunning corals and sponges adorned the crystal clear waters, bearing in mind this was before the ravages of El Niño. On my first dip a couple of days before, I had swum with graceful Manta rays as they meandered through the same gap with the current. We had been assured that larger predators (sharks) did not brave the shallows of these causeways. The theory was that the waters in the middle of the atoll were clear of such dangers, and I certainly do not recall any instances of shark attack in Gan's history.

Despite having been born in Trinidad, Ian surprisingly was not a strong swimmer. He had little if any experience of snorkelling with a mask, snorkel and flippers. As we made our way along the reef, which dropped away steeply into the abyss of the atoll at that point, we were caught short by an instantaneous turn in the weather. None of us had noticed the approach of the towering cumulus clouds and associated thunderstorm brewing. To be fair, these afternoon thunderstorms struck with alarming regularity each day, so we were somewhat remiss in not anticipating the storm. Within seconds, the intense rainfall around us started to obscure the visibility to the beach. Aware of Ian's inexperience, I yelled out to make for the shore, and to stay together. I set a deliberate steady pace in an effort to keep Pete and Ian following in my wake. At that moment, whilst looking through my mask to the sandy bottom about 10–12 feet below, I was aware we were not alone. Two sharks, around six feet in length, were swimming in synchronous formation directly below us. I was very relieved as they suddenly turned away apparently uninterested in our presence. I reached the shallows and stood up to catch my breath, and turned to Pete who had stuck to me like glue during the swim to shore. Alarmingly however, Ian was nowhere to be seen. Despite the thunderous rain that was still pelting down, I asked Pete to stay alongside me as we swam back into the atoll to find our skipper.

Visibility was barely ten yards at best as we headed back out. I was relieved when a couple of minutes later, I caught a glimpse of his thrashing arms beating the surface of the water ahead. I believe he could well have drowned if we had not come to his aid at that very moment. He was clearly in distress, and had swallowed a lot of water. I realised immediately that in his panic, he had thrown off his snorkelling gear; the very aids that would save him from drowning if only he had known. I had to yell at him to calm down. Forcing him to turn on his back, I linked one arm under his, and Pete did the same on the other side of his body. We then front crawled with Ian suspended face upwards between us, and made our way back to shore. I was exhausted as we reached the shallow water, at which point a revitalised Ian started to embrace me gibbering about how we had just saved his life. Aware of the fact that most shark attacks take place in water less than three feet in depth, and not entirely sure that our predator friends had cleared off for good, I ushered Pete and Ian onto the beach. Only then did I let them know about the sharks that must have been more than interested in Ian's shenanigans in the water a few minutes before.

The adjoining islands that made up the atoll were strung around like the links in a necklace. On the far side of the atoll, groups of isolated palm trees punctuated the horizon. There was much folklore about novice crewmembers new to the islands, who were tempted to take sightseeing boat rides provided by our RAF Marine Branch colleagues based at Gan. Primarily situated for the rescue of downed aircraft and their crews, in their spare time, this small unit used to offer rides to the neighbouring islands around the atoll. One such island across the other side from Gan was appropriately named Bushy. Legend had it that there was a disco on this remote spot where local girls provided additional entertainment. Charged with a couple of cases of beer, more than a few visiting aircrew had been left for hours at a time on Bushy with expectations beyond their wildest dreams. Once dumped on the beach, they would find nothing but sand and palm trees as they were directed towards the (imaginary) disco on the far side of the island. They would have no option but to drink the beer and wait for the boat crew to reappear. Howls of derision from the resident marine craft crews would add to their embarrassment.

Stepping across the causeway to the adjacent island of Hitaddu, there was a small RAF communications unit. It handled amongst other needs the long-range communications with aircraft and the link with headquarters in the UK. Fishing was a favourite pastime for the motley bunch of airmen stationed there. Uniform consisted of baggy empire building shorts and flip-flops, with scant regard to rank badges.

Their star attraction was a four metre square concrete pool that housed a bizarre selection of marine life from the Indian Ocean. About three feet deep, it was the permanent home for several species of shark and ray, barracuda, grouper and not to mention puffer fish, which if trod on could be fatal without prompt medical attention. The pool was not there purely for those interested in fish: it was also a source of great fun. Lashed together by assorted pieces of old rope, several sun-bleached scaffold planks lay alongside. The challenge was to ride a rickety old service bicycle along the sagging planks, which were hastily put in place to span the pool. Along with others in my crew, I took my turn and gingerly attempted the crossing. I don't recall anyone successfully crossing from one side to the other without falling in. It was great sport watching people eject themselves from the water whilst evading the perils of the pool. The chaps marooned at that desolate command post had a habit of finding many strange ways to make the hours and days pass quicker.

Addu Atoll taken from the F-4 on arrival – 27 October 1972. (© Crown)

We flew a Gan–Gan sector on 2 November 1972, refuelling our buddy tankers, as more aircraft were sent on their way to Singapore. Two days later, we launched again with another batch of our chicks one of which was crewed by our friends from the Fighting Cocks squadron. Straight after take-off, one promptly declared a Mayday. In the confusion that followed, we were recalled, dumped fuel, and landed back at Gan after about ninety minutes in the air. Meanwhile, the front canopy of 43 Squadron's Phantom had somehow become detached from its rails and deposited itself into the ocean below. Seated immediately behind the front windshield, the pilot was protected from the airflow to some extent, although noise made communication between him and his navigator impossible. The flight commander in the back was deluged with blast and buffeting from the open area of the cockpit in front of him. With three jugs (external fuel tanks) fitted, the F-4 was massively overweight for an immediate return and landing. Having no fuel dumping capability, the only option available to the Phantom crew was to burn off the excess fuel down to an acceptable landing weight. Unfortunately, this took the better part of nearly two hours, by which time the nav was battered virtually senseless and deaf. After landing, by which time we were well refreshed in the bar, the stricken jet would be in need of a replacement front canopy before any subsequent flight. To seek shelter from the sun, it was decided to tug the Phantom from the apron to the motor transport shed so that when the replacement canopy arrived, the engineers would be able to work in the shade. Sadly, this operation resulted in two perfect grooves from the wheels of the heavy jet along the length of one of the few metalled roads in Gan. Finally, in the second week of November, we refuelled our remaining chick to the Far East and left him to make his own way to Changi before we peeled off into Tengah.

We had a few days off before flying again, and so we were able to explore our new surroundings in Singapore. Boogis Street – long since razed – had to be visited, along with the night markets and hot spots. We drank Singapore Slings in The Raffles Hotel where the prices were a fraction of what they are now, and took in as many of the local sights as our poor military allowances would permit. On 14 November 1972, we took a theatre familiarisation flight to give us a feel for the air traffic control and geography around the area. We tracked north along the Malaysian coastline up to the Penang district, where we made an approach into the large base at Butterworth.

214 Squadron Victor K1 XA937 in the Far East. (© Crown)

On our return to Singapore, we flew into our sister base at Changi where our fighters were based. Over the next couple of days, we flew alongside our Phantoms on the local towlines, and participated in exercises with the neighbouring air defence fighters. I remember acting as a high-flying target for the local Mirage fighters, which failed abysmally to get anywhere near our cruising altitude. Despite her sluggishness on the ground, once in the air, the clean shape and superb crescent wing of the Victor was more than capable of hauling her to an altitude of over 50,000 feet. Although the fact that our aircrew equipment assemblies (i.e. oxygen system and cabin pressurisation) were only cleared up to 49,000 feet, we flew our aircraft to over 51,000 feet that day. Our nav radar was able to see through the rear view periscope the Mirage interceptors topping out and falling earthbound several thousand feet below and behind us.

We returned from Singapore courtesy of Transport Command once more in the whispering giant, a Bristol Britannia of 99 Squadron. I purchased my first Seiko watch, the preferred chronometer chosen by almost everyone on the detachment. Top of my shopping list was however a complete hi-fi system. Singapore was probably the best duty-free port in the world at that time in which to acquire the best in High Fidelity stereo equipment. My bargains included cabinet-style ScanDyna speakers from Denmark, a powerful Akai amplifier, and top of the range record deck. By the time my colleagues flew my 'presents' home, we might not have had much by way of possessions in our house, but we did have a stereo system that was second to none. The reality of such extravagance came back to haunt me however when I received my next pay cheque. Having drawn advances to pay for my new toys, Eileen was not well pleased when my pay for the whole of the next month came to £19.

Approximately halfway through the tour as a co-pilot, suitable candidates were offered an Intermediate Co-pilot's Course (ICC). This training was designed to improve the overall skills of the co-pilot who had only previously occupied the right-hand seat, by introducing him to the left-hand seat; i.e. the captain's seat. It was a prelude to promotion and captaincy. After serving on 214 for just under fifteen months, in February 1973, I began my ICC training. This was a significant step because unlike the ergonomically designed aircraft of today where all important controls and systems are equally accessible by either pilot, the same was not the case in the Cold War generation of aircraft.

The various systems of the Victor were positioned around the cockpit, with the result that the switches for certain systems like engine anticing and cockpit pressurisation were only available to the pilot in the right seat. All critical switching was deliberately located on the left-hand panels; designed to be functioned by the captain only. Although each pilot had his own dedicated throttles as these were placed on the consoles on the outside of each seat, the nose-wheel steering handle for example was situated on the left side of the front edge of the fuel tray. It could only be reached and operated by the pilot in the left seat. Therefore, it was only that pilot who was able to steer the aircraft during ground manoeuvring. The same applied to the very important brake parachute switch that deployed the braking parachute after landing (or aborted take-off). Having completed the course, the ICC co-pilot was qualified to occupy the left seat and act as captain, provided of course a suitably qualified instructor occupied the other seat. From that moment on, I would take every opportunity to fly with one of the instructors who would permit me to fly in the left-hand seat in preparation for my captaincy.

In late April 1973, I was programmed to participate in a Ghost trail recovering fighters from the Far East. Fortunately, I was crewed with Sqn Ldr Tony Banfield, our squadron QFI. I would progress through much of my remaining career crossing over with Tony in the training world as a QFI, and later at Boscombe Down as a test pilot. During the next seven sorties therefore, courtesy of Tony, I flew from the left-hand seat on five occasions. The first two sectors were transits through Akrotiri to Dubai in the Gulf. By the third sortie, I was feeling very confident in my new seat as we started engines on the ramp at what was then a desolate airfield – a far cry from its prominent international status today. A rickety old hangar behind me on the edge of the ramp looked decidedly unsteady on its rusting steel supports at each corner. Our Phantoms were already taking to the runway as I teased up the Sapphire turbojets in the soaring daytime temperatures. By the time my aircraft had started to move from its parking spot, a startled transmission from ATC informed me that I had just blown down the decrepit hangar behind me. Fortunately, there were no aircraft in it, nor had there been I surmised for some time. Imperative that I get airborne without delay to chase after my chicks, I disregarded the request for me to hold my position, and promptly took to the runway completing the checks on the roll. I never heard back from our hosts in Dubai, sensing that I may have done them a favour in the long term.

By the time we got to Gan, it had been dark for some time. Although deprived of the awe-inspiring seascapes of the idyllic islands nestled in their atolls, my approach to Gan for the first time in the left seat was still exciting. The approach lighting (apparently fully serviceable since my last visit) guided me effortlessly towards the concrete strip. I remember it being a black night with no clear horizon from the confines of our dimly-lit cockpit. After touching down on the relatively short runway, I streamed the brake parachute promptly. Deceleration was normal, and I allowed the jet to coast along the full length of the landing strip. I planned to turn the aircraft around through 180 degrees at the end of the runway and back track along its length to the turn-off taxiway. The brake parachute would normally be jettisoned on the runway when down to taxi speed.

As it was a late hour however, I felt it would be more considerate to keep the 'chute deployed and drag it back to the apron area and avoid the need to call out the recovery team. In order to prevent damage to the fabric, the technique was to ease up the power on the inner engines and use the jet efflux to keep it billowing above the tarmac. At the end of the runway, I was careful as I swung around to keep the wheels within the confines of the narrow runway. I was aware of my brake parachute trailing some 200 feet or so behind the aircraft's tail cone. In the blackness at the far end of the airfield, as I straightened the aircraft to start backtracking, there was a sudden jerk through the airframe. Looking quizzically at Tony to my right, and before I could utter a word, the aircraft shuddered a second time. Thinking that perhaps it was some sort of braking anomaly, I continued to taxi the aircraft via the turn-off and parked on the edge of the ramp. Momentarily increasing the power to tension the webbing, I operated the release so that the brake 'chute would fall backwards and settle just off the apron behind. As it could be gathered up in the morning, I agreed with tower to leave it until daybreak, and promptly shut down and put the aircraft to bed.

The following day as we reported to the flight line for a Gan–Gan sortie, the ground crew met us with a host of questions. We were asked quizzically if we had had problems on landing and in particular with the brake parachute. Temporarily forgetting about the jerking movements at the runway end, I said that all had been normal as far as I could recall. They invited us outside to take a look. On the ground, the mangled remains of our braking parachute were spread out. I looked at Tony and wondered what could have caused it to be ripped to shreds. Further inspection revealed that the dishevelled pile of webbing contained the tangled remains of splintered goalposts. All became clear as it transpired that the tugging that I had felt the night before occurred as a result of uprooting the goalposts from the football field next to the end of the runway. Needless to say, we were hardly flavour of the month with the footy enthusiasts at Gan Island. We kept our heads down as we passed through Dubai once more as we brought our Phantoms inbound, skulking back to Akrotiri as quietly as possible without attracting attention.

RAF Gan where I uprooted goalposts – 25 April 1973. (© Crown)

Before the month was out, I accompanied Tony Banfield again, this time on a Western Tankex that involved slipping through Goose Bay to Offut Air Force Base, Nebraska. Home of the USAF Strategic Air Command Headquarters, our American cousins treated us with their usual generous hospitality. Steak would never quite be the same again after I was introduced to the 20-ounce porterhouse. As we recovered to 'The Goose' on the way back, a change of plan (probably lack of handling facilities at the snow-bound RAF detachment) required us to route through Gander. On arrival at Gander, we were faced with desperately poor weather conditions. Newfoundland was enveloped in low cloud, and there were widespread horrendous winds and torrential rain. To make things worse, the wind was blowing directly across the runway in use, and the surface rain was pooling heavily. The landing that followed was quite eventful. After streaming the brake parachute, the swing from the sideways pull on the canvass almost took the aircraft off the side of the runway. Tony needed the full width and length of the runway to bring the aquaplaning jet to a halt. As there was no RAF support at the airport, we were fortunate on that occasion to have a crew chief riding the sixth seat. The following day, he was able to satisfy himself that we had not 'boiled' any of the tyres as a result of aquaplaning, and we recovered the aircraft to the UK without further ado.

The summer months flashed by with the usual mix of tanker receiver training on Towline 2, and the refuelling exercises for our various receiver types, colloquially known as Buccex, Litex, Harrex and Phantex towline training sorties. Further detachments were undertaken to Luqa in Malta and Akrotiri supporting yet more fighter trails. In September 1973, 214 Squadron was tasked to refuel a section of Lightnings to Tehran in Iran. Still very much under the control of the Shah, the Imperial Republic of Iran's Air Force was a well equipped service, thanks primarily to the Americans, but operated very much on British lines. The RAF's Lightnings were seen as ideal playmates for Iran's fighters, namely the Republic F-5. Arriving in Mehrabad Air Base close to the capital, I was immediately struck by the raw beauty of this impressive country. Situated about 8,000 feet above sea level, it was obvious that our gutless Mk 1 Victors were not going to be able to fly off with heavy fuel loads, despite the long runway.

Within forty-eight hours of our arrival, we were refuelling our Lightnings that were already pitting their wits against the western-trained Iranian F-5s. Once our tanks were depleted, we raced back to Mehrabad and promptly commandeered the swimming pool in the hotel occupied by our fighter pilots. Typically, our hotel did not have a pool, so we made the best of a bad situation by using theirs; that is until their squadron boss presented himself poolside. Still suited in his 'grow bag', he told us in no uncertain terms that we could now vacate the pool as his boys were about to appear after some hard flying. The special relationship that normally existed between the Lightning pilots and tanker aircrews certainly failed to materialise on this detachment.

Not since my IACE visit to Turkey had I witnessed such diversity of scenery in that beautiful country. The bazaars in Tehran were amazing, as we routed through endless passages and alleys crammed full with merchandise. I purchased the inevitable copper table, which only just fitted into Annie's Hatch in the back of our tanker. One of our more adventurous captains risked being beheaded by illegally procuring several bottles of brandy, which were decanted into demijohns lifted from Akrotiri on the way out. The contraband booze would prove to have considerable purchasing power in the crowded bazaars. The highlight of the visit however was a cultural evening in the British Embassy in the company of many local dignitaries, senior officers and ambassadors in Iran's capital. We had to restrain our crew chiefs from stealing the vast array of plaques and memorabilia that would have fitted in just fine with the spoils of war that adorned our squadron crew room back home. Servants bearing silver platters loaded with every conceivable spirit and mixes, hovered around the plush residence. Dressed in my favourite (only) light cavalry twill suit, I thought I presented a picture of sartorial elegance, until it was time to leave. Having drunk an excess of the complimentary drinks, I descended the grand steps at the front of the residence, stumbling halfway down. I attempted to stay upright, as my legs frantically tried to keep pace with my body. I ended up falling to my knees in the grit of the driveway, in the process ripping gaping holes in my suit trousers. Although I'm sure no one of importance witnessed my undignified departure, I'm embarrassed to say we lived up to our moniker as tanker trash that evening.

More major inter-service exercises followed in October during which time we intercepted a number of Bear contacts over the Iceland/Faroes gap. By January 1974, I had completed just two years and three months as a Victor co-pilot, and had accrued in excess of 1,000 hours. In February, I returned to the OCU once more to start the captains' course. I immersed myself in the books again, something which would characterise my career until retirement thirty-six years later. This would be an opportunity to finally prove myself as a crew commander, with the prospect of returning to my preferred 214 Squadron as a tanker force captain.

Chapter Six

The Sport of Kings

Captain – 214 Squadron, RAF Marham
May 1974 to January 1976

112 Victor course at No 232 OCU – February 1974. (© Crown)

After a spell in the ground school, I was soon back in the air in the left-hand seat, a position in which I was becoming increasingly at ease. My student crew spanned the first five ranks. My fresh-faced co-pilot was a pilot officer, and my nav radar was a flying officer, both junior to me as a flight lieutenant. However, as my AEO was a squadron leader and nav plotter a wing commander, both were senior to me. Wg Cdr Alistair Sutherland had been posted back to the Tanker Force and was assigned as the next squadron commander on 55 Squadron. After three dual sorties, on 8 April 1974, I operated as pilot-in-command of Victor B1A XH467 for the first time.

Three weeks later, I completed a final handling test in the company of OC 232 OCU, and joined my crew on a night-long celebration. The impromptu party went on until the early hours of the morning when some wag decided that we should have a musical interlude. Armed with my mouth organ, we rattled around the patch to retrieve each crewmember's choice of musical instrument. We composed and sang until dawn, soaking up the euphoria of having graduated as No 1 Group's finest tanker crew. I was able to catch up on some leave before reporting back to 214 Squadron on the far side of the airfield. Before the month was out, 2½ years after my first ranger to Akrotiri, I embarked upon my first crew solo deployment as a newly promoted captain to Cyprus. After five hours aloft and having coupled up with a pair of our in-theatre 56 Squadron Lightnings for a refuelling refresher, we were in the thick of it savouring the familiar brandy sours in the bar once more.

The next few weeks on the squadron allowed me to settle into the familiar routine of tanking our usual customers on the UK towlines. By early August, I was honing my formation skills as a new captain in the left-hand seat. We frequently planned tail chases on departure, which made the now-familiar snake climb procedure routine. Alongside other Victor tankers, I took every opportunity to accompany another tanker during descent and approach to landing. Based on the remote possibility of losing the primary airspeed indicator, it was a great excuse to use the other aircraft as a shepherd, and practise the accompanied let down back to base. I never did find myself in such a predicament, but I managed to fly these accompanied manoeuvres on both my second and third sorties back on 214.

The next rung on the operational ladder as a new captain was to get my receiver 'ticket'. In order to maximise the flexibility of a number of tankers in formation, our crews not only had to be qualified to dispense fuel as a tanker but also take on fuel as a receiver. All Mk1 Victors were equipped with a refuelling probe mounted over the cockpit, which meant that all squadron aircraft could receive fuel.

The ability to take on fuel as well as transfer it was at the core of flexibility within the Tanker Force. The whole process started with the two aircraft joining up after the snake climb or rendezvous. As the captain's seat was on the left side of the cockpit, the ideal station keeping position was echelon starboard: i.e. to the right-hand side and slightly astern of the lead aircraft. This offered the best field of vision to the receiver pilot. The windscreen structure and relatively narrow front and side windows, meant it was quite difficult to maintain close formation in echelon port looking across the cockpit whilst flying from the captain's seat. The tanker aircraft as formation leader would prepare for refuelling by trailing the centreline hose. To get the hose to droop at the correct angle, it needed to be filled with fuel, a task performed by the nav radar. The procedure also permitted the refuelling operator to 'prime' the hose to ensure all air was removed prior to transfer. With the tanker now ready for refuelling, the pilot would clear the receiver aircraft to move astern. This is where the fun started. The normal sequence was to reduce

The refuelling probe mounted above the cockpit transparencies.

power and allow the aircraft to drop back a couple of aircraft lengths, and then slide astern the tanker. Easing on the power once more, the ideal 'stabilised pre-contact' position was achieved by positioning the aircraft so that the tip of the probe sat in line with the trailed hose approximately ten feet behind the basket.

Adding a small knob of power to create a closure rate of 3–4 knots, the aim was to fly the aircraft up the line of the trailed hose and place the probe tip inside the periphery of basket. The spokes of the basket would then guide the probe into the central reception coupling. As the probe tip nudged forward over spring-loaded rollers, it was gripped with sufficient force to enable the basket and probe to move as one. This was referred to as a 'latched contact'. At the same time, the hose drum unit motor would wind in the hose, preventing any tendency for the hose to droop. Once seven feet of hose was wound on the drum, all conditions for the transfer of fuel were satisfied. As the vertically arranged traffic lights either side of the HDU fairing changed from amber to green, a steady flow of fuel was indicated, and fuel would pass into the receiver's tanks. At this point, the receiver's cockpit transparencies were as little as twenty feet from the tail cone of the tanker above, and frequently less. As the hose was pushed in, the HDU motor took up any slack so that a constant droop angle was maintained. The receiver pilot would then aim to maintain a stabilised in-contact position whilst taking on the required amount of fuel.

The hose was marked with white bands at ten-foot intervals to assist the pilot in judging his longitudinal position. As the hose was pushed in so that forty feet of hose remained trailing from the tanker's HDU, the receiver pilot's aircraft was at the ideal refuelling position. A

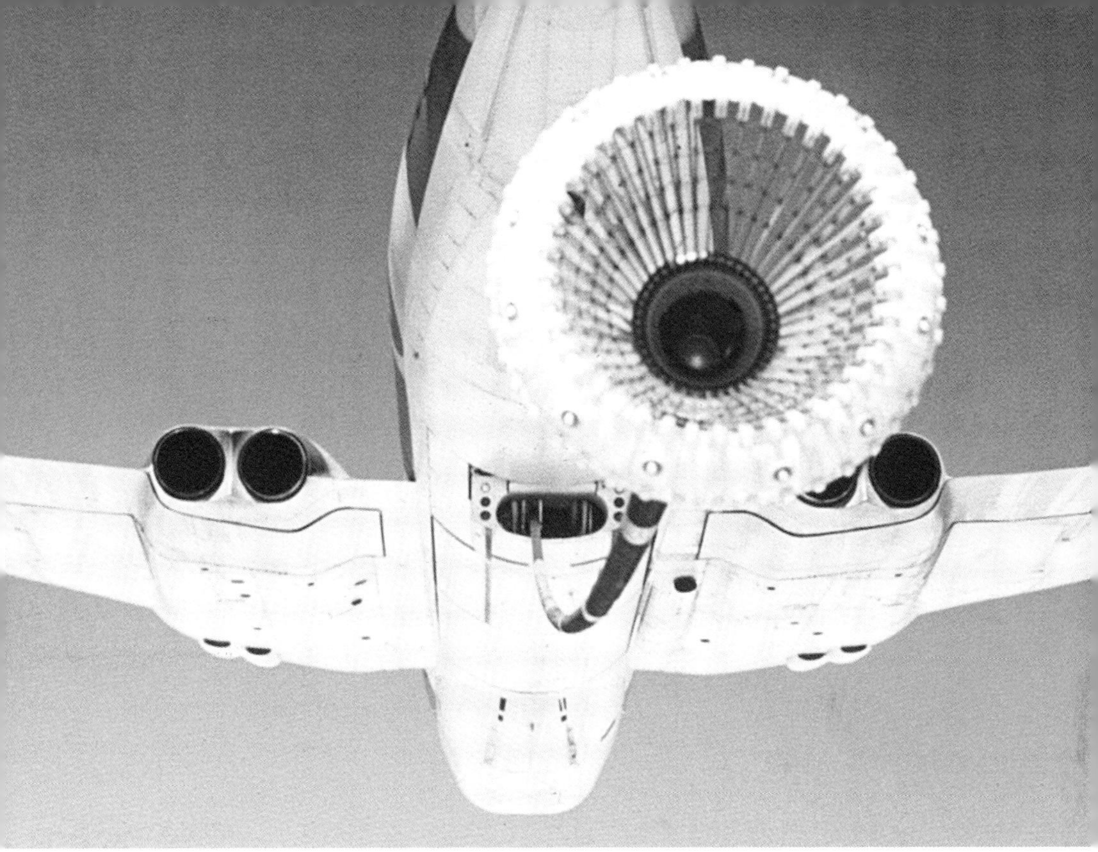

Stabilised 'pre-contact' position: probe tip ten feet astern the basket.

View from co-pilot's seat of the stabilised 'in-contact' position.

lip of the HDU carriage. A serving carriage traversed the entrance to the hose drum from left to right as the hose was wound in to keep it neatly coiled on the drum. This carriage attained a position approximately two-thirds towards the right-hand side of the HDU opening – another visual cue that the correct fore-and-aft position had been achieved. At this stabilised position in close contact, the receiver aircraft was able to gently manoeuvre laterally and vertically within acceptable limits of what was referred to as the 'cone of safety'. Fore and aft position was maintained by slight adjustments on the throttles to keep the orange band at the mouth of the HDU. If the receiver aircraft dropped back, the basket would stay attached to the probe assisted by the drag from the airstream on the webbing around its periphery. At the same time, the coiled hose would feed out from the drum to enable the fuel transfer to continue. When ready to break contact, the pilot would reduce power slightly and allow the aircraft to drop back slowly, whilst following the extended line of the drooping hose. The hose would feed from the drum until it reached a mechanical stop on the serving carriage at full extension. The arrested hose would then impart a tug on the basket that would overcome the geometric lock at the reception coupling, allowing the rollers to release the probe tip. As basket and probe separated, the receiver aircraft would position back onto the starboard wing of the tanker. Once the area behind was clear, the hose was wound in and the post-tanking checks completed.

Not for the faint hearted therefore, the art of receiving fuel, particularly in such a large aircraft, was a massive undertaking and one that demanded considerable skill and discipline. My receiver training began four months after my arrival as a new skipper. The aim was to keep the wings aligned with the lateral plane of the tanker ahead, and maintain the same perspective fore and aft by making small changes of power. The biggest mistake whilst 'prodding' (pilot speak for the process of making contact) was 'chasing' a moving basket as the approach to contact was made.

Focusing on the basket usually meant losing the big picture, which often resulted in the receiver pilot's inputs becoming erratic. Invariably, this would lead to over-controlling and the aircraft becoming unstable – not ideal when so close to the tanker in front. Floodlights illuminated the under surfaces of the tanker to permit refuelling to be accomplished at night. Night prodding was even more difficult as fewer visual references were available to the formating pilot. Furthermore, it became even more difficult when flying on 'black' nights where no clear horizon was apparent, and especially when executing turns whilst in contact. A phenomenon exists when there is disagreement between what the inner ear senses and what the eye sees, which is very confusing and can be unsettling for the formating pilot. During refuelling, it was not unusual to sense that the aircraft was rolling in one direction, despite having just rolled the wings level after stopping a turn. Referred to as 'the leans', it was absolutely imperative to ignore the confusing messages, and concentrate on keeping station with reference to the aircraft in front. Practice was the only pre-requisite in developing the required skill and confidence.

My receiver training during August and September 1974 consisted of ten sorties during which time I made ninety-three 'dry' prods (no fuel transferred) and two 'wet' contacts (fuel transferred). A quarter of these contacts were made at night. One of the wet contacts was a 'maximum onload' where I received 25,000 lbs of fuel during one single transfer. The task simulated a critical refuelling during an operational trail where the aircraft would be required to fill to full. I found the whole process of receiver training as a pilot challenging, yet thoroughly enjoyable. The satisfaction of accomplishing a series of nicely controlled contacts without incurring the wrath of the seasoned rear crew was instantaneous and a personal confidence builder. Prodding was without doubt, as far as the receiver-trained tanker pilots were concerned, the sport of kings.

A pair of Victors 'buddy refuelling'.

However I did receive a rude awakening just prior to my final night solo-prodding sortie. On 12 September 1974, I was called out as the standby skipper on the familiar Operation Dragonfly. This was my first opportunity as a new captain to intercept an inbound intruder. Blasting off in my combat-readied tanker, I was accompanied by four other crewmembers with whom I had not flown before. As soon as the gear and flaps were retracted, an engine fire audio warning filled my bone dome earpieces. Placed prominently on the coaming directly in front of the pilots' field of view, one of the red engine fire lights was illuminated brightly. I called for the engine fire drill, eased back on the throttles to level off, and put out a Mayday call. I positioned over the north Norfolk coast while the crew went into their immediate actions. After my co-pilot had pressed the fire extinguisher button, a few seconds later, the fire light went out confirming the fire had been extinguished.

With engines paired in close proximity in each wing root, the standard operating procedure was to shut down the adjacent engine as a precaution just in case of secondary damage. This was accomplished without delay. We were laden with a full fuel load, and flying on two engines had not only handling considerations, but also performance limitations with only half engine thrust remaining. Fuel dumping was the next priority therefore in order to get down to an acceptable landing weight. This would also make control easier on approach and shorten the stopping distances associated with landing at a heavy weight. With the emergency drills completed, I set up for an immediate return to base to put the aircraft back on the ground as quickly and safely as possible. We touched down back at RAF Marham in just fifteen minutes.

The potential for disaster became apparent as we evacuated the aircraft. I was flabbergasted to see fuel coming out of every orifice. To make matters worse, the wheel brakes – overheated from the heavyweight and faster than normal landing – were billowing smoke in close proximity to the leaking fuel. On a positive note, Marham's ever-ready fire crews in their tenders were now surrounding us. We backed off onto the grassy area by the side of the runway and left our firemen to get on with their job. In a moment strangely reflective of my Chipmunk cowling emergency, we were delighted to see a crew bus arrive, and thought we'd be whisked off to operations to get out of our sweaty flying overalls. Not so! The crew transport deposited us by XA936, a second standby aircraft, and without further ado, we were told to get airborne ASAP. Operation Dragonfly was still effective, and there was clearly to be no pat on the back followed by a few beers in the bar. With my heart still pounding at nineteen to the dozen, we clambered aboard our new steed and launched once more in pursuit of the Russian Bear.

A tri-service major exercise followed a few days later in the form of Northern Merger. I flew two consecutive missions on 26 October and spent nearly eight hours in the air. The following month, my crew picked up our second lone ranger, this time to RAF Germany. Recognised as a real jolly, the operational reason behind this lone ranger was to give the crew the experience of planning and undertaking an unaccompanied deployment to RAF Gütersloh. Having flown across the lower part of the North Sea, we provided a couple of hours refuelling training for the Lightning F-2s of 19 and 92 Squadrons. After shut down, I was dragged, bone dome in hand, across the ramp to a waiting two-seat Lightning. Much to the chagrin of my co-pilot, I had secretly arranged a ride with one of my old Cranwell counterparts.

Within twenty minutes, we fired off Gütersloh's strip in full burner and headed for the remote German countryside. Keith Hartley was to become a good friend over the years, as we both subsequently graduated from ETPS into the world of test flying. What I did not know that day was that Keith would become one of the most widely acknowledged experts on the supersonic Lightning over the next three decades. Keeping it just below the speed of sound, I flew the T-bird around the famous Möhne Dam and after barely fifteen minutes at full chat, we were spearing back into the circuit having burnt the best part of four tonnes of fuel. The whole weekend after this exhilarating ride was spent on cloud nine. Happy hour in the mess bar that Friday evening seemed to last about eight hours from what I could remember. On Saturday, we were treated to a drunken crawl around the married patch where a different meal course awaited us at each house. Armed with a barrel of Norwich Ales that we had smuggled in Annie's hatch on the outbound flight, we returned the hospitality on Sunday lunchtime by inviting our hosts to the mess for some real ale. Before we departed for Marham on Monday morning, we serviced our new friends in their thirsty Lightnings with a final refuelling on the Germany towline. I

Climbing into a Lightning T5 at RAF Gütersloh – 4 October 1974.

had a whole new perspective of RAF Germany after that fantastic weekend.

It would be six months before I was lucky enough to land another Germany ranger. The flight over to the towline on this occasion went without a hitch until about halfway through the refuelling when we lost an alternator. Although three remained, there were potential problems with taking this aircraft into Germany, and so whilst we were still able to finish the tanking session with the Lightnings, I asked my AEO to call No 1 Group HQ to advise them of our predicament. However, not about to lose such a fabulous repeat engagement, I hatched a plan to fly back to Marham after the refuelling, with a view to returning immediately using the squadron hack, XH667. I knew that the two-pointer, limited to daylight tanking only, would not be needed over the weekend. Accordingly, with the refuelling complete, we raced back to base at limiting Mach number. Bag dragging between the pans, and seeking the assistance of our ground crew to swap over our liquid cargo in Annie's Hatch, we were airborne once more bound for RAF Germany after a record turn around. We made happy hour in good time and settled into yet another great weekend of entertainment.

The officers' mess at Gütersloh was a majestic building. Accentuating the front elevation was a corner turret-like structure that housed at its upper level a small octagonal-shaped room. Apparently, this room was a favourite hideaway for the elite Luftwaffe fighter pilots based there during the Second World War. Tales of their prowess in their Me109s washed down with copious quantities of fine German lager no doubt echoed into the early hours of the morning. Gütersloh's commanding officer was none other than Field Marshal Hermann Göring, the iconic German fighter ace. Apart from the superior air created by his considerable stature, Göring would often hold court with his adoring protégés, and was well known for his quotations and boasts.

Directed to this remarkable little room by our RAF fighter pilots of the seventies, I noticed the well-worn benches around its periphery and imagined the proud and cocky Luftwaffe pilots who had listened attentively to their esteemed leader. In the low ceiling, a crooked oak beam spanned the walls. A staggered cut in its centre was cleverly carved so that the one half would support the other when hitched up to the ceiling. It was at this point that one of our colleagues recounted the tale of a particular meeting between Göring and his young pilots. Pontificating in his usual manner, he was reported as saying that, "If I should ever tell a lie, may the beams of this ceiling creak". At this juncture, and anticipating the moment, some bright spark pulled surreptitiously on a handle by a floorboard at the edge of the room. This handle was connected to a concealed cable that held up the ceiling beams. A pull on the cable enabled the split beam, hinged at either end, to lower from the ceiling resulting in a noticeable creaking noise. How amused Göring was at this response from his underlings is uncertain, but it is a delightful anecdote. Certainly in March 1974, one was still able to operate the creaking beam, and I have no reason to doubt the validity of the tale.

As one would have imagined, the fighter pilots of the German air force were afforded all the privileges that came with their illustrious position. By all account, they feasted like princes and were treated like royalty. The public rooms in the officers' mess shouted opulence, and the RAF personnel took pride in maintaining the décor of this unique building. One particular aspect of decoration however did fall fowl of one particular RAF commanding officer during the seventies. The toilets were situated in the basement, and were reached via a staircase from the main entrance hall. In the lavatories, there were large chromium-plated handlebars positioned either side of the urinals attached to the walls. You could only imagine our German cousins grasping the bars while hurling into the porcelain after a gluttonous meal. A certain previous CO had been so offended that officers might behave in such a manner, that he had the 'straining bars' removed. Fortuitously the subsequent CO had seen fit to restore the toilets to their former glory. Sadly however, most of the glorious murals that had adorned the remaining walls of the gentlemen's room had been lost forever.

In the intervening months, I was able to consolidate my experience through frequent exercises and trails. Akrotiri and Luqa featured regularly, and always provided interesting flying and great fun. My confidence as a receiver pilot grew with recurrent prodding practice, although the pressure to make contact on those important brackets during an operational trail never failed to raise the blood pressure. Within a year of joining the squadron, I had amassed over 200 contacts, around a quarter of which were made at night. Operation Dragonfly missions punctuated the regular training, although it seemed that the Russians were testing our defences less aggressively throughout this period.

On 2 June 1975, I landed my first Western Tankex as a captain, transiting once more to Goose Bay, Labrador. The next day, we flew a Goose-Goose trip, during which a maximum offload was given to another Marham tanker returning direct from Offutt Air Force Base (AFB) to the UK. On 4 June, we made the four-hour transit to Nebraska where we had forty-eight hours off. On arrival at the base, I offered to drive the rental car, not realising it was of course an automatic. Parking on a verge outside the Ponderosa Steak House on our first night, I was somewhat red faced when spinning the wheels so fast in the soft ground that it sank to the axle; I was glad of a five-man crew (and crew chief) to push the saloon out. Having just got accustomed to the cold beer, it was time to return to base two days later. This involved my first operational maximum onload over Newfoundland from a fellow Victor tanker. In the refuelling bracket, I took on board 45,000 lbs of avtur in one go, a contact that lasted over twenty-five minutes. I was more than relieved to hand over the aircraft to my co-pilot and take a break as we coasted out from the eastern seaboard to cross the Atlantic. After nine hours and five minutes, we landed back on familiar turf at Marham.

Ironically, a particular sortie on 17 July 1975, only five weeks after the transit home, deserves more than a passing mention. Although large transfers of fuel between Victor tankers were not unusual, especially on Operation Dragonfly, Marham was tasked with a specific exercise on this date identified as Exercise Big Suck. I forget the background for this; perhaps it was called for following modifications in the probe, its many shims and seals, or other elements of the refuelling system. Nevertheless, I was scheduled to fly on towline 5 off the Norfolk coast and rendezvous with another Victor K1. The aim was to receive a maximum onload of 50,000 lbs, change places, and transfer it all back to the other aircraft. In any deployment where a flight of tankers launch from the same base, it would take the order of two hours or so to burn off that amount of fuel to create the space in the tanks to then receive such a maximum transfer. Furthermore, a transfer of fuel of this magnitude would take approximately thirty minutes in duration. Although the centre hose was capable of transferring fuel at up to 2,500 lbs per minute, this suggested that a 50,000-lb transfer could be accomplished in around twenty minutes. In reality, as the aircraft's fuel tanks are filled to full, a back pressure develops in the diminishing tank space above the fuel. This results in a considerable reduction of transfer rate as the tanks get close to full. Interestingly, as the Victor nears its maximum all-up weight, the controls appear 'heavier', making even small corrective inputs in the elevators and ailerons increasingly difficult and tiring. Apart from the considerable length of time in contact whilst receiving fuel, the sheer concentration and skill required is quite exceptional. Clearly however, No 1 Group needed to establish and prove that specific capability. The pilot in my right-hand seat that day was Flt Lt Steve 'Biggles' Biglands, our AAR instructor on 214 Squadron. The next time that I would take on a maximum onload of that amount would be during the celebrated Black Buck 1 mission in the South Atlantic during the Falklands War. By pure coincidence, I would be refuelling with Biggles on that occasion too, albeit under a very different set of circumstances. Someone was indeed thinking outside the box in 1975.

The Russians seemed to have stirred the hornet's nest once more during the latter months of 1975. Along with my armed escorts, we intercepted several Tupolev Bear 'Delta' and 'Foxtrots' not to mention the occasional Tu-16 'Badger' and M-4 'Bison' long-range bomber and reconnaissance aircraft. As I write this some time after the end of the Cold War, it seems these ancient long-range recce aircraft are pursuing something of a renaissance as the Tupolov Bears are being seen once again prowling around the fringes of the UK's airspace in 2015.

M-4 'Bison' intercept, Exercise Strong Express, 26 September 1972. (© Crown)

The Mk 1 Victor behaved itself generally very well during the five years that I flew it, and I have only fond memories of my tenure on 214 Squadron. Apart from the incidences mentioned, and a couple of other engine failures neither of which occurred at critical phases of flight, I had few other scares. On 14 August 1975, I did have a repeat of the nasty engine fire experienced a year earlier, again during the climb. This turned out to be a mirror image of my previous situation where after shutting down the engine, and its adjacent engine, I managed to disperse around 40,000 lbs of aviation kerosene over the Norfolk countryside, before landing my smoking jet within fifteen minutes of taking off. The magnificent Marham fire crews dealt with my predicament with their usual aplomb, and we retired to the bar without delay on that occasion.

That aside, I can say that I always felt totally secure in the great Handley Page aircraft. It was always going to be a wrench leaving such an iconic aircraft that I had grown very fond of. Although designed as a bomber, the Victor B1 had been modified to fill the gap created by the demise of the Valiant tanker, in the role of air-to-air refuelling. The fact that it adapted to this unique role so readily from an engineering point of view as well as operationally was directly attributable to the superb Handley Page design. However, plans had been well in hand to upgrade the basic airframe and engines. From the mid 1970s, the vastly superior and more capable Victor K2 started to arrive at Marham. For the time being however, I had to say farewell to the faithful Mark 1 Victor.

Each year in the RAF, an individual's progression as an officer and pilot had to be assessed by one's immediate supervisor. Officer qualities and flying ability topped the important sections of the Form 1369. However, there was an opportunity to state on this form up to three preferred postings once the current tour expired. This 'dream sheet' bid rarely became reality, but the majority of pilots did aspire to one particular choice of posting – the exchange tour. The RAF, in company with the rest of NATO's air forces, participated in such an exchange programme. Its aim was to give the successful candidate the opportunity to serve in the armed forces of one of the other member nations to promote a mutual understanding of each other's operations and procedures. Options available for tanker pilots who had completed a successful captain's tour were limited, although there were two in existence during the 1970s. Both appointments were within the United States Air Force (USAF). The first was established at Pease AFB in New York State on the eastern seaboard, and the second at Mather AFB in California. I had lodged my bid for an exchange tour in the States as the first preference on my dream sheet for the previous two years. No one was more surprised therefore when my squadron commander appeared without notice at our quarter one evening. The boss informed Eileen and I – under the strictest confidence – that I had been earmarked for the Californian exchange tour. He seemed as excited about the appointment as we were, and said that he just wanted to see the reaction on Eileen's face as he gave us the great news.

My last flight on Victor K1s just before Christmas gave me one last chance to run in ten more contacts in the company of a sister 55 Squadron aircraft, bringing my total number of prods to around 250. With 1,700 hours under my belt, I would take my next flight on the mighty Boeing Stratotanker into the blue skies of Northern California on my 27th birthday on 30 March 1976.

Last flight in Victor K1 RAF Marham – 23 December 1975. (© Crown)

After-landing drinks with OC 214 Squadron (left). (© Crown)

Chapter Seven

California Dream

904th Air Refuelling Squadron, Mather AFB, California
May 1976 to November 1978

KC-135A Stratotankers of the 904th AREFS Mather AFB –1976.

The flight in a RAF VC10 to Washington DC was a first for our three-year-old son. Although excited to begin with, after we had been airborne for barely half an hour, he announced to Eileen that he needed the toilet. As he looked around the cramped lavatory, he calmly stated that he wouldn't be using that loo. Interestingly, he still remembers the unusual rearward-facing seats of that RAF transport aircraft. To this day, he always prefers to sit facing rearwards in a train. Before taking up my appointment as an exchange officer, I was required to attend a briefing with the British Defence Staff in the embassy in Washington DC. The various meetings gave me a good feel for what I could expect at my new base. By far the most enlightening was the discussion with the financial staff.

To my great surprise, after an explanation of how my pay and allowances would be administered, I was asked if I would like to take not only a non-repayable grant, but also an interest-free loan to help us get started in California. I thought initially there must be a catch, but the stone-faced accountant calmly explained that most exchange officers did indeed take both. I needed no further encouragement, and duly slid a bundle of American dollars into my briefcase and signed on the dotted line. I liked this tour already.

In the meantime, Eileen not surprisingly opted to go shopping downtown. She soon found the prospect of looking around DC quite daunting, and despite clear blue skies, she was not prepared for the biting arctic winds that day. Having been dropped off by a cabbie, they were making their way towards the shops when the gusts threatened to blow them off their feet. At one stage, Eileen was holding onto railings and hanging on to Richard for dear life. An office worker in an adjacent building saw their plight and took them inside to protect them from the fierce elements. They were even offered a hot drink. Having decided to rendezvous at the Monument, and suitably fortified, Eileen decided to head off to our meeting point albeit somewhat earlier than planned.

On arrival at the Monument, high winds had closed the obelisk to visitors for the first time in years. Nevertheless, a very considerate staff member allowed them to wait just inside the lobby area. Half an hour later, they decided to go back outside so that I would be able to see them on my arrival. Delayed by the briefings at the embassy, I turned up considerably later than expected. In the days before mobile phones, I had been helpless to let her know of my predicament. I was somewhat surprised on my arrival to find them huddled in the back of a patrol car like a pair of criminals.

For the third time that day, our freezing solitary waifs had been rescued, this time by the splendid Washington Police Department. Two of the city's finest cops had gallantly protected my forlorn family from the bitter cold and had invited them to keep warm in the back of their ride. I think this was a defining moment for Richard who has ever since shared a special interest and affection for American cops and their 'Black and Whites'. A cab ride soon had us back in our hotel on the Potomac, where we took refuge from the weather, and counted our bundles of crisp dollar bills like criminals on the run! Our opinion of the kind American citizens of Washington that day could not have been higher, although the English accent no doubt helped.

Following our arrival at Mather in Northern California, the incumbent exchange officer had meticulously planned a frenetic week for our handover. Jim Uprichard (known to everyone as 'Updick' from our earlier days on 214 Squadron) had cultivated many service and social contacts during his tour at Mather. Together with our wives, Jim and I bounced from one social function to another every night that week. During the day, Updick trailed me around the many associated squadrons that made up the 320th Bomb Wing, introducing me to hundreds of new people that I would eventually be working with. We were all staying in the temporary living quarters while our allocated married quarter on base housing was being cleaned inside and out. Appropriately, our allocated home on base housing was at 135 McCall Drive. Situated on the far side of the airfield, the ranch-style bungalow had spacious lawns all around, which provided great playing areas for Richard. A covered port between the house and garage provided shelter for

Eileen and Richard with a Sacramento PD 'Black and White'.

bikes and toys and protection from the sun's rays. Base regulations required that we kept the grass cut and watered frequently to suppress the possibility of fires, a considerable risk in the dry hot summers. Fears of rattlesnakes and other reptiles were unfounded as we rarely saw such critters. The drive across this massive airfield between base housing and my place of work was about five miles or so, and in between was desolate scrubland. The pale sandy and largely featureless landscape was interrupted near the housing area by the emerald expanse of the Mather AFB Golf Course. All through the year, the lush shades of beautifully manicured fairways and greens stood out like an oasis in a desert. Water provided from its own natural well ensured superb playing conditions throughout the year, despite the fact that on our arrival in 1976, California was entering its sixth year of continuous drought.

First on the agenda for me during that week was the need to get a car. The city of Sacramento, California's state capital, was just a handful of miles outside the main gates. Jim took me to the city, and suggested Howe Street would be the place to go. Along its dead straight two-mile length, motor dealerships and car lots of unimaginable size displayed thousands of vehicles. Prices in 1976 were ridiculously low by UK standards; gas was currently selling for 55 cents per US gallon, approximately 25p per imperial gallon at today's prices. Armed with my wad from Washington, the choice was bewildering. Jim's only advice was to get something big and comfortable in view of the mileage that we were likely to cover over the duration of the tour. Air conditioning was an absolute necessity given the climate. Although not particularly exciting or glamorous, Updick suggested I consider buying a station wagon. He, on the other hand, had fulfilled a life long's ambition in owning a Mach One Mustang: the archetypal American muscle car. However, he had regretted not having something more spacious and comfortable when he'd driven elderly parents all the way to the Grand Canyon and back in it. With this advice in mind, although not entirely convinced, I set about the task of finding a suitable car.

Almost immediately, like love at first sight, I was irresistibly drawn towards a sky blue Pontiac Firebird. In the Californian sunshine, this archetypal roadster sporting a striking eagle motif across its enormous bonnet oozed appeal. My advisor smiled sardonically. Unlike my lowly MGB, which fit like a tight glove, this convertible was spacious, and was built to accommodate someone who was 7 feet tall. It drove like a dream; the six-litre engine accelerating it to the Californian speed limit of 65 mph in around five seconds. With a wry smile on his face, and reiterating that I had not listened to one iota to his advice, I reluctantly stepped from my dream car and widened the search.

Before long, I settled unbelievably on a Ford station wagon that was valued at a ridiculously low price, but whole-heartedly approved by Updick. Ironically, America was finally coming to its senses and joining the rest of us in trying to reduce its consumption of fossil fuels, and especially petroleum. It was three years since the (first) oil crisis, and unlike the Europeans, they had not fully embraced the smaller more energy-efficient automobile, or 'compact' as it was known in the States. Encouraged by the low cost of petrol, I rather shamefully followed the American mantra and bought the gas-guzzler on the spot, handing over a chunk of my recently acquired greenbacks.

The spacious bench seat more than adequately accommodated the three of us in the front. With the second row seat folded down, there was about 8 feet of flatbed in the rear. Many a time, whilst traversing the States, we would pull into a KOA (campgrounds of America), and crawl into our sleeping bags and rack out in the back. The rear folding door could be dropped like a tailgate, especially useful when stopping for BBQs at picnic sites. We never travelled without our matching Coleman's one-gallon thermos flask full of water, cool box stocked with ice and basic food necessities, and a tray of Schlitz beers of course. The powerful automatic never seemed laboured, even when we crossed the Rockies, and with gas prices so affordable, fuel consumption was not a factor. As Richard set eyes on my new acquisition, he proudly christened it the 'CarBus', an affectionate nametag that stayed with us for the next three years.

Before taking up my position on the squadron at Mather, I had to attend the combat crew training school for conversion onto the USAF tanker. The 4017th CCTS at Castle AFB was situated a couple of hours away down the Sacramento Valley. Although Monday through Fridays would be spent at the school, I was able to drive back to our new home each weekend to be with my family. Unfortunately, this meant that Eileen was thrown into the deep end back at Mather, and she had to fend for herself for much of the four months after the Updicks left. After ground school, I got to fly the Boeing Stratotanker KC-135A for the first time on 30 March 1976. The similarity with the Victor in that the KC-135 had four engines ended there.

A similar age to the Victor, the Stratotanker had been in service for about twenty years. It had distinguished itself in particular during the Vietnam War, and was regarded as a durable and capable tanker. Although at ease with its size, the cockpit layout, instrumentation and handling characteristics were drastically different from the Victor. We had no need of bone domes for routine flying, something that I had become very accustomed to wearing. As a result, much of the communication on the flight deck was by normal voice across cockpit, more akin to flying an airliner. A development of the Boeing 707 civilian transport, I learned quickly that much of the tactical navigation (departing from and arriving into airfields for example) was the responsibility of the pilots. This was a far cry from the way that the Victor was navigated, where I had been used to following the directions of my two navigators. Once familiar with the on-board navigation systems and associated flight instrument displays, I quickly adjusted to my new cockpit environment.

I was pleased to see that Strategic Air Command (SAC) also liked to fly its tanker aircraft around in formation, although not as tightly grouped as those in the RAF. On my second trip, I found myself positioned as No 2 in a three-ship minimal interval take-off, or 'MITO'. I was beginning to realise that the Americans are really fond of using initials and mnemonics; something that I was going to have to get used to quickly. On take-off, I followed another KC-135 after a fifteen-second interval along the runway – quite an eye opener. The take-off thrust of the KC's engine was augmented during the heat of summer by what was known as water methanol injection. Unfortunately, its use had the effect of producing streams of black smoke in the jet exhausts, and resulted in much reduced visibility for the following aircraft during MITOs. An interesting aspect of the water-meth system was that if there was a failure of injection at full power, the sudden loss of significant thrust was virtually indistinguishable from an actual engine failure. As early as my sixth training sortie on 22 April 1976, I was faced with this dilemma. At around 100 kts, there was a loss of thrust from my No 3 (starboard inner) engine, which resulted in an immediate swing to starboard. At such a critical stage, there was no time to assess whether it was an actual engine failure, or a loss of water injection. As it happened, and in the view of my instructor, I made the only safe decision at the time and chose to abandon the take-off. By mid May, I had accomplished all of the dual instruction training sorties, and had completed successfully the final check ride in the presence of the standardisation and evaluation (Staneval) checkers. With around seventy hours on type, I took to the air three days later as a rookie aircraft commander for the first time with my own crew. Co-pilot Jay Miranda and navigator Al Lovejoy shared my flight deck, whilst a fresh-faced teenager with pink cheeks called Ricky Geiger successfully refuelled a B-52 from the boom operator's compartment in the rear of the cabin. The relief on the face of our crew instructor pilot (IP) Ricky Stevens was evident as we disembarked from tail number 64-14831. My crew had safely undertaken our first refuelling mission in a USAF tanker with an RAF aircraft commander in charge. Looking at the smiles on our faces as we disembarked the aircraft, I believe my American crew were just as pleased as me after landing back at Castle AFB without bending the aircraft.

A couple of weeks later at Mather AFB, I took up my appointment with the 904th Air Refuelling Squadron (AREFS) as the assistant operations officer; essentially a flight commander in RAF parlance. Although normally established for an officer of the rank of major (equivalent to a squadron leader), I was still a flight lieutenant. I was very much treated as a major however, and many of the crewmembers of my equivalent rank of captain rank addressed me as 'Sir'. I shared an office with the other ops officer as two flight commanders might on an RAF squadron. My counterpart was a soon-to-be-

CCTS crew: co-pilot – Jay Miranda, nav – Al Lovejoy and boomer – Ricky Geiger.

promoted lieutenant colonel, and a graduate of the USAF Academy. He wore the very prominent silver signature ring that was the hallmark of its graduates. They were referred to as 'ring knockers' because of their annoying habit of tapping their ostentatious ring on the desk. The majority of the squadron deliberately avoided my colleague because of his officious nature. This worked very much to my benefit. Because of our open-door policy, if visiting crewmembers could see that he was in the office, they would invariably come back later when I alone occupied the room.

The assistant ops officer's position also meant that I was the face of the refuelling squadron at the morning 'stand-up' meeting that started each working day. I was frequently called upon to represent the squadron boss. Apart from standing out because of my RAF khaki uniform from the rest of my blue-suited USAF colleagues, I was out-ranked markedly at these briefings. There must have been a dozen or so half colonels, and three or four full bird colonels present at each morning meeting. Although somewhat daunting to begin with, I actively took to this role with enthusiasm and was soon accepted as the 'Limey pilot from the British air force' as they loved to refer to me. I always felt from the outset that the Bomb Wing commander seemed to admire me; he would always hear my point of view and opinion whenever I had to speak on behalf of the tanker squadron commander.

Another bunch of exceptional guys in the 904th were the boom operators, or 'boomers' for short. At their head was an imposing figure who stood around 6 ft 3 inches tall, bald as a coot, his chest adorned with several rows of medal ribbons. He afforded me great respect, and always addressed me as 'Sir' – unusual for one of the very senior enlisted ranks. This senior master sergeant always sported a sizeable Cuban cigar, in the days when no one batted an eyelid about such matters. On the other hand, his sidekick was a

In my office at the 904th AREFS operations block at Mather AFB.

very boisterous and rotund joker by the name of Master Sergeant Sondrini. His style was somewhat more relaxed and familiar; on entering my office (invited or not) he would greet me with "What's the shakes lieutenant?" These very experienced boomers were the lifeblood of the squadron, and were well respected by all. They were afforded the privilege of a small crew room off the side of the mission planning room to which one had to be invited. 'The Boomers' Bar' was suitably equipped with an outsized fridge that contained enough beer to keep a regiment going.

After my first escorted introduction to the bar, a junior boom operator was given the responsibility of ensuring that, at 3 pm each afternoon, my personal six-pack would be pulled from inside the fridge and placed on top to 'warm'. These beers were the Brit's personal allocation, and no one was allowed to interfere with them. That said, as we started early each day because of the hot climate in California, we tended to finish early. Accordingly, from about 4 pm in the afternoon, the Boomers' Bar was the preferred meeting place to 'shoot the breeze' as my American colleagues would say, and drink an ice-cold tinny (or in my case – a warm one). The presence of the 320th Bomb Wing was proudly advertised on a prominent boarding outside the operations block. Not so noticeable however was the cheeky addition of the '+ 1 BRIT' just after the '1,650 SAC Professionals' below the shield.

The squadron buildings were typically low lying and devoid of windows. The ultra-efficient air conditioning kept the place as cold as an icebox. Indeed, the temperature of the rooms was often far too cold for me, although I soon adjusted to it. A spectacular

The 320th Bomb Wing billboard outside operations.

totem pole stood guard by the main entrance. It was adorned with wooden badges of the lodger units, positioned from the ground upwards. Little did I realise that there was a standing competition in place between the various units on the wing. The whole shebang was treated very seriously, and competition was intense. Points were accumulated for just about any achievement in the monthly rankings system. It was in fact several months before I realised that the various symbols of bald eagles, steely gauntlets and missiles etc.

representing the different units actually moved up and down the pole according to each unit's performance. However, as well as gaining points for one's unit, deductions could also be made. After several stoppages by the base cops for exceeding the airfield speed limit, I had apparently accumulated quite a few negative points on my own. Accordingly, I was personally responsible for the 904th's logo position, which invariably was nearer the bottom than the top of the totem pole.

Finally, I got the chance to fly with the characters that Jim Uprichard had introduced me to four months earlier. More importantly, I wanted to get back on board the KC-135 and establish my credibility amongst the troops on my new squadron. Despite nearly five years of AAR experience with the RAF, the environment within the USAF was markedly different. Whereas the RAF's tanker force was specifically designed around the support of air defence fighters defending the UK airspace, the USAF's refuelling aircraft were primarily dedicated to SAC in support of the long-range bombers like B-52s, affectionally referred to as 'Buffs' (big ugly flying f*****s). Accordingly, virtually all B-52 bomber squadrons were co-located with sister KC-135 tanker squadrons. Mather's modest SAC unit, although small, boasted no less than two-dozen B-52s supported by a similar number of KC-135s. The size of the 904th alone in terms of airframes made it roughly equivalent to two of Marham's Victor squadrons, i.e. two-thirds of the entire RAF's tanker force. Apart from our primary role in support of our sister squadron of B-52s, we did provide a considerable amount of refuelling for other bombers in SAC, the fighters and mud-movers of Tactical Air Command (TAC) and the transport aircraft of Military Airlift Command (MAC).

The voluminous tomes covering every conceivable aspect of SAC's operation of tankers were mind-boggling. Luckily for me, my squadron colleagues gave me a long leash in those early days. In order to satisfy the squadron acceptance check, my first two sorties were flown in the company of a squadron instructor pilot. Captain Dave Pasero was one of the intriguing characters that had been introduced to me by Updick during the handover. We struck up a wonderful relationship immediately, and he was to become a good friend and colleague, as indeed had been the case between him and Updick. Pasero (as he liked to be called) was a rough diamond. On more than one occasion, he would invariably spend the night at our quarter racked out on the sofa still in his uniform, usually after imbibing huge quantities of gin. His tipple was Tanqueray, and needless to say, mine also to this day. The only difference between the two of us was that he liked his gin 'straight up'. After one particular happy hour on Friday night, he awoke on the Saturday morning, just as I was brewing a coffee. I offered Pasero a mug, but he declined the offer, and glugged down the neat tumbler of Tanqueray beside him that I mistakenly assumed to be water.

Our first mission involved refuelling F-15 Eagle fighters of TAC in one of the designated refuelling areas over Southern California and neighbouring Arizona. Whilst in the refuelling area, Pasero suggested I take the opportunity to join our boom operator in his pod at the rear of the fuselage to monitor the refuelling. Unlike the flexible hoses of the probe and drogue system employed by the RAF's tankers, the flying boom was a rigid protuberance lowered in the air stream at the rearmost extremity of the fuselage.

It carried two elevons near its end, which were controlled by the boomer enabling him to 'fly' the boom in the lateral and vertical planes. With the receiver aircraft positioned in a stabilised position astern the tanker, the boomer could then press forward on his hand controller. This had the effect of telescoping a sliding inner sleeve of the boom. The extending section was then 'flown' towards the slipway of the receiver's receptacle, usually situated on the spine of the aircraft. As the boom nozzle entered the slipway, it was guided by the slipway doors and channelled into the receptacle to form a locked contact. Under guidance from the associated electronic circuitry, fuel could then be transferred from the tanker, through the inner sleeve of the boom, into the receiver's fuel tanks. Any lateral, vertical, or fore and aft movement of the receiving aircraft's position relative to the tanker could be followed by the flying boom, so long as it stayed within a safety cone. If the limits of this cone were encroached, the automatic safety features would trigger a disconnection whereby the extended boom would rapidly retract inside the outer boom structure. At this point, the boom operator would promptly fly the boom up out of harm's way to clear the receiver aircraft.

I have lasting memories of this first refuelling session. The beautifully elegant F-15s were carrying a particularly stunning sky blue livery. Never having had the privilege of vacating my seat in-flight whilst flying the Victor, as long as there were three pilots on the crew in the KC, there was always an opportunity to accompany the boomer in the rear of the cabin. After that date, I always tried to make sure I carried my camera for the superb photo opportunities that so frequently presented themselves. During my tour, I even got the chance to fly the boom on rare occasions, under strict guidance of an experienced

The KC-135A refuelling boom – fully extended position.

boom operator of course. As the boomers used to say, in what other profession could you be paid to lie on your belly and pass gas?

I have often been asked which of the two refuelling systems was the better: the RAF's probe and drogue or the USAF's flying boom. Each has its advantages and disadvantages. As I reflect on the ruggedness and durability of the flying boom refuelling system, I'm reminded of a remarkable story that was related to us whilst under training at Castle AFB. The boom operator instructor who mentored my young boomer Ricky during our conversion course was Senior Master Sergeant Sandy McClendon. Sandy was an experienced boomer who had seen active service in Vietnam. The KCs were used extensively throughout the war in South East Asia. Apart from supporting long-range bombing operations with B-52s from Guam and other bases across the Pacific, they were involved frequently around the fringes of the war zone where they were used in support of fighter/bomber sweeps. Sandy's crew had been part of an operation providing refuelling for F-105 Thunderchiefs striking at the heart of the enemy. The 'Thud' was a multi-role single-seat fighter/bomber, and was used extensively during the Vietnam War. Capable of carrying a wide range of munitions and bombs, its only limitation was that it had only one engine.

As their tanker was about to go off task during one mission, they intercepted a Mayday from a stricken jet returning from a strike. This particular Thud had been caught in the melee and suffered massive flack damage, with fuel leaking from just about every orifice in its airframe. What's more, the damaged engine was losing power, and the pilot was having difficulty staying aloft. If Sandy's tanker had waited at the safe recovery towline until the stricken jet cleared the hot zone, it was likely that both aircraft and pilot may have been lost. In a selfless act of bravery, the KC crew commander headed his aircraft straight into the hot zone making a beeline towards the damaged fighter/bomber that would not have been able to keep flying for more than a few minutes.

Against all odds, and avoiding narrowly being shot down themselves, the tanker rendezvoused in the nick of time with the Thud. Barely able to make contact because of its deteriorating engine, the Thud pilot just managed to manoeuvre his sluggish jet to a position under the back end of the KC-135's refuelling boom. He had neither spare power from his ailing engine nor controllability from damaged controls to hold position longer than a few seconds. Seizing the moment, and without waiting for the properly stabilised conditions, Sandy skilfully flew his boom and captured the fighter's receptacle. Fuel started to flood into the receiver's tanks. Sandy could see the jet was leaking fuel from the obvious battle damage, and soon, the Thud was helplessly slipping back and approaching the extension limit of the boom's safety cone. An automatic disconnect seemed inevitable, with obvious disastrous consequences. Thinking on his feet, or should I say belly, Sandy yelled at the Thud pilot to hang in there, and expect to be towed. Totally contrary to normal operating procedures, he instinctively isolated the safety limit switches. At full extension, the mechanical stop prevented any further boom extension, and the boom's latching device became geometrically locked within the receiver's receptacle. As the boom effectively became a rigid tow bar, the tanker was now dragging the hapless fighter through the air. The Thud pilot was just able to keep his aircraft under control behind the tanker as he was towed away from the war zone to more friendly skies.

Arriving over his safe haven in Thailand, the linked aircraft were flown to the airfield's overhead, where Sandy reactivated the safety circuits. Immediately, the refuelling boom retracted and flew up to clear the receiver aircraft. The Thud dropped back and down with the lack of thrust from the useless engine. The relieved fighter jock completed a classic 'dead stick' landing using the emergency profile adopted after an engine failure. A very appreciative F-105 pilot was overjoyed to set his jet down not only in one piece but also in friendly territory. He regarded it a small price to pay as he bought the beers for his tanker crew for the rest of the night. Sandy and his crew were justifiably rewarded with medals for gallantry, and Ricky and myself knew we had been in good hands whilst at Castle AFB.

The KC-135 was a very capable tanker. With a zero fuel weight of around 100,000 lbs, it had room in the tanks for just over twice that weight in fuel bringing the maximum all-up weight to 301,000 lbs. Much larger offloads than those with which I was familiar in the Victor were possible whilst flying the KC-135. Indeed, it was not unusual to transfer the order of 75,000 lbs to the fuel-thirsty B-52 Stratofortress and the brand new B-1 Lancer strategic bombers of SAC. Flow rates during transfer of around 5,000 lbs per minute (twice that of the Victor's HDU) were achievable. Moreover, much of the cabin space behind the flight deck was free to accommodate passengers or freight. Pallets of seats meant we could seat around fifty passengers on trooping runs.

On more than one occasion, I flew the aircraft with dozens of dependants from Mather

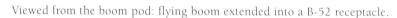

Viewed from the boom pod: flying boom extended into a B-52 receptacle.

on orientation flights. These were short flights of around a couple of hours, invariably routing over the edge of the Sierra Nevada, flying around Lake Tahoe and concluding with a circuit of the San Francisco Bay area at an altitude of about 10,000 feet. Typically, with such vast resources, the USAF was well placed to extend these treats to service families, and they were always very much appreciated. Contrast this with the security precautions that so restrict such practices today. A large side cargo door enabled us to carry a variety of spares, including replacement engines if necessary. In the freighter role, I operated the KC-135 into bases all over the western and southern USA. As well as our neighbouring USAF bases like Travis and McClellan in Sacramento County, these flights took me to Vandenberg and March AFB in Southern California, Tinker AFB in Oklahoma, Warner Robbins in Georgia and Buckley Field in Colorado to name but a few. All in all therefore, it was not only a very capable tanker, but also a remarkably flexible cargo and passenger airframe.

Aside from the SAC bombers, which were our primary customers, it was not long before I added the other large aircraft of USAF's inventory to the list that demanded the services of our tankers. E-3 AWACS communications and control aircraft and the cargo planes of MAC were sporadic customers. C-130 Hercules and C-141 Starlifter were frequent stablemates, but perhaps the most awesome of all the big boys was the C-5 Galaxy. The bow wave from this goliath had the effect of pushing up the horizontal stabiliser of the tanker as it closed up for contact. The longitudinal trim wheel either side of the centre pedestal would rotate furiously as it trimmed the aircraft in a vain attempt to keep the KC-135 level. On a particular test flight in early May 1977, I transferred 70,000 lbs of avtur to a C-5 (affectionally known as Big Mac for obvious reasons), only to be informed he would be back for two further refuellings some hours later. His mission was part of a proving concept to keep the C-5 aloft for fifty-six hours.

Much like my AAR experiences in the RAF, I found it more interesting and rewarding to refuel the fighter types. Regular customers from TAC included the F-4 Phantoms, F-105 Thunderchiefs, A-10 Warthogs and F-111 Aardvarks; all of which I had the pleasure of refuelling over the areas of Arizona and New Mexico. Rather more unusual were the aging F-100 Super Sabres flown in the mid seventies by the Air National Guard units. The first of the 'Century Series' fighters, Super Sabres distinguished themselves as the real workhorses in the Vietnam War. Ironically, these jets, like those of the US Navy, used a probe and drogue arrangement for refuelling. To achieve this, a short hose with a basket attached was strapped onto the end of the boom before departure.

On 26 October 1977, I called in a flight of six F-100s. As they joined on my port wing, I could not help capturing the moment on camera: these iconic aircraft illuminated by the low-setting sunset against the backdrop of the rugged landscape of New Mexico. In mid November 1976, I was refuelling over the Edwards Test Center supporting the development trials of both General Dynamics F-16 and McDonnell Douglas F-15 air defence fighters. The fly-by-wire Fighting Falcon as it became known, and the F-15 Eagle were both new generation fighters. Nearly forty years on, both aircraft types are still flying and have been very successful exports, employed in many air forces around the world.

The Red Flag exercises held over the mountains of Nevada gave first-hand opportunities for fighters and bombers to operate within simulated enemy environments. Offensive aircraft could pit their wits against each other in simulated combat conditions, and ground-attack fighter/bombers got the chance to drop live ordnance against designated targets. Well placed in Northern California to provide pre-strike refuellings, the tankers from Mather were often in demand. I frequently refuelled ground-attack aircraft loaded to the gunnels with live ordnance before they went on to drop their loads on targets in Nevada.

On one such mission, I had the task of refuelling a flight of eight F-105s. Their aim was to attack a specific target as an eight-ship formation to impart a massive combined strike as one. Having passed fuel to three aircraft, I was aware of a fluctuating oil pressure on my No 4 engine. The rules (probably somewhere in SAC Regulation 60-4) as regards refuelling following the loss of an engine were particularly clear: don't! I cleared the aircraft from astern onto the wing where the other four jets were awaiting their turn. I called the lead Thud to take a look behind my affected engine, just as the oil pressure dumped to zero. I asked the chicks to ease out a little, while I shut down the No 4 and took stock of the situation.

My conscientious navigator immediately announced his intention to call SAC's headquarters to inform them of our predicament. However, I promptly stopped him in his tracks and told him to sit on his hands. With nearly half of our offload complete, our all-up weight was not a factor, and we could hold altitude easily on the remaining three engines. Bearing in mind the importance of our receivers' mission, I put it to my crew that we could continue refuelling once all checklists were complete. My young co-pilot, whose eyes by now where as big as saucers, would have gone along with any of my decisions. After allaying the nav's fears at my deliberately contravening an air

Edwards AFB Test Center with YF-16 prototype – 16 November 1976.

force regulation written by some jam stealer in Omaha, he reluctantly went along with my plan. The boomer, happy as Larry in his pod, could not have cared less. I briefed the receivers about our asymmetric condition, and advised them to be cautious as I reconvened the refuelling. The remainder of my fighters were duly filled to full. On leaving to pursue their target, the flight leader made his appreciation very obvious that we had helped him save the day, and I cleared my nav to call SAC HQ that we had 'just' lost an engine and were returning to base. I could sense that my co-pilot was secretly in awe of my 'interpretation' of the rules in order to get the job done.

Arriving in the circuit at Mather, the backlash started. I was unaware that following the loss of an engine, the duty Staneval IP would be required to check our approach speeds and other data prior to landing. Each unit had a section of senior instructors responsible for training, and standardisation and evaluation of the line crews across the wing. Three top tanker and bomber crews made up this elite section within the 320th Bomb Wing. The regular crew dogs generally feared them. They kept themselves to themselves, which rather defeated any chance they had of embracing a positive training environment. This rather draconian policy had long since been eradicated in the RAF. They even wore a bright yellow neckerchief under their flight suits, rather than the mundane green cravat that the whole of the remainder of the squadrons wore. I was surprised therefore to be called on the second radio by the chief pilot of Staneval whilst we were setting up for landing, that we must relay our landing data for their checking. I was dumbfounded. This was the first time that I was alerted to the 'Big Brother' attitude that prevailed in the USAF.

By the time we had finished arguing the toss, and almost ready to put the aircraft on the ground, the IP suggested I overshoot to give us more time to confirm the figures. My reaction was that this instruction only made more potentially dangerous what should have been a straightforward asymmetric approach and landing. The weather was glorious, the afternoon sun still high in the sky, and the wind virtually non-existent. Knowing that I would have to perform the full stop landing, I quickly re-briefed the co-pilot and gave him control so that he might get the opportunity to perform a three-engine go-around in these ideal circumstances. His face lit up at the prospect of flying an asymmetric overshoot that few other skippers would offer him. We went around to satisfy the ego of the Staneval IP who was clearly trying to cover his backside. After completing another circuit, I took control for an uneventful asymmetric full stop landing.

Back in the mission planning room, the IP briefly questioned why I had not followed to the letter of the law the appropriate SAC regulation. I vented my frustration at him for having to ask for my landing data to be checked after such a relatively benign occurrence. I then explained to him that instructing a pilot to execute an abnormal go-around when on three engines was only likely to exacerbate the situation. The 'God' of our Staneval section was clearly not used to having his authority challenged. Essentially, we agreed to disagree, but at least I had given him an insight into the RAF way. After all, that was the purpose of having an exchange officer in his midst. Secretly, I believe the Staneval pilot was envious of the unfettered reign afforded RAF aircraft commanders, and this particular guy always gave me a wide berth after the incident.

On 8 September 1976, I landed my first temporary duty overseas trip. After positioning to March AFB in Southern California, I attended the mission briefing which covered every minute detail and planned contingency. The number of briefing officers present in comparison to our Marham 'low key' briefings was mind-boggling. Dozens of splendidly prepared overhead slides were presented one after the other, outlining the take-off sequence, formation procedures, fuel brackets, timings, comms plans and so on. My first trail was awe-inspiring. It was made up of two separate formations of six KC-135 tankers and eighteen A-7 Corsair receivers: forty-eight aircraft in all. Two days later, I launched as the No 3 tanker in a stream of six KC-135s from March AFB. My formation coasted out and joined up with our Corsairs before setting course to Hickham Air Force Base in Hawaii. Each tanker then rounded up its trio of chicks to form the independent cells. I can still visualise the sight of the two cells ahead, stepped down at 500 feet intervals, as we headed due west over the Pacific. Perhaps it was true – the Americans always do everything bigger and better. A little over six hours later, I had my first view of the massive Pacific Air Force's base at Hickham Field, and of course, the adjacent naval base at Pearl Harbor.

My crew on this occasion included another crew commander by the name of Captain Palco. Under his guidance, we set about booking a room at the Hale Koa (the USAF services hotel on Waikiki beach). After a bit of horse-trading, Palco managed to secure the penthouse suite on the top floor. We had only three days in Honolulu, but that was enough to get acquainted with Waikiki beach, my miserable attempt at surfing, Mai Tai cocktails at happy hour, and an introduction to the best eggs Benedict breakfast at the beach restaurant. The second free day was taken up by a visit to the superb memorial at Pearl Harbor, a day I shall never forget. Looking down from the viewing platform at the semi-submerged gun emplacements of the sunken warships was chilling – especially when the casualties numbered so prominently in the disaster. The USS *Arizona* alone lost 1,177 officers and crewmen. On the way home, we used the KC's passenger capability to airlift some thirty military passengers stateside.

As soon as I felt settled in the KC-135, I set about getting a ride in one of the B-52s of the 441st Bomb Squadron. Although the thought of flying this Boeing behemoth did not particularly appeal to me, I knew that if I did not take this unique opportunity whilst at Mather, I would certainly never get the chance again. Usually, the Buffs were lined up across the ramp from the tankers, and so I had become used to their menacing presence. On the day of my introductory flight, as I walked out with my host crew, I became aware for the first time just how imposing the Stratofortress was close-up. The massive airframe settled on the stubby gear units situated at the four corners of its lower fuselage. Towards the forward fuselage just aft of the cockpit area, 'stretch marks' of wrinkled skin ran diagonally from top to bottom. It appeared that the front end was sagging under the strain of its own weight.

Even then in 1977, this stalwart of Strategic Air Command had been in service for over twenty years, and as I write, it is planned to keep the type for a further twenty years or so with recurrent in-service upgrades. The bomb squadron's B-52s were largely 'G' models, and so relatively new marques; more easily recognised by the shorter flat-topped fin. Once aboard, I sat on the jump seat located centrally in the relatively spacious cabin, although characterised by split-levels. Behind the pilots up front, the nav team was located down below in the 'hole', and the electronic counter measures (ECM) operator and rear gunner sat up and to the rear. This seating arrangement meant that the pilots and defensive rear crew had seats that ejected upwards whereas the navs' seats fired downwards. The consequence of this particular emergency escape design was not lost on the navigators, especially during take-off, flight at low-level, or during approach and landing.

Pearl Harbor Memorial, Hawaii – September 1976.

From my position, I could observe the pilots and see much of the forward instrument panels. I recall being transfixed on the bank of engine gauges: eight across, displaying the various engine parameters in vertically aligned rows. The aircraft commander in the left-hand seat seemed to have his hands full with eight throttle levers, particularly during the take-off roll, which seemed to go on for an eternity. Strangely, once airborne, the nose attitude seemed to dip in contrast to the normal pitch-up attitude of conventional aircraft. I had witnessed this many times on the ground at Mather as these lumbering giants used every bit of concrete to get airborne, and then stagger into the climb with their noses pointing down rather than skyward. This aircraft seemed to be at variance with the normal laws of aerodynamics.

The part of the mission I was most keen to witness was of course the air-to-air refuelling from one of my own squadron tankers. For this stage of the flight, I had managed to cajole the skipper (much against his instincts and training) to let me occupy the co-pilot's seat. As we closed in on our tanker, I got a feel for the unconventional handling characteristics of the B-52 for the first time.

The poor response to control inputs quickly made me aware of the inertia of that vast aircraft. As aileron was applied through the control column, it took three or four seconds before the aircraft responded and started to roll. Equally, it was very 'heavy' longitudinally, and small pitch inputs made to maintain a smooth formation position had little effect on the pitch attitude. Although quite heavy at increasing weight, the Victor was nevertheless very responsive to control inputs, and I felt almost detached from this aircraft when faced with the sluggish response of the Stratofortress. However, I settled before too long in an acceptable close-astern position just behind and below the KC's refuelling boom. Not confident enough to let me handle the refuelling whilst in contact, the skipper then took control for the actual contact and transfer of fuel. The following navigation exercise was relatively boring for me, and our return to Mather concluded with a landing off a straight-in approach.

As if to add a little spice at the end of my flight, there was a testy crosswind of about 15 knots as we set up for landing. To my surprise, the Buff has a very interesting feature whereby the four landing-gear trucks can be rotated by a large rotary knob on the centre console, when faced with landing in a crosswind. In conventional aircraft, the nose is pointed into wind to create a 'crab' manoeuvre to prevent the aircraft drifting off the extended centreline whilst on final approach. Just before touchdown, an opposite rudder input removes the angle-off to realign the aircraft fuselage with the centreline of the runway. In this way, there are no excessive side forces imparted to the landing gear as the wheels touch the tarmac and the landing rollout accomplished.

View from the B-52 co-pilot's seat astern one of our KC-135 tankers.

In the B-52, the aircraft is also flown in a wings-level attitude with the nose conventionally pointing into wind to counteract the effect of a crosswind. However, using the gear-offset facility, the wheel units are rotated by the same amount as drift angle (i.e. to align them with the runway centreline). The aircraft can then be flown onto the runway whilst the crab angle is maintained, as there will be no side forces on the gear and tyre assemblies as they touch the ground. The aircraft then tracks along the centreline during rollout, albeit with the aircraft's nose pointing off to one side. At slow speed, the knob on the centre console is then returned to zero which has the effect of turning the wheels back into fore and aft alignment. At least that is how it's supposed to happen.

I was horrified as the co-pilot prepared to enter the gear offset at about five miles finals. Finding the knob 'frozen', he twisted in his seat and applied his size 10 boots to the rotary control to free it. With the knob now free to turn, the landing gear was set to the required offset angle. The touchdown and landing rollout was normal, although I felt decidedly uncomfortable as the aircraft tracked sideways along the centreline with the nose pointing off the side of the runway. As the jet slowed to a walking pace, the co-pilot once more turned the knob to straighten the landing gear units for normal taxi configuration. Approaching the turn-off point, the captain then applied a nose-wheel steering input on his tiller to manoeuvre off the active runway.

With the wheels now aligned, the aircraft responded initially by turning through about 45 degrees, when it seemed as though we were suddenly starting to drift towards the outside edge of the taxiway. At that point, there was a very loud metallic 'twang'. In danger of going off the taxiway into the bundu, the skipper felt he was losing control, and braked sharply to a halt. We decided to call it a day, shut down the engines, and vacated the aircraft on the taxiway. As I made my way down the steps and walked under the nose of the aircraft, I became aware of the forward left truck, whose wheels were pointing almost 90 degrees to the left of the aircraft's centreline. Clearly, the twang had signalled the failure of one of the cables designed to operate the front left gear offset function. In the crew wash up, there was much ribbing of the heavy-footed co-pilot, whose actions must have been at least partially to blame for the failure.

By September 1977, approximately midway through my exchange tour, I began an in-house instructor pilot upgrade (IPU), which would permit me to undertake regular crew checks on squadron personnel. My instructor was a superb aviator by the name of Norman Gerity, an old KC-97 tanker man. My conversion was completed over the course of six sorties, and sealed with a check ride overseen by the Staneval checker with whom I'd crossed swords previously. Fortunately all went well, and I soon found myself doing additional IP flights with my squadron colleagues. It also put me in a position to fly with the wing's executive pilots who often ran out of currency because of their onerous ground duties. This included flying a competency check on the 320th Bomb Wing vice-commander before the month was out.

In the new year on 17 January 1978, I was Pacific-bound once more this time deploying initially to Beale AFB in Northern California. Beale was about a couple of hours north of Sacramento, and was home to the superlative yet mysterious SR-71 Blackbird. Always housed within their camouflaged hangars, these illusive reconnaissance jets were only seen as they were departing or arriving on a mission. Interestingly, this was one of the few

USAF aircraft that I would not get to refuel during my exchange tour. Due to the specific grade of fuel that this Mach 3 aircraft used, the Blackbird required a dedicated marque of tanker: the KC-135Q, or 'Q' model. I had got to know Beale from my trips to the KC-135 simulator as part of my upgrade with Norm Gerity. Incredibly, this fixed-base sim was located in a train – yes train – which in turn was operated on the national train grid by none other than USAF personnel.

My memory of the journey up to this desolate part of Northern California is punctuated with visions of the numerous rattlesnakes, usually flattened on the roads by traffic. On this occasion, we were assembled for the usual pre-trail briefing prior to a major deployment called Coronet Crane. During the inevitable multi-slide presentation, my name was listed as the aircraft commander of the sixth KC-135 in a cell of six tankers. Some joker of a colonel whose show this was, called out the skippers' names in turn, and concluded by announcing to the amusement of all, "and bringing up the rear, a limey from the British air force. God help us all."

Once airborne, I surveyed the formation stretching into the distance ahead. Bringing back memories of my first trail to Hawaii, I had a grandstand view looking down on five other tankers, each with a brace of F-105 Thunderchiefs. With my own crew in tow this time, we had the usual three days to wind down in Hawaii. On this occasion, we took the opportunity to tour around the big island in a rental car. My haunting memory of this experience was of my colleagues encouraging me to take on the treacherous surf on a number of spectacular remote beaches. Fighting well above my weight, I stupidly plunged into the surf in one cove, where the breakers were about 6 feet high. I soon found myself out of my depth in the raging swell, and being slammed under the water into the sandy bottom below. The wind was knocked out of me, and gasping for breath I was only just able to drag myself to the beach. I gave the surf much more respect after this event.

During 1977, the co-pilots on the wing flew barely six or seven times each month. In the same way that the RAF had to cut back on flying hours following the fuel crisis of 1973, the USAF was coming under increased scrutiny from the Pentagon to make savings. It was decided to supplement their limited flying hours by permitting SAC's co-pilots to fly the aircraft they had trained on. In the case of Mather AFB, the nav training school used T-37 basic jet trainers to familiarise their students during low-level navigation exercises.

The T-37 was the equivalent of the RAF's Jet Provost basic trainer. It was universally known as the 'Tweet', shortened from 'Tweety Bird' on account of the high-pitched scream that its two tiny jet engines made. The programme was given the obligatory and cumbersome description of Accelerated Co-pilot Enrichment Scheme, shortened to 'ACE' of course. Once authorised, our squadron co-pilots got checked out on their former steed and, on an opportunity basis, earned extra hours in this noisy little jet. Not wishing to miss out on adding another type in my logbook, I pointed out to my boss that I really ought to be supervising my boys by checking out on the Tweet as well. Before too long, I took every opportunity to fly with the guys, albeit in the capacity of an observer. Apart from the incredible noise, the jet reminded me of the JP 3, and its performance was very similar. I took the chance to demonstrate my aerobatic sequence RAF-style, and relished the opportunity for my subordinates to impress me with their familiarity and former skills in the aircraft.

One area that did intrigue me however was their reluctance to practise stalling, and more importantly, spinning. I soon became aware that the RAF's training approach to recognising and recovering from these abnormal flight regimes was very different from that of our American counterparts. I like to think that by demonstrating the proven recovery techniques from out-of-controlled flight, my sessions in the T-37 with our ACE co-pilots helped fill some of that void and restored their missing confidence. Our shared experiences in the clear skies over the mountainous Pacific Coast Range were sheer joy, and I believe very beneficial to our mutual relationships within the refuelling squadron.

By way of the T-37, my neighbour next door in base housing was one of the pilots who instructed the student navigators on the nav school. Sam was a very smart and likeable officer, who thought that he was God's gift to flying. His zany young wife Carla had a habit of sauntering into our quarter on a weekend carrying an oversized jug full of strawberry daiquiris whilst we were still in bed. However, they were superb neighbours and always entertaining company at our many BBQs and parties. On this particular afternoon, Sam arrived home and immediately engaged me in conversation on our front lawn. He could barely contain his excitement as he proceeded to tell me about an incident earlier that day. Essentially, he had forgotten to lower the undercarriage as he came into land. I should say that the gear was so short in the Tweet that you felt as though your backside was scrubbing the ground in the flare, even with the wheels down. Sam explained how his landing had been so smooth, and that he had barely noticed that the gear was still up. As the jet skidded to a halt on the runway, it was only as they stopped in a cloud of dust that Sam realised the error of his ways. As they climbed out and stepped onto the concrete, there were very few visible signs that anything was amiss. According to Sam, there was so little skin damage under the fuselage that he suggested he might well be in line for an award, perhaps even a medal. He seemed a little perturbed when I pointed out that had he remembered to lower the undercarriage, he might have avoided this potential accident altogether. A few beers later, Sam was still convinced he was the best 'stick and rudder' man in the USAF.

In November 1977, I was tasked to refuel the B-1 Lancer, again very much in its infancy at the time. On that occasion, I transferred no less than 75,000 lbs to the secretive swing-wing bomber. On completion of that task, I was alerted by ATC to the presence of the NASA B747. This specially converted jumbo was fitted with a tripod structure mounted on the upper fuselage, designed to carry a complete space shuttle. I remembered watching the news reports of the initial un-powered approach and landing trials of the shuttle earlier that year.

Conducted from the Dryden Flight Research Facility, these trials were designed to prove the post re-entry handling and performance capabilities of the future space shuttle. The B747 would carry its load piggyback style to altitude, and then air-launch it from the tripod. A full test programme was underway in preparation for the orbital missions a few years later. On this particular day, it just happened to be ferrying one of the shuttles on its back in our vicinity. Inevitably, I asked if I could take a closer look as I realised this might well be a one-off opportunity. In the event, I was able to brush shoulders with the combo from a distance of about two miles. Annoyingly, despite my efforts to carry my camera on most flights, I had not brought it along on this occasion, and so I only have my vivid memories of the rare encounter.

On 31 January 1978, I embarked upon another temporary duty overseas, the unforgettable Coronet West 18. The deployment saw the delivery of the last three F-4 Phantoms to the Republic of Korean Air Force (ROKAF). We would proceed via Hickham AFB in Hawaii, and then across the International Date Line to Andersen AFB, Guam. Being a Brit was a diplomatic issue; I would therefore be involved only as far as Guam. The remaining pair of tankers would then position with the F-4s to Kadena AFB on the island of Okinawa some 400 miles south of Japan. From Kadena, a single KC-135 would accompany the three jets on their final leg across the Korean Strait into the ROKAF airfield, Taegu Air Base in South Korea. Because of the complexity and duration of some of the legs, my close friend and IP, Norm Gerity augmented the crew as mission coordinator.

We left March AFB in Riverside County as a flight of three tankers with our three chicks. The flight to Hickham was largely uneventful, and our three brand new F-4s looked resplendent in their glistening ROKAF livery. The section leader of the three fast jets was a larger-than-life character and full colonel in the USAF, whose name appropriately was Bull. Whilst in formation over a beautiful blue Pacific, I took time out with the boomer to get a few snaps of our friends astern. As I called the chicks astern our tanker, the F-4s lined up in echelon port and starboard behind the tanker, and the results were stunning. Finally, all three settled in line abreast just astern of and below the lowered boom. Just then, Colonel Bull called his wingmen to ease out a little, at which point he rolled his own jet over to the inverted position, and posed once more between his colleagues belly-up. With no worries in the world, and all the fuel they could possibly want on tap, they were happy bunnies.

The following day, I flew for the first time across the International Date Line, losing twenty-four hours in the process. However, some distance west of the Hawaiian Islands, one of our Phantoms developed a problem which dictated that he return to Hickham. As we'd been airborne for some time, an unaccompanied return for the fast jet would have been risky. Norm decided that one of the other tankers should accompany him to assist with the navigation, and more importantly, to provide any additional refuelling should he need it. That left two KCs with the two remaining F-4s to press on to Guam. Some 47,000 lbs of fuel was offloaded to our chicks during this eight-hour flight.

The island of Guam is the largest of the Mariana Islands about 1,500 miles south of Tokyo. Captured by the Japanese after Pearl Harbor, it was only retaken by the US forces after much fierce fighting. After establishing the island as a United States territory, Andersen AFB was built as a garrison and remains a hugely important air base in the Western Pacific. Twin runways almost 11,000 feet long with parallel taxiways dominated the new airfield. Its expansive aprons were capable of supporting hundreds of aircraft. As I flew the approach into Andersen, I was mesmerised by the sheer numbers of B-52s and KC-135s alone; dozens of them in elongated lines. This was not to mention the plethora of visiting and resident transport aircraft. It was from here that bombing missions were mounted during the Vietnam War from the mid-sixties all the way through to 1973. Once on the ground however, it was Norm Gerity's mission to introduce me to Kobe beef.

F-4 Phantoms over the Pacific en route to South Korea – 31 January 1978.

To this day, I can still remember my first encounter with that delicious steak. According to Norm, the animals are sourced from hand-reared cattle in Japan, and the meat is recognised around the world for its superior taste and tenderness. I could not agree more. With the loss of one of our F-4s, some replanning was necessary which would significantly affect my involvement. It was decided to press on with the pair to Okinawa, essential to keep the show on the road. This was accomplished on 2 February, whilst the tail-end Charlie was repaired at Hickham AFB. In the event, on the next day, we flew the revised plan by launching from Kadena and initially headed back towards Guam to rendezvous with the rectified jet. After a successful link up, his accompanying tanker landed at Kadena. We were then joined by our pair of chicks and continued as a four-ship over Okinawa towards the intended final destination of Taegu Air Base in South Korea. Miraculously, all lost time had been made up, and it seemed our scheduled arrival would be on time for our ROKAF reception committee. I was not expecting what I saw on arrival at Taegu.

This part of South Korea is desolate and the landscape largely featureless. It was several degrees below zero, and although fine, the biting winds made it feel as cold as hell. Open machine-gun emplacements were situated around the airfield at frequent intervals, and shivering soldiers manned live weapons. After an impressive run-in-and-break by our three F-4s, we followed our playmates to the ramp to the obvious delight of a modest welcoming party. After a brief reception, we were ushered into what resembled a fairly sparse crew room, where some snacks and refreshments awaited us.

Not having planned to be on Korean soil, I became acutely aware of my flying suit – adorned with my RAF brevet – clearly at odds with those of my fellow crewmembers. One by one, the diminutive ROKAF fighter pilots came up to me and stroked my wings in recognition, albeit with expressions tinged with curiosity and wonderment. Weirdly, in the corner, an enlisted airman had been given the task of providing some music on this auspicious occasion. This consisted of a portable record player, and an assortment of early American rock and roll vinyl records, which had been played to destruction.

We were whisked off to our accommodation soon after, and I contemplated how I would get through the next three rest days without attracting too much attention. To say that the social scene was somewhat limited would be overstating the case. To all intents and purposes, it seemed to me that the whole country was still on a war footing. Curfews were in force, restricting movement about the city in the evening. After a couple of days, we could not get out of the place fast enough. Successful in avoiding an embarrassing diplomatic incident, on 7 February 1978 I flew our cold-soaked KC-135 direct to Guam. We returned to Hickham the following day and recovered to March AFB the day after for debriefing. Coronet West had been an eye-opening trip across the great Pacific Ocean. It gave me an insight into the massive capabilities of the United States Air Force, and it was truly inspiring to visit its astonishing bases spread across that part of the Pacific region.

In May, we were joined on the squadron by one of the USAF's first female pilot graduates. I flew with our new pilot on several occasions, and have to say her ability was somewhat limited by her rather diminutive stature. The KC-135 was quite a handful at times, especially when flown under asymmetric power, and some of the control forces and particularly rudder forces were considerable. After a couple of circuits tagged on the end of a refuelling detail, she would find the physical demands of coping with engine-out procedures quite demanding.

There was considerable pressure all the way down from the Pentagon to ensure these pioneering military lady aviators made the grade. Our co-pilot certainly did make the grade and became a well-liked crewmember within the squadron. I cannot recall whether or not she completed the upgrade to aircraft commander however. Just over a year after returning to Blighty, I was able to offer her a ride in a Jet Provost whilst instructing in Yorkshire. It may have been on that occasion that I learned one of her colleagues from the original female graduate course had been unfortunate enough to become pregnant. I hesitate to think how the Pentagon dealt with that revelation.

The Giant Voice navigation competitions waged against the RAF bombers of No 1 Group were needle matches to say the least. In July 1978, I flew a number of these competition flights in company with our own B-52s. The routes tested the skills of their nav teams as they completed celestial nav legs, terminating in simulated bomb runs on calibrated sites across the northern states. During this bombing competition, the 320th was expecting superior results from their best crews as usual. The mission planning room was festooned with banners and decorations, in anticipation of the expected USAF victory. At the allocated hour as the final results were pouring in, just as we were gathering to devour the not-inconsiderable amount of beer drafted in for the occasion, all went horribly wrong.

The RAF's Vulcan crews had pipped them to the post, and unbelievably, the Wing staff cancelled the planned celebrations. Trying hard not to gloat and reveal my true colours, I rounded up a few of the tanker boys who had refuelled and supported our bomber counterparts, and we secured a stash of booze for our own party. I have never seen such poor losers in my whole career. Coincidentally, I had to shut down an engine during one of these competition sorties, and contrary to regulations (for the second time), I still managed to refuel my sister B-52 so that he would not have to abort his bombing run. Less than two weeks later, I had a very similar incident with the No 4 engine (on a different airframe), necessitating a jettison of some 20,000 lbs of fuel to get down to landing weight. Apart from these incidents, the faithful Stratotanker was a remarkably reliable aircraft.

Each year, in May all the exchange officers got the opportunity to get together and share experiences at Maxwell AFB, Alabama. The main aim underpinning the week's activities was to integrate the RAF types with the international students attending the USAF Staff College. Needless to say, the educational benefits were far outstripped by the social antics of the British interlopers. I was fortunate to attend two of these wonderful encounters, and we chose to drive the 2,000 miles to Alabama, using a different route out and back each time. In 1977, we went through the southern states via Texas (and the Alamo), and returned along the length of Route 66. This involved a lot of family singing, as we drove through the melodic sounding Oklahoma City, which really was 'oh so pretty'. However, although I loved the desert, Eileen was not so fond of Flagstaff, Arizona, and the rest of those desolate places. Despite this, we did 'get our kicks, on Route 66'.

The next year in May 1978, we drove across the mid west for a change of scenery. On this occasion, we arrived at the temporary living quarters to find the biggest bowl of fruit and a beautiful bouquet of flowers. Major Lance Bodine and his wife Linda had put in a special request to host my family, as he had just learnt that he was to be assigned to Mather AFB shortly afterwards. On the first night of our stay, Lance and Linda invited us up to their magnificent house at Blue Ridge near Montgomery. I think we were all mesmerised by Lance's love of the Wild West.

The walls were strewn with pieces of driftwood, bleached skulls of longhorn cattle, cowhides, and a host of branding irons and other paraphernalia. Hunting rifles and Winchesters were in abundance, displayed on wall racks all over the place. They apologised, as the evening meal was prepared, as they only had venison to offer us. During the stopover that night, not only did our families gel, but also Lance and I bonded in a way that augured well for our future working relationship as operations officers at Mather. After a fabulous week, which included Maxwell being assaulted by a Tornado, we set off once again for California, this time along a northern route. We stopped briefly at the iconic Wild West towns of Cheyenne and Laramie. This brought back childhood memories of early TV shows about cowboys and Indians, or should I say cowboys and Native Americans. The scenery through Colorado, Wyoming and Utah was spectacular. I do admit to feeling a little vulnerable however as we drove across the prairies known as the High Plains in the foothills of the Rocky Mountains. Assaulted on both sides by unbelievably threatening skies, lightning bolts were spearing into the ground only a hundred yards away. We pressed on towards Salt Lake City on a dull rainy morning with the intention of making a brief stop at the Mormon Tabernacle.

Having slept in the back of our CarBus at night to maximise the travelling time, we were starting to look like a hippy family. Unshaven, and looking rather scruffy, I was beckoned by a sympathetic guide who seemed to take pity on us. We were given a personalised tour around the Celestial Room, before being left momentarily to wonder at the magnificent surroundings inside the temple. In our ignorance, we inadvertently almost strayed into the inner sanctum, when we were intercepted by the guide who ushered us 'non-believers' away. The last leg of our momentous journey took us through Reno, Nevada, after which we high-tailed it back to Mather just in time for me to return to my squadron.

A few weeks later, Major Bodine thankfully replaced the operations officer with whom I had shared the office for the majority of my tour. At work, Lance looked like the archetypal USAF officer. His hair was shaved close to his scalp like the academy cadets I'd seen at Colorado Springs a few years earlier. His uniform shirt and trousers had creases that you could cut yourself on, and his patent leather shoes gleamed in the Californian sunshine. He was a true gentleman, and was universally liked by the officers and enlisted men.

Off duty however, he turned into a huntin' shootin' fisherman who was never without a Stetson on his head, a pair of faded denim jeans riding over a pair of genuine cowboy boots – and the mandatory beer in his hand. Their house, much like the one we had visited in Alabama, was like a wrangler's retreat. It was located in the El Dorado Hills, about twenty miles along Highway 50 to the east of Mather AFB. Eileen, Richard and I had visited their remote spread, affectionately referred to as 'Bodine's waterin' hole', many times since their arrival. Whenever we drove there together after work, Lance would ensure that we always had a 'road beer' en route to stave off the thirst.

Approaching the house, he would get me to call Linda on the CB radio using the

Entering Salt Lake City with Temple Square on the right – May 1978.

'handle' Lance had given me 'The Country Squire'. The purpose of the call of course was to prompt Linda to pull the iced tumblers from the freezer and fill them with copious amounts of gin and tonic. On the walls around the house hung the rustic memorabilia we had seen before. In Lance's study, and in pride of place, stood a chest with dozens of pigeonhole drawers that no doubt once adorned a pony express office. On top was a collection of bronzed cowboy figurines. Displayed on the wall above however was a magnificent array of a dozen or so lever-action Winchester rifles, arranged in a fan. This short-barrelled carbine was the weapon favoured by those on horseback because of its ease of handling, and was immortalized in many of John Wayne's movies.

In the balmy evenings, we would relax on the decking, accompanied by Lance's black Labrador Guinness. Down the valley to the west twinkled the sparkling lights of California's capital city, Sacramento. Lance had served his country as a decorated pilot during the Vietnam War, but I have never met anyone before or since who knew how to balance that vocation with the art of relaxing away from the office.

In October 1978, I was fast approaching the end of my tour as an exchange officer. I completed my last instructional sortie on the KC-135A performing a check ride with the vice-commander of the Wing. Just as my predecessor Jim Updick had been hosed down after completing his last flight, I was met by Mather's fire crews in the customary manner after shutdown, and targeted by the firemen's hoses. A large contingent from the whole Bomb Wing joined our post-flight celebrations as champagne corks popped all around.

The six-month extension that I had managed to add to my original tour of duty ensured that I was able to serve almost three years as an exchange officer with the USAF in Northern California. Our last few days were spent crating up our belongings from the base accommodation, and preparing for the journey home. After handing over the base hiring, we were invited to spend our last week with Lance and Linda at their pad in the hills. They decided that we would have one last meal together – steak of course. The idea was to have a quiet evening to enable us to say our personal farewells in the comfort of their lovely home. Around mid-evening after supper, I mentioned to Lance that I thought I had seen car headlights on his drive outside. The ranch was miles from the nearest neighbour, and so he assured me that this was unlikely. To our total surprise, about twenty minutes later, the whole squadron poured through the front door carrying packs of Schlitz and Coors beers. It was a wonderful send-off in the company of so many of our friends and their wives, with whom we had forged real friendships over the previous three years.

Lance had saved one last surprise for us that night. With cowboy hat pulled over his eyes, and cigar hanging from the corner of his mouth, he called everyone to order and started to say how much our two families had enjoyed the previous year. They had been terrific friends during our tenure together, and Richard in particular absolutely hero-worshipped Lance and everything that he stood for. He still harbours the special gifts of a rattlesnake's rattle and Indian arrowheads that Lance gave him. After his monologue, Lance said that he had always been touched with the close working relationship that had developed between the two of us, and had always been thrilled at the way I shared his interest in

After a watery reception from Mather's fire crews – 5 October 1978.

the American culture, and the Wild West in particular. In wanting to bestow on me a present that he knew would always remind me of the Bodines, he reached up and handed me one of his prized Winchester Model 94 carbines.

The year of manufacture of this gun pre-dated 1964, which made it one of the more collectable handmade models. I was gobsmacked. I did not have time to reflect upon the ramifications of returning to the UK with a firearm, not to mention a couple of cases of shells. I'd cross that hurdle later. Never had we felt so privileged to have the opportunity of spending the best three years of our lives in such a wonderful place and in the company of such a great bunch of genuine friends.

Having checked with the sheriff of Sacramento that I intended taking my Winchester to the airport on our departure, all he was concerned about was whether or not the gun belonged to me. I informed him that it had been given to me as a gift, to which he responded impassively that as it was indeed my gun, I could take it wherever I wished. Accordingly, along with our suitcases piled on a baggage trolley, I strolled into the Sacramento airport terminal with my firearm casually slung over my shoulder. Could you imagine this happening now even in the United States at an international airport? What happened next really took the wind out of my sails.

Standing next to me in the queue at the ticket desk was an American dressed like an outdoorsman character from the movie *Deliverance*. Sporting a hunting rifle with telescopic site, his weapon must have been nearly twice the length of my carbine.

Somewhat indignantly, he scoffed at my Winchester, muttering something to the effect that my gun was just a toy. Somewhat taken aback by his effrontery, I stood my ground and responded that if it was good enough for John Wayne, it was good enough for me. As I got to the front of the queue, the check-in attendant took our tickets. Seeing the rifle over my shoulder, she asked politely and in a matter of fact way if I would like my gun placed in a box. Yes, they had boxes for rifles at the check-in desks.

Two other RAF officers, their wives, and a host of our friends from Mather turned up to see us off at the airport. Standing with quite a crowd of people in the terminal, I was summoned by a lady carrying aloft a billboard displaying my name. I was somewhat bemused albeit delighted to be the recipient of a telegram, no doubt containing a heartfelt farewell message. All became clear, however, as the smartly attired messenger started singing a suitably worded ditty aimed at yours truly. The boys on the squadron had the last laugh as usual.

Amidst many tearful goodbyes, we reluctantly made our way to the departure lounge, and finally onto our waiting airliner. The sound of John Denver's *Leaving on a Jet Plane* was playing on the PA system in our United Airlines jet as we departed Sacramento Airport. Eileen, Richard and I had tears streaming down our faces.

We flew via Denver, Colorado to the nation's capital once more. I had to attend a formal debriefing session at the British embassy, and submit a final report summarizing

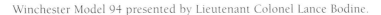

Winchester Model 94 presented by Lieutenant Colonel Lance Bodine.

my views on the suitability and effectiveness of my particular appointment within the exchange programme. I was not about to deny another candidate such a prized posting, especially one who came from the home of the Tanker Force. Our last day in Washington was spent touring around a few of Washington DC's monuments, and took in a visit to the John F Kennedy Eternal Flame at the Arlington Cemetery. Interestingly, we managed to link up once more with our next-door neighbour Carla, of strawberry daiquiris fame!

We boarded the familiar RAF VC10 once more for our Atlantic crossing. The November cloud was on the deck at Brize Norton, and we had to make three go-arounds before the Shiny Fleet skipper could see the runway and return us to British soil once more. Depression set in instantly, as the miserable cold wintery weather made us think that life would never be the same again. Some time later, after meeting up with another former exchange officer, we shared notes and mused over our deflated feelings at the end of that wonderful exchange posting. His poignant observation was summed up as follows: they reflected on their USA experience as BC and AC – Before California and After California – it seemed appropriate.

At the Arlington Cemetery, Washington DC – November 1978.

Chapter Eight

Bird Strike!

2 Squadron, 7 Flying Training School, RAF Church Fenton October 1979 to June 1980

Having completed arguably one of the best possible postings in the RAF, I was in a quandary as I contemplated my next assignment. All of the evidence pointed to the fact that I was well overdue a ground tour, as I had completed three consecutive flying tours to date. The hot contenders were perhaps staff jobs at No 1 Group HQ RAF Bawtry or Headquarters Strike Command (STC) at RAF High Wycombe. My first thought was somehow to stay flying. On my last dream sheet, I somewhat reluctantly requested Central Flying School (CFS) and instructor training as a means of staying in the cockpit. In recognition of a job well done apparently, my sponsors at the British Defence Staff in Washington, responsible for overseeing my last annual report had fortuitously supported my bid. Soon after leaving the States, I was given a provisional course date in April 1979 to attend the CFS Course at RAF Leeming.

Before this could happen however, I would be required to attend the Refresher Flying Squadron (RFS) course, also at Leeming. This course was originally designed for senior officers who, after completing ground tours, needed their flying skills refreshed before taking on station or squadron flying appointments. As a result, RFS was essentially a no-pressure course, where the approach to flying was to refresh rather than test dormant flying skills. In my case, it was probably aimed at eradicating those annoying American flying habits and non-standard radio terminology that had become ingrained in my flying after three years in the States.

The RFS instructors were all experienced QFIs with previous tours on various flying training schools. Designed around twenty-five hours of flight time, about a third of it was flown solo. The Jet Provost marques that I'd flown previously at Cranwell were T3 and T4 aircraft, so it was nice to get my hands on the T5. The JP 5 had the same Viper engine as the Mk 4, and so performance and speed were similar. However, it did have an electrically operated canopy, and it was pressurised. This resulted in a much quieter cockpit and superior environment in which to instruct. After a very enjoyable two months, I felt suitably 'refreshed', and ready to embark upon my flying instructors' course.

In April 1979, I took to the air once more in the sluggish JP 3A, and set about the black art of instructing – CFS style. The routine consisted of learning the methodology of presenting the exercise to a student using the ubiquitous white board in the confines of the briefing room. This was followed by flying the instructional sortie in the right-hand seat with the QFI acting as the 'student' in the left-hand seat. The intensive course resulted in about 100 hours of largely enjoyable flying. During the latter stages of the QFI course, the emphasis was back in the JP 5, which included the best bits: spinning, aerobatics, low level and formation.

In order to appreciate fully all aspects of the spin, we were required to demonstrate to the student not only the entry and onset of the incipient spin and its recovery, but also the fully developed characteristics of the stabilised spin through eight complete turns. The actions necessary to exit the spin consisted of a very specific order of control inputs, which had to be precise in their application to ensure prompt and effective recovery. Having sat through the full eight turns, I 'pattered' my way through the standard full recovery.

However, on this occasion, the aircraft failed to respond to the final forward stick input to unstall the wings. Furthermore, the spin seemed to be 'tightening'. The rotational speed in fact increased, and this was compounded by an unusual increase in speed of about 20 knots above the normal spinning speed. I seem to recall that this exercise was started at an altitude of about 20,000 feet. By this stage, we were descending rather rapidly through 10,000 feet. Fortuitously, my QFI recognised this worsening situation as a 'high rotational spin', a manoeuvre with which I was unfamiliar. Shouting the words "I have control", he immediately took control of the spinning jet and proceeded to apply the standard spin recovery actions once more, albeit with considerably more aggression. So abrupt was his forward elevator input to unstall the wings, we nearly flipped inverted, until he pulled back in the opposite direction that left us pointing vertically downwards. The speed was now increasing at an alarming rate of knots.

In the normal course of events, if a spin was not recovered by the time the aircraft was passing 5,000 ft above the ground, it was mandatory to eject. This separation from the ground was necessary to permit an adequate margin for the Martin Baker seat to complete the ejection sequence, eject the pilot safely, and allow time for the parachute to fully deploy. We were rapidly approaching that 'base level' as our aircraft bottomed out. We called it a day, and flew back to base. In the post-flight rigging checks, it was found that the stick forward input was only resulting in about two-thirds of the expected elevator movement – considerably less than that required to unstall the wings in the spin recovery.

As a newly certificated 'B2' QFI, the choice of posting was complicated by the fact that I had recently been promoted to the rank of squadron leader. This would have warranted my taking over one of Training Command's JP squadrons. However, it was considered prudent that I earn at least the next rating of instructor qualification in order that I would have credibility as a QFI in command of a squadron. Accordingly, I was sent to RAF Church Fenton in order to generate more instructional experience before taking over 2 Squadron at RAF Linton-on-Ouse. In the event, I was delighted with this outcome as Church Fenton had only just been re-activated from its former care and maintenance status. This meant that we were exempt from the dreaded command inspections until such time as the station had sufficient time to become fully operational once more.

Once checked out as competent-to-instruct by the base Standards Flight, I took on my first students in mid-October 1979. These two 'studes' were diametrically opposed in terms of ability. One took to flying like a duck to water, and it did not surprise me to see him perform with distinction during the Falklands War three years later. The other student was more methodical and measured, and progress steady rather than spectacular. My two charges were already part way through the syllabus; both students were proficient in the basic flying skills. Luckily for me therefore, I went straight in at the deep end and low-level flying.

JP 3A XM414 on the apron at RAF Church Fenton – October 1979.

The sixth instructional sortie with my second student turned out to be quite memorable. The JP 3 was a superb trainer, and flying low level at 250 kts and 250 ft agl was demanding for the student yet hopefully great fun. This particular low-level exercise took us into the Pennines of North Yorkshire. These hills and steep-sided valleys offered up a great training ground in which to teach the skills of low-level flying techniques. John (not his real name) seemed to be reasonably settled, and was progressing albeit steadily with the demands of map reading and flying the aircraft at the same time. Bounding over one particular ridge, he lowered the nose to follow the nap of the earth in order to maintain his height above the ground. As we descended into the valley floor, the grey leaden skies were suddenly filled with a mass of large black birds.

The flock must have contained several hundred crow-like birds. Without warning, and in a vain attempt to avoid them, John pushed hard on the stick to dive under the wheeling flock. With less than a few seconds at best before we hit the ground, I instinctively snatched at the control column and pulled the nose up. It was inevitable that we would impact at least one of the birds, if not more, but this seemed eminently more desirable than flying into the deck. As the aircraft pitched up, a gut-wrenching bang was heard as one of our feathered friends smashed into the nose section right at the base of the canopy on the student's side. The impact was so hard that the majority of this large black bird found its way between the skin of the nose and the underside of the canopy structure, and into the cockpit. It smacked John fairly and squarely in the face, which was thankfully protected by his clear visor.

Simultaneously, the physical jolt of the impact caused the sliding canopy to run backwards about eight to ten inches. Our cockpit was now open to the elements, and the noise of the slipstream rushing by at about 300 mph was deafening. I looked to my left to see John's visor covered in bird remains, and his body rigid with shock. I dared not move the throttle of our single engine in case any birds had been ingested through the intakes. Any throttle movement might have caused a compressor surge with the possibility of a flameout. I tried in vain against the thunderous noise to attract my student's attention. This proved to be fruitless as John was only able to give a good impression of a stunned mullet. Fearing he might have been rendered temporarily unconscious from the full-frontal attack, I turned my attention to the problem in hand. Climbing with a fixed throttle setting, I eased the aircraft up to about 4,000 ft, and simultaneously traded speed for height to reduce the ambient noise level. I punched out a Mayday call on the emergency frequency 'Guard' to seek assistance and let air traffic control know of our predicament. I got a call back immediately on the safety frequency and called for a vector towards the nearest airfield: as it happened, Linton-on-Ouse some 30 miles to the south.

With time to take stock, I realised for the first time that the forward edge of the open canopy, which had a rigid metal frame member, was now positioned directly over the top of my bone dome. I discounted the option to try and close the hood in case the structural damage might cause it to fly off the rails. On the other hand, any option to eject was now out of the question because of the presence of the canopy structure directly above our seats. A further look at the engine parameters confirmed at least that it was apparently unaffected, and it was running faultlessly at about 90% rpm. My priority was to get the aircraft back on the ground at the earliest possibility and render first aid to my stricken student.

The controller positioned me directly to the extended centreline of the runway at Linton. I eased the throttle back for the first time when within gliding distance of the airfield (in case the engine failed), and dropped the flaps and gear when I was convinced I could make the runway. After landing, I stop-cocked the engine and climbed out to give some room for the attending emergency services. Once the splattered remains of the offending bird had been scraped from his visor, signs of life returned to my cohort's face. He slowly regained his senses, and was able to climb over the side with assistance from the fire crew.

A couple of hours later, John was given a clean bill of health by the station doctor, and we reflected with some humour at the chain of events. After some on-the-spot repairs by a couple of airframe engineers, our aircraft was declared serviceable, and we (I) flew us back to Fenton. I'm pleased to say John was back in the saddle the next day as we resumed his training with no apparent detrimental effects.

Even the quick learners had their weaknesses however. The following month, along with my 'ace' student Mike, we detached to Edinburgh Turnhouse so that we could take advantage of the superb low flying in the Scottish Highlands. A typical sortie profile would consist of thirty minutes or so navigating along pre-determined legs, to a final sector known as the IP to target run. The IP or initial point would be an easily recognisable geographical feature (e.g. a small lake) from which to start the final run-in towards a simulated target. This section would require precise flying where a specific heading would be flown for a nominated time (say forty-five seconds) at which point the target would be 'splashed'; simulating the release of bombs or weapons.

I briefed Mike that I would demo the first IP to target run so that he could observe the workload and sequence of events. My selected run took me around a ridge and then I dropped into the bottom of a steep-sided valley to pick up the IP and run towards the target for a simulated attack. On overflying the target, I had to roll and pull into a maximum rate turn to starboard to keep clear of high ground beyond the target site. My student who had flown the majority of the low-level route so far seemed to be performing well, albeit he seemed a little more subdued than normal. Whether or not this had something to do with the beers we had consumed in the B&B the night before remained to be seen.

However, engrossed with the run in, I duly pattered the important aspects of flying accurately on heading and speed, and getting him to look ahead to visually identify the IP. I splashed the target and aggressively threw the aircraft into a 90-degree bank turn towards the exit route whilst pulling about 4 'g' to ensure a safe separation from the high ground. As I pulled hard, out of the corner of my eye, I suddenly became aware of Mike throwing up his breakfast into a flying glove. We left the rest of that exercise until the next day.

One of the great attractions of the QFI's job was the incongruous mix of teaching the benign exercise of 'effects of controls' one minute, and then the much more demanding exercises of formation flying, aerobatics and low level the next. It was sheer fortune that my last three months at Church Fenton were spent entirely in the rather sportier JP 5. By definition, this meant teaching the advanced exercises in the company of those students who were nearing the end of the syllabus. I like to think that I was able to gain the confidence and respect of most of my students at Church Fenton.

Settling down for a quiet evening at home in Haxby one night, Eileen and I were suddenly aware that a minibus load of students had pitched up raucously, unannounced and uninvited. Mirroring the command exercise Taceval, I quickly realised this was a test scenario set up by the students on a targeted instructor – me. My credibility and reputation would rest on whether or not I could produce sufficient beers to satisfy the self-promoted examiners. I'm pleased to say I passed with flying colours, and no doubt Eileen rustled up some grub for them in the process.

They all went off at close of play in great spirits satisfied at the results of their no-notice exercise, as we set about clearing up the mess left behind. They clearly did not forget the hospitality we gave them that night. At my tourex, the students on 2 Squadron, on the occasion of their graduation, requested that Eileen should be centre stage in a tree-planting ceremony. Such an honour would normally be bestowed on the station commander's wife. Our boys had decided to dispense with tradition, and bestow the privilege on Eileen – quite a compliment. Whilst Eileen deftly manoeuvred her silver spade and deposited a token pile of earth into the prepared hole, I flew my last sortie in a diamond-four formation overhead; a fitting end to my year in training command.

Chapter Nine

"Is There a Phoenix in the House?"

Pilot Leader – 57 Squadron
October 1980 to March 1982

While my masters at RAF Barnwood vacillated over my squadron commander's appointment, I must have received five or six different posting instructions. I had accepted that my immediate future as a flying instructor lay within the training world. This meant pitching myself against all those hundreds of QFIs vying for relatively few executive positions, in a very big competitive pool. I was not surprised therefore to receive a phone call from my desk officer in the summer of 1980. I was expecting to hear that I'd finally been allocated one of the training squadrons in the Vale of York. He did surprise me however when, out of the blue, he informed me that there was a position available on the Tanker Force for a squadron QFI.

He asked me outright if I would be interested in returning to RAF Marham. The position was that of pilot leader on 57 Squadron. Although the thought of returning to 'El Adem with grass' did not necessarily appeal to me initially, it was an opportunity to avoid being tarred with the QFI brush in Training Command – possibly for the rest of my career. Was this my chance to escape? After all, I'd only applied to CFS as a means to keep flying and avoid the dreaded ground tour. I was being offered yet another flying appointment, in a role with which I was more than familiar, and a squadron executive position to boot.

However, a problem I foresaw was that we had just bought our first house at Haxby five months earlier. How would Eileen react to the possibility of having to up sticks and move home for the fourth time in less than two years? Her close friend advised her in a defiant manner to 'tell him you're not going'. After all, we had barely settled into our lovely new home. Seeing that I was quite tempted by the offer, in her typically unselfish way, she did not hesitate to give me her full support and encouragement. Perhaps she understood that I was not truly committed to the prospect of spending the rest of my career in a training environment. On a positive note, we (Eileen) would not have to go through the demeaning process of scrubbing a married quarter from top to bottom and facing up to the scrutiny of some officious service housing official. In the event, one of my instructor colleagues stepped up fortuitously and asked if he could rent our property, an offer that was particularly timely and mutually beneficial to us both. In no time, we were loading our worldly goods into a removals lorry yet again, and set off once more to the remote East Anglia.

By October 1980, I found myself in the familiar hands of 232 OCU where I was crewed up with another team. The Victor K2 tanker was a very different animal from the lethargic

Mk 1. Fitted with the Rolls-Royce Conway-201 bypass engines, the aircraft had nearly twice the amount of thrust, and an impressive performance to match. With around 123,000 lbs of avtur in the fuel tanks, this was a much more capable tanker. A number of familiar faces were still to be found on the OCU. One of the staff navigator trainers was Mr Victor himself: Sqn Ldr Ernie Wallis. Ernie had the distinction of having spent virtually the whole of his career at Marham, and was the undisputed expert on the Victor's refuelling role equipment. Little did I know that less than two years later, Ernie and I would be crewed together in a very different set of circumstances in the South Atlantic.

I'm pleased to say the course went well, and after only three instructional sorties in the company of a QFI, I soloed with my student crew on 23 October 1980. Unlike the Victor Mk 1 OCU, the Mk 2 conversion course provided the student crews with a full tanking qualification. After a couple of weeks, in airframe XM715, I refuelled a bunch of Jaguars, Phantoms, and Buccaneers on one of the near-by towlines. Who would have thought that I would find myself taxiing that same Victor K2 at Bruntingthorpe Airfield some thirty-two years later. In the following trips, I was re-introduced to the snake climb procedure, formation flying and accompanied descents, all familiar from my 214 Squadron days.

I reported to OC 57 Squadron in early December 1980. I was aware that my new boss, Wg Cdr Graham Curry, was an experienced tanker man and ex-OCU QFI. But I had not had the opportunity to get to know him before. We discussed my new role as pilot leader, one tailored to the training and supervision of the squadron pilots. What I did not expect was the offer of a free rein with which to run my office in any way I felt appropriate.

Immediately, I felt happy with my new appointment, and felt sure I had made the right decision in returning to Marham and the Tanker Force. My first flight on 57 was a squadron acceptance check, and not surprisingly, Graham Curry occupied the adjacent seat. We refuelled a pair of Jaguars on an accompanied cross-country, before bashing the circuit on our return to Marham. The sortie was probably one of the most convivial check rides in the whole of my career, and it cemented a genuine liking and respect for my new boss. I was already thanking my lucky stars that I had managed to make a home run from the confines of Training Command. A month later, I flew on my first Ghost trail with Phantoms to Palermo (which had replaced the former transit base of Luqa in Malta).

I settled quickly into the familiar role of air-to-air refuelling once more. Within a month or so, I had renewed my receiver training qualification, and it was great fun to be back in the saddle and participating in the Sport of Kings once more. The familiar Operation Dragonfly, the code name for the protection of the UK airspace, now flew under the banner of Operation Tansor, a thinly disguised reference to a 'tanker sortie'. Barely a month had passed before I was called upon during a Phantom refuelling to respond to a no-notice Tansor Mobile, to intercept the ever-present Russian Bear intent on testing the UK's defences once more. Some things had clearly not changed at all since my departure from 214 five years earlier. More Tansor callouts followed, and on 17 April 1981, my crew intercepted no less than three Bear 'D's loitering in the Iceland/Faroes gap. It was a frenetic time as we were launched later the same day after another callout, and once more again the following morning. Welcome back to the Tanker Force.

A 57 Squadron Victor landing and streaming at Palermo – February 1981.

Around the same time, I touched base with my old friends The Fighting Cocks, and trailed a pair of 43 Squadron's F-4s through Palermo to Akrotiri. During the latter part of April, I took part in a Pirate trail in support of a pair of Buccaneers. We accompanied our chicks across the pond before leading them into Goose Bay in Labrador for a scheduled stopover. Two days later, we escorted the Buccaneers across the southern edge of the Hudson Bay before casting them off to make their own way to the Canadian Forces Base at Cold Lake, Alberta. By the time we had landed back at The Goose, aircraft unserviceabilities grounded two of our tankers, my own included.

Marooned in one of the coldest places imaginable, the other skipper (and new partner in crime) Flt Lt 'Badger' Brooks and I set about amusing ourselves in the only way we knew. Over the next seven days, we invented several new cocktails, which were given a variety of monikers. Not surprisingly, I remember only one – the 'Goose Bay Sponge', although don't ask me to recall its contents. The evenings were spent consuming huge quantities of Molson Canadian lager, otherwise affectionally referred to as 'mole skins'. It really went down well with the huge steaks that we grilled on the BBQ outside. Little time could be spent tending the steaks however, as more than a minute or so spent in the sub-zero temperature outside ran the risk of freezing to death – literally.

After forging some great relationships with the Canadians in the mess, and particularly air traffic controllers, Badger and I decided to give them a treat as we finally departed, one week later than expected. Leading the 'Phoenix Formation', I cleaned up after take-off, and Badger stuck to me like glue in close line astern. We executed a flat figure of eight around the airfield and flew through on one final pass. Calling for spool up, I applied full power, and we pointed skyward in an energetic climb before coasting out to the east. The boys in the tower thanked us for the impromptu show, and wished us well on our return to Marham. Less pleased were the squadron engineers who were taken aback by the not-inconsiderable fatigue count that Badger had placed on his airframe.

Always willing to appear on the air-show circuit, I took a K2 to the International Air Tattoo at Greenham Common in June 1981. After a terrific weekend, we crewed up on the Monday morning to fly our Victor back to Marham. As I taxied out, ATC asked us if we had anything special planned for our departure. Not wishing to be a party pooper, I asked them if I could be cleared for a steep climb after lift-off. Unlike the stately Mk 1 Victor, the performance of the Mk 2 was exhilarating, especially with a low-fuel state. I quickly agreed with the crew that I would hold the aircraft down after lift-off, get the gear up and flaps in, accelerate to about 250 knots, and then pull up into a steep climb. There was nothing inherently foolhardy about this procedure, and it was guaranteed to give an impressive display to the spectators on the ground. Furthermore, as we had flown in with only sufficient fuel for the short transit home, we were very light. During the weekend, I had run into one of my former students from Yorkshire, Chris Newrith. Not only was he a good student, but also a talented cartoonist. Chris' artistic talents captured our mugshots, along with our impressive departing steed.

'Big T' (wearing sunglasses) and crew caricature, International Air Tattoo – June 1981.

With clearance to take off and approval for the steep climb, my co-pilot Mal High poured on the coals and the aircraft lurched off like a scolded cat. Once clean, I pulled up the nose and started to zoom skywards. At the same time, ATC instructed me with an alarming instruction to 'stop your climb at 3,000 feet'. Fearing a confliction with another aircraft,

I had no alternative but to push over paying careful attention to the limited negative 'G' capability of my aircraft. From a rate of climb at over 5,000 ft per minute, it was inevitable that I would overshoot my cleared altitude, which I was rapidly approaching. The ballistic effect took me to about 4000 ft, and I frantically called ATC I had gone through my cleared level, but was descending back to 3,000 ft. Back in the office however, during the sustained zero 'g' push, four engine oil low-pressure lights illuminated, and both main hydraulic reservoir levels temporarily indicated fault conditions. My AEO was on the edge of his seat for a couple of minutes while things slowly returned to normal, and one by one, all warning lights extinguished. The ATC controller apologised profusely for issuing a lower cleared altitude at no notice, but complimented me on yet another spectacular departure.

By July, my QFI qualification was endorsed with a 'certification to instruct' on the Victor, which came with a right-hand seat conversion. Thereafter, I was in a position to perform routine currencies and recurring checks on the pilots of 57 Squadron. Another Western Tankex in August gave me the chance to put myself to the test once more by receiving a 25,000-lb onload from another K2, whilst flying non-stop from Marham to the Strategic Air Command Headquarters at Offutt AFB. After four days in Nebraska, we returned through Goose Bay, where I was able to inflict on yet another crew the delights of the Goose Bay Sponge. The following day, we set out once more across the Atlantic, having enjoyed another memorable stateside visit.

No 57 (Phoenix) Squadron was one of the best squadrons in which I had the pleasure to serve. Socially, it was nothing less than brilliant. Whenever a squadron member entered the bar, a cry of "Is there a Phoenix in the house?" was usually heard. The mandatory response from any 57 Squadron members was of course "You bet your burning ass there is".

It seemed that we had more BBQs and fancy dress parties that year than on any other unit I'd served. Boss Curry and his attractive wife Sonia laid on one particularly memorable French-themed party in their married quarter one evening. What the Curry's did not bank on was the arrival of Badger and Midge Brooks, John and Olive Foot, and Eileen and myself of course, intent on deliberately lowering the tone of their bistro evening. As Graham opened the door, the look on his face showed a mixture of surprise and trepidation. Eileen, Midge and Olive were dressed as French tarts: dresses that were slit to the thigh, fishnet tights and high heels. Although I say it myself, they looked absolutely stunning.

In order to enter into the spirit, we sported moustaches, berets, and we wore jeans and t-shirts as opposed to lounge suits, which was probably expected. The whole effect was topped by strings of onions that were slung haphazardly around our necks. Before the boss could jokingly shut the door in our faces, the six of us pushed our way inside. The reaction from the guests initially was one of shock and horror, until everyone saw the harmless humour in our Gallic intrusion. Far from trying to undermine Graham and Sonia's hospitality, we were only intent on lightening the atmosphere. Before long, everyone saw the funny side, and I'm sure the Currys took it as a great compliment. The mood changed instantly, and I like to think we contributed towards the whole success of the evening.

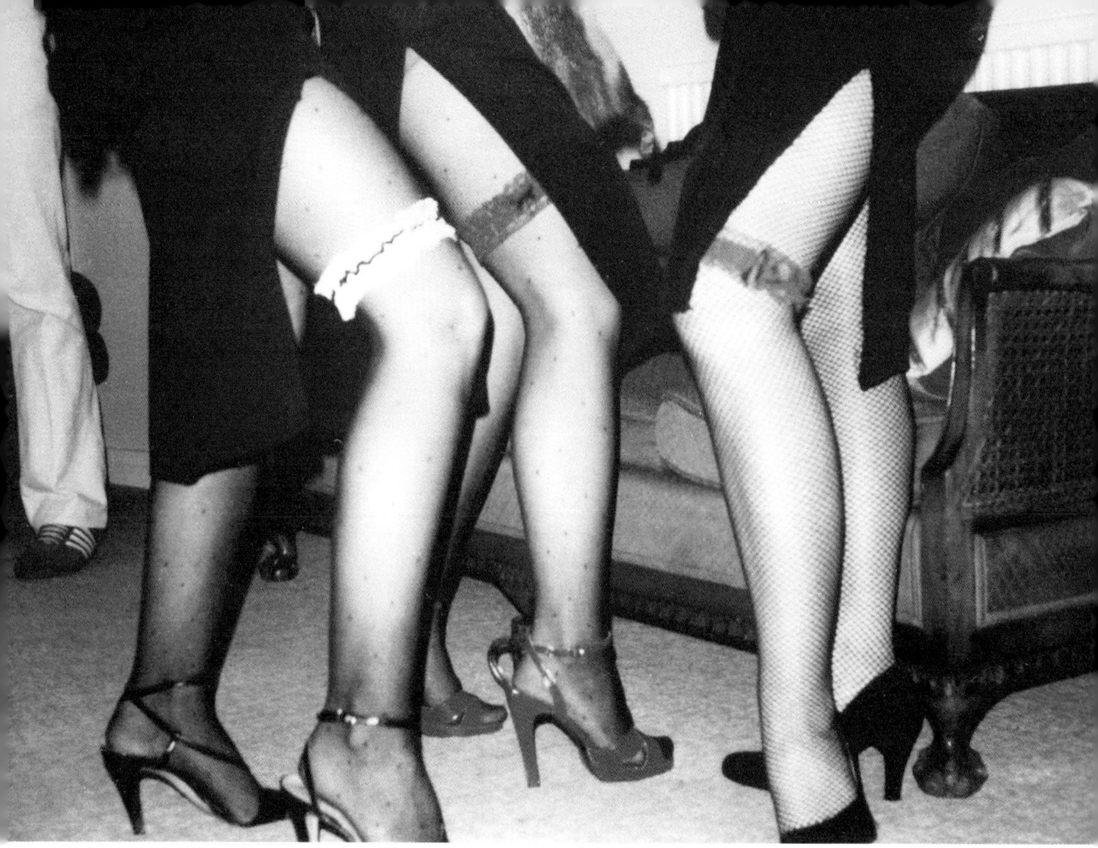

Three French 'tarts': Midge, Eileen and Olive.

By January 1982, I had clocked over 3,000 hours flight time in my logbook. As pilot leader, my position put me in the firing line for a number of dubious flying duties; one in particular was the honour of flying with our air officer commanding No 1 Group. On 7 October 1981, I had the pleasure of accompanying Air Vice-Marshal Mike Knight on a Phantom towline, to give him a tanker familiarisation flight in the Victor K2. Responsible for the overall air defence of the UK, the AOC exercised control over the Tanker Force at RAF Marham, and hence his interest in being familiar with its aircraft and crews. Stuck behind a desk for much of the time, I had heard that our AOC liked to mix it with the troops and get back into the cockpit. I approached this opportunity with some reservation, but in the event, it was an absolute pleasure to fly with this senior officer. He immediately put me at ease, and I soon learned that this was a man completely at home in an aircraft – even one in which he was not current. He had a very direct no-nonsense approach to flying, but underneath lurked a gentleman with a sense of humour. This was a short but enjoyable introduction to a man whom I would grow to admire before my time on tankers was through. Interestingly, it would not be the only time that I would have the privilege of flying with AVM Knight.

By coincidence, our commander-in-chief Queen Elizabeth II had made one of her frequent visits during January 1982. As Marham is the nearest RAF Station to the Queen's residence at Sandringham, the Royal family is no stranger to the home of the Tanker Force. I was honoured to represent the tanker aircrews of 57 Squadron, and it was a pleasure to be introduced to Her Majesty as she undertook a tour around one of our hangars.

A couple of months later, Eileen and I were delighted to receive a much-coveted invitation to attend a garden party at Buckingham Palace. However, in the spring of 1982, things were beginning to take a sinister turn far away in the South Atlantic. Furthermore, and unbeknown to me, I was about to get yet another posting change. As it transpired, our monarch would require my services elsewhere at the time, and we unfortunately were not able to attend.

The station commander Gp Capt Price introducing Her Majesty to my crew – January 1982.

Chapter Ten

"Superfuse" – The Black Buck Legacy

Flight Commander –55 Squadron
April 1982 to December 1982

I was getting used to random calls from my desk officer at the Air Secretary's Branch. Once more without warning, I received a call during March with very little notice that I was about to be posted as flight commander onto 55 Squadron across the waterfront at Marham. At least we would not have to move house and go through the laborious process of handing over yet another married quarter with all that entailed. During this period, the Vulcan force was being phased out, and a number of Vulcan pilots had been cross-trained onto the Victors at Marham. By sheer coincidence, the majority of these bomber 'pukes' as we used to irreverently call them had been inadvertently pooled into 55 Squadron.

The limited knowledge of tanking operations and lack of experience in their new aircraft became a problem during that period of increasing tension – hence the reason for my posting. Not at all pleased to leave 57, I had even less enthusiasm in joining 55, especially as it was now top heavy with 'triangle heads' (a reference of course to those pilots who had previously flown the Delta-winged bomber). Nevertheless, as the RAF was not a democratic organisation, at least in those days, I duly marched across the apron and assumed my challenging new executive position on 55 Squadron. The date was 1 April 1982, and I had to assume this was pure coincidence rather than mischievousness on the part of my desk officer.

My first days on 55 Squadron were quite frenetic, what with getting to know many new faces and adjusting to the environment on an unfamiliar squadron. However, Marham seemed to be awash with an increasing number of unusual external agencies. The backdrop to this was the unsettling Argentine presence on the island of South Georgia in the distant South Atlantic. Night refuelling qualification was not normally maintained in the Tanker Force at that time, and all of a sudden, there came through a directive to get all our squadron pilots current once more in the art of receiving fuel at night. Rumours started to circulate amongst the cleaners who used to sweep the hangar floors – always the best source of information if you needed to know what was happening.

My first sortie on 55 Squadron consisted of a brief rush up to the nearest towline off the coast of Norfolk where I made ten hurried contacts on another tanker at night. That done, I was duly summoned by the station commander Group Captain Jerry Price, to a meeting in the ops block well into the evening of 11 April. Inside the briefing room, I was met with the rather unusual sight of a couple of NCOs on the floor fiddling with a structure that resembled a Meccano framework. I then saw what I knew to be a pair of

F-95 cameras, the type used in photographic reconnaissance (PR) aircraft. It transpired they were constructing a prototype of a PR rig, which was to be assembled inside the Victor's nose section. It was intended to locate the rig in the bomb aimer's prone position between and just forward of the pilot's ejection seats. Angled so that the cameras were aligned with the nose-cone transparencies, our modified tanker could then be used as a long-range PR aircraft. It quickly became clear that we were about to gain a new role.

The station commander went on to shed some light on the proceedings. Victor squadrons had undertaken the photographic role in the past, although to my knowledge, this was at high altitude for ground mapping and survey purposes. What was envisioned here was a requirement to take pictures at low level. No one at Marham was either current or qualified for such a task in the tanker. Having recently been instructing in Training Command, which included low-level flying, it was considered that I was perhaps the most qualified skipper at Marham to put the aircraft though its paces. Interestingly, we were directed to maintain a veil of secrecy over our clandestine task. In order to spread the experience from the outset, I was to fly the first sortie with Sqn Ldr Martin Todd, my counterpart on 57 Squadron. The main aim was to become familiar with flying the Victor

Nose transparencies used for the photo-reconnaissance F-95 camera fit.

at low level, and to assess the aircraft's handling characteristics and suitability for the PR job. On 12 April 1982, with authorisation to take the Victor down to around 250 ft agl, we flew the first modified aircraft fitted with the camera rig. This included letting down over the North Sea and making simulated attacks on Flamborough Head to uncover any potential handling problems and develop a set of appropriate operating procedures.

On our return, after debriefing, Gp Capt Price suggested I personally handpick my own crew for the follow-up flights. On returning to the squadron, I sought out my specialist crewmembers from those experienced aircrew that at least were known to me. Flt Lt Glyn Rees (the boss' co-pilot); Sqn Ldr Ernie Wallis ('Mr Tanker' himself as my nav radar); Flt Lt John Keable (Ernie's navigator team partner and nav plotter leader on 55 Squadron), and Sqn Ldr Mike Beer (a trusted friend and a highly capable air electronics officer). I took a third skipper along on my next flight, Sqn Ldr John Elliott (55's other flight commander).

During this flight, I functioned the new F-95s taking vertical and port-oblique camera shots as we flew at low level past disused airfields acting as simulated targets. We circumnavigated the Hebridean Islands, and neighbouring Scottish coastline making pretend 'attacks' on coastal features. Together, we made up the trio of PR qualified crews for whatever Strike Command was about to throw at us. Yet another development took place at that time with the arrival of radar specialists from 27 Squadron, the Vulcan Maritime Radar Reconnaissance (MRR) unit. Over the next few days, the radar equipment in the Victors was 'tweaked' to improve its capability – more akin to that standard fitted to Vulcan MRR aircraft. Guesting nav radars from 27 Squadron were to become frequent additions to the tanker crews, adding their unique specialist MRR experience to the ever-flexible tanker crews.

By the end of the second week of April, there was talk of a full-blown Argentine military invasion of the Falkland Islands. Even so, few amongst us had any idea of the exact location of the Falkland Islands, and most people thought they were situated somewhere west of the Scottish Highlands and Islands. Intelligence briefings on the increasing tension in the South Atlantic followed. Expectant aircrews were drafted into the ops block for briefings on escape and evasion techniques. Our attention was really focussed when at the end of one briefing, we were all given a will form which we were required to fill in. We had not seen such an escalation towards a war footing before, and it seemed the bubble was about to burst.

The Falkland Islands are situated 400 miles off the southernmost point of Argentina, and nearly 8,000 miles from the UK. Positioned roughly halfway to the Falklands by either sea or air, Ascension Island was identified as a potential forward operating base (FOB) for Britain's planned activities in the South Atlantic. Fortuitously, the airfield facilities on the island would be able to serve the MoD's interests in providing a vitally important airhead when mounting any future RAF air operations. In 1982, Wideawake Auxiliary Airfield (often referred to by its 3-letter code – ASI) was a little used airport whose sleepy facilities Pan Am maintained. The name was derived from the equatorial Sooty Tern that surrounded the island in astonishing numbers. Colloquially, it had always been referred to as the 'Wideawake' because if its incessant calls. The single long runway would be more than capable of supporting No 1 Group's Victors, enabling them to operate to the very limits of their performance capabilities at maximum all-up weight. The single parking apron was a concern however; it might limit the number of aircraft that Ascension could park at any one time.

On 18 April 1982, I launched with the first wave of tankers bound for our new base in the middle of the South Atlantic. In order to transit directly to Ascension without stopping en route, each Victor took on 30,000 lbs of fuel from a buddy tanker whilst rounding the Iberian Peninsula. Shortly after Ernie Wallis' radar picked up the island's craggy outline, we caught our first view of this remote volcanic outcrop.

Problems associated with operating from this isolated location immediately became apparent. The air traffic control facility was established for just two resident controllers. They would soon face the prospect of handling vastly increasing numbers of aircraft movements. Within days, this matched those of Chicago O'Hare, the busiest airport in the world. Although in its past, Ascension had harboured significant numbers of troops (particularly during the Second World War), it was not geared up for the rapid influx of flying units and supporting personnel that flooded in during April 1982. The RAF's transport fleet, including Hercules and VC10 aircraft, had already been preparing the way with supply runs to set up the basic infrastructure for future operations. Nimrod MR1

Landing 'into Ascension' (© www.chrisfrenchart.co.uk)

surveillance and reconnaissance aircraft had been despatched to Ascension to ascertain the Argentinian land, sea, and air presence and capabilities. The next group to arrive on the island would be a significant proportion of air-to-air refuelling tankers in the form of Marham's Victor K2s.

After landing, my crew assembled under XL511's front fuselage. I couldn't help but notice the triangular windows in the nose of my steed, behind which were hidden the newly acquired F-95 cameras. Spirits were high as we looked around at the intriguing backdrop of Ascension's foreboding landscape. The ramp was bathed in glorious sunshine, and the beer tasted good.

My first impression was the barrenness of the landscape. Ascension's single runway runs from north-west to south-east across the southernmost part of the island. Guarded on the south side by extinct volcanoes, and on the north by increasing high ground and yet more volcanoes, the runway nestled in-between. On the surface of the airfield away from its apron and runway, there was evidence all around of volcanic activity. Closer inspection revealed abundant quantities of pumice stone, gritty volcanic dust and copious amounts of black lava and clinker.

From our vantage point on the airfield, there was one patch of greenery on the horizon, the uppermost section of the appropriately named 'Green Mountain'. At close to 3,000 feet above sea level, this was the highest peak on the island. By virtue of the fact that its crown frequently sat in the base of the afternoon cumulus clouds, the moisture that formed at least supported some vegetation. Much of this greenery owed its presence

From left to right: Ernie Wallis, Mike Beer, Me, Glyn Rees and John Keable – 18 April 1982.

least supported some vegetation. Much of this greenery owed its presence to the early settlers who introduced various plants and trees to the island. Norfolk Island pines for example were planted, and a small copse was nurtured to make available straight and sturdy trunks: ideal for mast replacements. Another peculiarity of Green Mountain was a small artificially constructed dewpond at its summit, which was surrounded by a small yet dense bamboo forest.

Other than these isolated examples of vegetation, the majority of Ascension's surface had been decimated by volcanic activity over the centuries, leaving a predominantly featureless landscape. The names of the geographic scars that littered the surface of this largely inhospitable island spoke for themselves: 'Devil's Ash Pit', 'Devil's Cauldron' and 'Devil's Inkpot' to name but three! 'Comfortless Cove', one of the former drop-off points for sailors with incurable and contagious diseases like yellow fever, provided a stark reminder of the severity of life under sail in years gone by. A number of similar isolated cemeteries bear witness to this day of the stricken sailors left stranded at their final resting place around Ascension's coastline.

Despite its harsh terrain, the inland areas supported a variety of wild life and birds in particular, including waxbills, canaries, mynas and partridges. Its coastline attracted many more species including Wideawake fairs (sooty terns), boobies, boatswain birds, frigates and gannets. The most spectacular visitor to Ascension's beaches however was the green turtle. Every two to four years, these magnificent creatures swim all the way from Brazil, their normal habitat, to lay eggs at the very beaches on which they were born. Soon after our arrival, we would all make an excursion to the beach at night to observe this endangered species, as they dragged their huge bodies along the sand and gouged out a nest to lay their eggs. They appeared to be crying as they tried to clear the sand thrown up into their eyes by their flippers as they scooped out great swathes of sand. By the time they had filled in the nest to cover the newly laid eggs, and laboriously made their way back to the surf, they looked completely exhausted. It was truly one of nature's most fascinating sights.

Despite the fact that the base had retained a distinctly American flavour, there was still some evidence of British influence. In the heart of the island's capital Georgetown stood the striking former Royal Marines' barracks in all its splendour. A colonial-looking building was at the centre of this small community. It was flanked by the inevitable cricket pitch – which would have served as a parade ground – and a quintessential English church complete with spire and bell tower. A veranda surrounded the main bar area in the upper floor, which served as the main meeting place for the expats on the island. The 'Exiles Club' as it was known was a focal point for the handful of Cable and Wireless employees and BBC World Service personnel who manned the relay station there. We were graciously offered honorary membership to this delightful club, which even boasted a rather shabbily maintained full-sized billiards table. At the well-equipped open bar, an honour system operated where chits could be signed in return for any amount of liquid refreshment. There was no better vantage point on the island in which to share banter amongst good friends and like-minded colleagues. We watched the sun go down on many occasions, and transfixed our glare on the receding sun in an effort to catch a glimpse of that infamous green flash on the point of sunset.

From the outset, the support facilities at Wideawake Airfield were limited to say the least. There were no buildings from which to operate within a reasonable distance of the aircraft. On 19 April in the relative cool of the morning, the first task was to erect the tents that would serve as our operations and engineering complex. Situated immediately adjacent to the ramp, with the jet pipes of our aircraft less than fifty yards away, we started constructing the 'tented operations complex'. The canvas brown tents merged well into the featureless volcanic ground. Several tents were grouped together to fulfil the specific needs of the separate sections; flying clothing, safety equipment, intelligence unit, engineering trades and a Tactical Communications Wing. The medical centre tent had a roughly prepared board in front, on which was painted '5557 MASH – Victor Battle Fleet' echoing the enduring American TV series *M*A*S*H* which portrayed the exploits of the mobile army surgical hospital. The largest complex of tents served as a combined operations centre and associated aircrew-briefing area. A separate section was set aside so that the various needs of the Victor, Vulcan, and Hercules units could be coordinated and mission plans formulated. As soon as we had completed the construction of the ops complex, we were using it for the briefing and execution of the first task of the Falklands Campaign, which now went under the overall codename of Operation Corporate.

The aim of the first mission was to make a reconnaissance sweep around the South Georgia area, and provide a radar plot of the potential enemy surface vessels in that part of the South Atlantic. These tasks were designed to provide the much-needed intelligence for the small task group in the South Atlantic led by HMS *Antrim*. Sent ahead of the main task force, *Antrim* had the job of deploying an advance party of troops to repossess

Wideawake Auxiliary Airfield tented operations complex – April 1982.

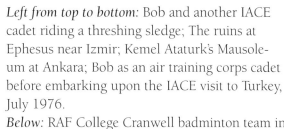

Left from top to bottom: Bob and another IACE cadet riding a threshing sledge; The ruins at Ephesus near Izmir; Kemel Ataturk's Mausoleum at Ankara; Bob as an air training corps cadet before embarking upon the IACE visit to Turkey, July 1976.

Below: RAF College Cranwell badminton team in February 1970. Bob was the team's captain (front row, second from right); College Hall at RAF College Cranwell.

Opposite page clockwise from top left: Last 214 Squadron flight on 23 December 1975; Summer Ball 1975; Bob and Richard debriefing; Flight with news reporter from *Birmingham Evening Mail*, 28 May 1975; No 5 Mess Dress dining-in night, July 1973.

Left: Bob in flying suit at base housing.
Below left: With a KC-135A.
Below right: On the jump seat;
Bottom: Tuxford family on the ramp at Mather AFB.

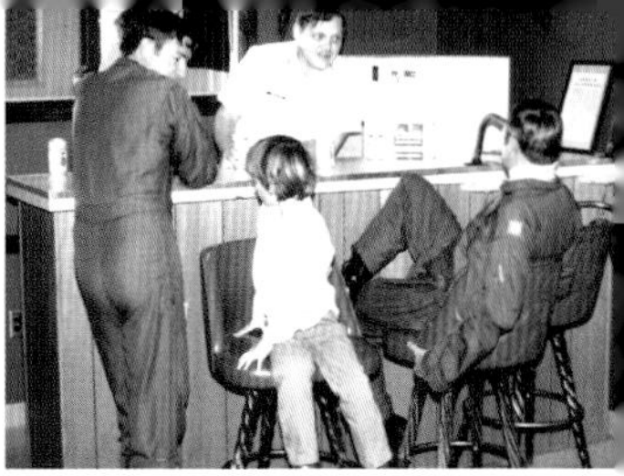

Above left: Bob & Eileen dressed for a formal dinner engagemer
Above right: Richard in the Boomers Bar with three squadron pilots.
Left: The Totem Pole showing the relative performance of the 320th Bomb Wing units: 904th Air Refuelling Squadron in thir place.
Below: Tuxford family with Lance and Linda Bodine – Novemb 1978.

Opposite page: USAF receivers in contact with KC-135A boom.
Clockwise from top left: KC-135A Flying Boom fully extended; F-16 Fighting Falcon; F-15 Eagle; A-10 Warthog; F-111 Aardvark; B-1 Lancer-1; C-5A Galaxy.

38885
U.S. AIR FORCE

HIGH SPEED BOOM
HIGH SPEED BOOM

Clockwise from top left: Eileen and Rich at Grand Canyon, Arizona – May 1977; Bob and Richard at Santa Barbara, California – June 1976; Elvis' birthplace in Tupelo, Mississippi – May 1978; In Yosemite, California – May 1977; On the Pacific Coast Highway, California – June 1976; Touring on Cannon Beach, Oregon – October 1978.

Above: Aircrew posing by the 57 Sqn 'Phoenix', RAF Marham – winter 1981.

Left: 57 Sqn up a gum tree at Pissouri, Cyprus – February 1981.

Below left: Bob's crew at the IAT '81, Greenham Common – June 1981.

Below right: Bob and Eileen at a 57 Sqn vicars and tarts party.

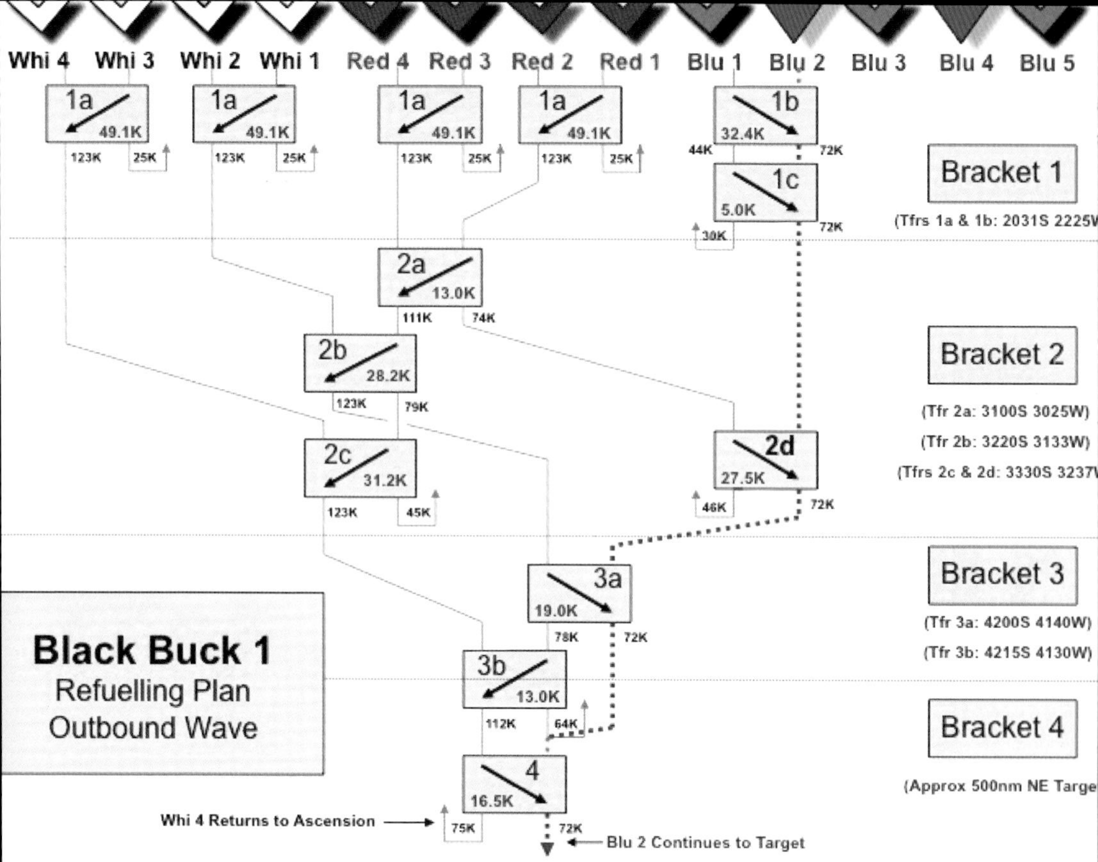

From top to bottom:
Black Buck 1 refuelling plan – Outbound Wave; Black Buck flying badge; Vulcan on ramp.

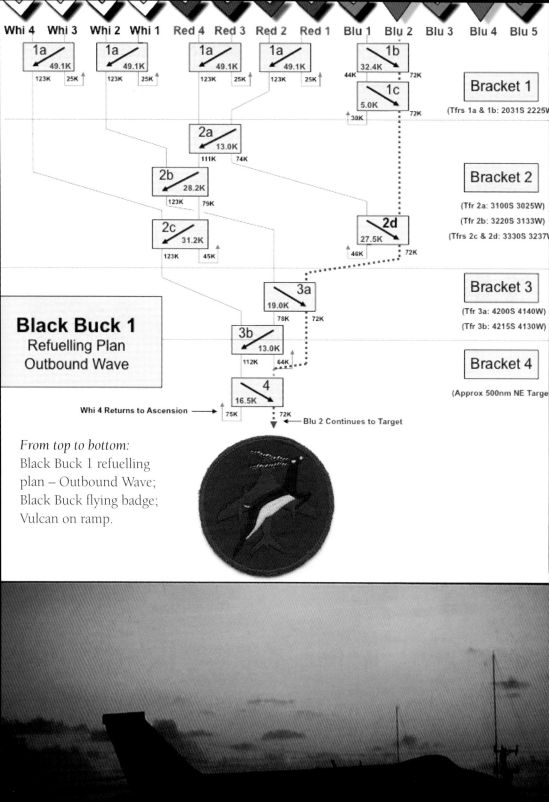

Above: RAF Marham Operation Corporate Awards, December 1982. From left to right: Sqn Ldr R Tuxford (AFC), Sqn Ldr E.F. Wallis (QCVSA), Sqn Ldr R.J. Russell (MiD), Flt Lt J.N. Keeble (QCVSA), AVM M.W. Knight AOC No. 1 Gp, Flt Lt G.D. Rees (QCVSA), Sqn Ldr M.E. Beer (QCVSA), Gp Capt J.S.B. Price (CBE [Mil]) RAF; Marham station commander and the first air head commander, Ascension Island 1982.

Left: The AFC presented by HM the Queen at my investiture at Buckingham Palace – December 1982.

Below: Memento of Black Buck 1. A photo of XM607 signed by Martin Withers' crew.

Top: The Lightning T4 gate guardian at Boscombe Down.
Below left from top to bottom: 50th Anniversary of ETPS: reunion with 1983 course colleagues. From left to right: Darcy Dunn (RCAF), Andy Mechling (USN), Chris Glaeser (USAF), Bernard Foron (FAF) and Bob Tuxford (RAF) – 5 June 1983; ETPS students versus staff cricket match at Boscombe Down, July 1983.
Below right: Eileen and Richard with ETPS Hawk T1 XX341 at Greenham Common, July 1983.

RAF tanker trials aircraft 1984-1987.
Above left: VC10 K3 tanker.
Above right: TriStar K1 tanker.
Below left: 57 Squadron Victor K2 tanker.
Below right: Hercules C1K tanker.
Bottom: Vulcan K2 tanker.

B Squadron heavy aircraft receiver trials 1984-1987.
Above left: Hercules C1K vs Victor K2.
Above right: Nimrod MR2 (P) vs Victor K2.
Left: Nimrod MR2 (P) vs VC10 K3.
Below: TriStar K1 vs VC10 K3.
Bottom: Hercules C1 vs TriStar K1.

Opposite page: AAR trials in contact. *Clockwise from top left:* Victor K2; Victor K1; TriStar K1; VC10 K3; Hercules C1K.

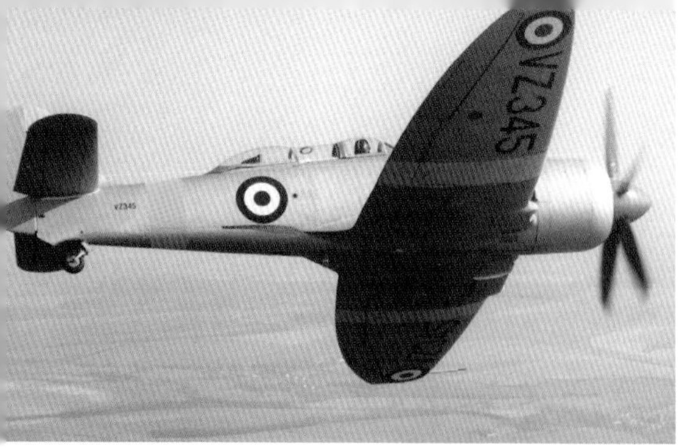

Clockwise from top left: Sea Fury T20 VZ345. Apprentice restoration project; Comet 4C XS235. Role: navigation and avionics test bed and overseas trials support; Harvard IIb KF183. Role: slow-speed photo-chase; Basset CC1 XS765. Role: crew transport.
Below: Navajo Chieftain C1 ZF622. Role: crew transport (Replacement for Basset).

From top to bottom: The 2-stick F-16 that Bob did not get to fly; Flight crew (from left to right): Bob Tuxford (trials project pilot and senior test pilot); Robin Tydeman test pilot; flight engineers Terry Smith and Ron Hendricks; ZD950 on the ramp at Edwards AFB test centre, July 1986.

Clockwise from top left: Spooling up the Spey engines on Nimrod MR2 XV226, 24 May 2015; VC10 K4 ZD241 at full chat on 26 May 2014; Taking XM715, a Victor K2 (and veteran of the Falklands War), down the runway on a fast run on 30 August 2015; Full power run in Canberra BI Mk 8/Mod 6 WT333, 1 November 2014.
Below: A pairs run-in JP4 XP672 on 25 August 2013.

the occupied island of South Georgia, 800 miles east of the Falkland Islands. Every Victor on the island would be needed to ensure the success of this far-reaching mission. The outbound wave consisted of five K2s which would deliver the 'probe' aircraft (the designated aircraft which would undertake the radar sweep) to the target area. On completion of the task, this aircraft would return to Ascension.

However, the demands of the long-range search pattern meant that the returning Victor would need a further refuelling in order for it to reach the island. A second recovery wave of four tankers would have to launch part way through the mission in order to rendezvous with the returning probe aircraft for a final refuelling. This RV was located approximately 150 nm off the Brazilian coast so that in the event of failure to take on fuel, the probe aircraft could make an emergency landing at Rio de Janeiro. To lessen the odds of this diplomatically awkward option, four tankers were planned in the recovery wave so that two tankers would be on offer at the rendezvous, dubbed the 'Rio RV'. A failure in the refuelling equipment of one aircraft could be overcome by the presence of a second tanker on hand.

The tanker planning team briefed the complicated refuelling plan, and overhead projections depicted the cascading refuelling brackets and fuel transfer information. Each crew navigator was given an A4-sized copy of the refuelling plan, produced from the sole photocopying machine that had been hastily despatched from the UK hours before. So that each tanker crew could step in and replace any of the other assigned tankers, a complete set of navigation plans and refuelling options for every tanker sortie had to be carried by all crews. It was quite a surprise when the briefing officer announced that my crew was allocated the probe slot. This critical role had to be flown by one of the three MRR/PR qualified crews; this meant that Sqn Ldr Todd and Sqn Ldr Elliott would have to be prepared to take my place in the event my aircraft fell down. At question time, I asked the intelligence officer to inform us where our own fleet would be located during the southbound leg. The response was less than helpful, and highlighted the lack of current and timely intelligence. Basically, we would not be privy even to the disposition of our own fleet, let alone that of the enemy. Once airborne, all of the rendezvous and join-up procedures would be made in radio silence; we could not afford to broadcast our departure from Ascension. The Argentine military had submarines and reconnaissance aircraft that might well be monitoring radio calls. On completion of the main brief, the individual crews separated, and the respective formation leaders covered every detail in respect of timings, start sequences, and formation changes and procedures.

Feeling somewhat apprehensive about the night ahead, I set off to the aircrew feeder with my crew for a pre-flight meal. The activity on the adjacent ramp was hectic as our ground crews moved engine starter units next to those aircraft that would start first. Engineers were finishing off their last-minute preparations, and airmen were cleaning windscreens in anticipation of multiple refuellings. The number of tankers was starting to grow to the point where the ramp was becoming seriously congested.

Sixty minutes prior to off-chocks, we drifted across the clinker to our waiting aircraft. At the allocated time, the combine started engines, disturbing the night with a cacophony of noise and dust. As I moved off to take my turn in the taxi sequence, we were dealt a

Victor K2s on the ramp at Wideawake Auxiliary Airfield – April 1982.

cruel blow. As soon as the aircraft moved, the newly fitted Carousel inertial nav system dumped, possibly as a result of not being completely aligned. Needing at least thirty minutes to re-align, the chance of our recovering this equipment – an absolute necessity for the aircraft flying the probe slot – fell to zero. We were desperately disappointed to lose the prime slot as the ops controller immediately re-allocated one of the 'short out' slots to us. In my place, John Elliott picked up the reins and took on my probe slot. On a positive note, I traded a potential fifteen-hour sortie for one of the short four-hour details. Our new task would consist of giving just one maximum offload to one of the other K2s and return directly to base. Or so I thought.

As the first section of the outbound wave of Victors groped their way down runway 14 at sixty-second intervals, Operation Corporate mission number one was well and truly underway. I took to the runway in turn and reluctantly settled into my supporting role, still cursing the inertial nav kit. To add insult to injury, Sqn Ldr Steve Stevenson (our guest MRR specialist nav radar) was seated uncomfortably atop the offending Carousel housing bolted to the cockpit floor. This modification had dictated the removal of the sixth seat, which would otherwise have offered him a little more comfort. He was now just along for the ride. Once joined up, we maintained a loose formation until nearing the first refuelling bracket around ninety minutes into the mission.

En route to Bracket 1 where the first refuelling was planned to take place, I took on an un-scheduled 21,000 lbs of fuel from a reserve Victor that had been launched because of delays on the ground. So early in this first mission, there was a feeling amongst the planners that there might not be enough fuel in the formation to get the probe aircraft to the search area and back. With fuel now to spare, I continued to the designated first refuelling bracket. Around 600 nm south of Ascension, my crew accomplished our first successful fuel transfer during Operation Corporate. The 45,000 lbs of fuel passed to my buddy filled his tanks to full: around 123,000 lbs of avtur. The whole process took around twenty-five minutes.

Our return to Ascension went without a hitch, and we duly parked XL163 on the ramp and retired to the debriefing tent. Eager to get an update on the state of play from the ops team, I was somewhat taken aback to be informed that my crew would be required to fly again. What I had not realised was that some of the crews who had arrived earlier that day were not sufficiently rested to participate in this first mission. Before long, we boarded a second K2 that night, XL188, and I led a four-ship snake climb and set course for the Rio RV.

As part of the recovery inbound wave, our task was to meet John Elliott's aircraft on his return from the sweep around South Georgia. The rendezvous with the probe aircraft went like clockwork, and the refuelling was flawless. John Elliott's crew returned safely after fifteen hours aloft, an achievement for which John and his crew would receive a Mention in Despatches. Five crews, including my own, flew in excess of eight hours in support of both outbound and inbound recovery waves. The squadron engineers and ground crews had worked miracles by turning aircraft around, refuelling them, and presenting them for further service in record time. The general feeling amongst the whole detachment was buoyant. A precedent was set, and a blueprint for every subsequent mission that required air-to-air refuelling over the South Atlantic had been established.

The next day, a second MRR task was ordered to identify the Argentine fleet disposition to the north of the Falkland Islands. My role in support of MRR-2 was in the so-called 'long-out' slot. This involved taking on 46,000 lbs of fuel at the first bracket, and then transferring 38,000 lbs to the probe aircraft at the second bracket. The flight time was in excess of 8 hours, all during the hours of darkness. Apart from losing the No 4 generator, the sortie was relatively straightforward. Small refinements to the refuelling plan had been implemented following the lessons learned on MRR-1, and as a result, the whole operation went according to plan. Not surprisingly, it was followed up by a third task generated less than twenty-four hours later on the night of 24/25 April. MRR-3 saw the tankers fly south to a point 200 nm from the eastern extremity of East Falkland Island. The missions were becoming more onerous in terms of distance flown, sortie duration, number of in-flight refuellings, and the number of tankers required. We had embarked upon an intense flying rate never seen before by our aircrews, ground crews, and especially, our aging Victor airframes.

A brief period of respite followed. In the wake of the success of the maritime reconnaissance missions, our masters at home were already planning the next chapter. At least my crew got to enjoy the facilities of the Exiles Club for a few days, even though the late-night treks back up the hill from Georgetown to our block were fraught with danger. The South Atlantic Fleet was still harboured off the coastline, and from the veranda of the Exiles, we were aware of the continued preparations amongst the ships at bay. Choppers filled the skies as stores and munitions were continuously redistributed throughout the participating vessels: cross-decking as it was referred to. So hasty had been their departure from the UK that although most of the victuals, ammunition, weaponry, equipment and most importantly – thousands of cases of beer – were there, it was all in the wrong ships. One of the vessels was undergoing some superstructure work as welders' torches flashed away day and night. SS *Uganda*, a former cruise steam ship, had been requisitioned for use as a hospital ship, and was receiving the final touches to her helicopter landing platform before heading south.

With the numbers temporarily swelled in the bar one particular night, there was an incredible feeling of anticipation and expectation. I remember meeting one of my old 97 Entry cadets from Cranwell, a Harrier pilot who had sailed to Ascension with the Fleet. I had not seen him since our graduation from the college twelve years before. The veranda was standing room only as word spread that there was to be a sunset parade on the adjacent cricket ground. The makeshift drill square must have witnessed many a splendid spectacle as the sun fell over the yardarm in that remote corner of the British Empire.

Suddenly, the Exiles Club was packed to the gunnels. Realising that such an historic gathering might never again be repeated, I feverishly took photo after photo of the evening's activities. Crawling on all fours around the perimeter of the parade ground, I was determined to capture every conceivable snapshot of that momentous occasion. The sight and sound of immaculately turned out Royal Marines was sensational. Resplendent in their service dress lovat-green uniforms complemented by green berets, the marines carried their musical instruments with pride. At the head of five columns were the

Sunset Parade Ascension Island – April 1982. (© Peter Wallis)

snare drummers leading a fully equipped band. Anyone would have thought they were practising for a Sunday parade, rather than about to embark on the first major British military action for decades. Pounding the very ground where their predecessors had paraded centuries before, these brave soldiers generated an overwhelming sense of pride in everyone.

I was so privileged to witness the event. My photographs would provide a perfect record of that historical moment. That is – until I decided to check the counter on my Canon SLR. At forty-five, the number of captured images seemed too good to be true: standard rolls of celluloid film in those days supported thirty-six exposures only. You can imagine how completely exasperated and desperate I felt as I realised that I had failed to load a film into my camera. Disappointed beyond belief, I concentrated on soaking up the atmosphere of that wonderful occasion. As the sun slid gracefully over the horizon, a solo marine trumpeter played that haunting melody of the last post. The realisation that these men were about to depart for the icy cold waters of the South Atlantic Ocean the next morning did not escape anyone's attention. As the light began to fade, there was barely a dry eye on the packed veranda of the Exiles Club. Ground and aircrews alike spontaneously burst into a rousing chorus of 'Don't Cry for Me Argentina'. I could have sworn that our dulcet tones must have been heard as far away as Port Stanley!

Ascension seemed somewhat quieter after the departure of the task force. Activity on Wideawake Auxiliary Airfield however continued to gear up at an alarming pace. It was five days since I had last flown, and interestingly, four more Marham tankers had arrived on the crowded ramp by 29 April 1982. Clearly, things were about to change with the arrival of the first sinister Vulcan B2. It did not escape the attention of my fellow flight commanders that these B2s were also equipped with refuelling probes, a very clear signal that we were about to take on yet another 'customer' within the context of the South Atlantic operations.

Shortly after the arrival of the tin triangles, Marham's tanker crews were assembled

Vulcan B2s arrive on Ascension Island – 29/30 April 1982.

yet again inside the draughty briefing tent. For the first time in my experience, we sat side-by-side with our counterparts from the Vulcan Bomber Force. The night of 30 April/1 May 1982 would mark a turning point in the course of the Falklands Campaign. Specifically, it would signal the commencement of offensive air operations against the Argentine invasion forces. In what was seen as an audacious move, the chief of the air staff had sanctioned a conventional bombing raid by a single Vulcan bomber on the Argentinian-held airfield at Port Stanley, East Falkland Island. The buzz of excitement in the briefing tent was intense as the scene was set for Operation Black Buck. Victor and Vulcan crews listened intently as the scenario unfolded. Three sections, comprising Red, White and Blue would form the outbound wave. Four tankers would make up each of Red and White sections, whilst a further three K2s would support the primary Vulcan and its airborne reserve in Blue section. Five tankers, including an airborne reserve aircraft, would make up a second inbound wave. These tankers were needed to meet the post-attack Vulcan at the well-proven Rio rendezvous. As in the MRR missions, the offer of two refuelling hoses at the bracket for the Vulcan's final refuelling would reduce the potential for failure in the event of a single HDU malfunction. The fuel plan was designed to ensure that all tankers in both outbound and inbound waves would have sufficient fuel to be able to return to Wideawake after their final refuelling, albeit with operationally acceptable minimum fuel reserves. I was allocated one of the medium-length sorties, and so could be expected to be airborne for around eight hours. At least, that was the plan.

After the short walk across the cinder track, we boarded our aircraft. Shortly afterwards, the night air was suddenly charged with the sound of fifty-two Rolls-Royce Conway and eight Olympus engines bursting into life. I teased my fully laden aircraft onto the taxiway from the crowded ramp, and joined the sequence of aircraft snaking their way to Runway 14. Red-1, commanded by Sqn Ldr Martin Todd, led the thirteen-ship snake climb between the volcanoes into the black South Atlantic sky. The deafening sound of the mighty four-jets as they struggled to get airborne must have been a spectacular sight. Ascension had not seen anything like this before.

Without delay, the next priority for each airborne tanker was to prove the integrity of its hose drum unit. Although trailing the hose would not guarantee that it would trail again two hours later, at least the early detection of a fault might avoid such complications later. To White-4's horror, this turned out to be the case as his nav radar found that their centreline hose would not budge from its housing. This was the last thing we expected, or wished for, so soon after take-off. Flt Lt Steve Biglands, having launched as Blue-3, slid across to White section and assumed White-4's position, which coincidentally elevated his role from airborne reserve to that of primary outbound tanker: the probe slot. The task would then fall upon him to be the last Victor at the southern-most point to refuel the Vulcan prior to casting him off seven hours later.

A more sinister situation was beginning to develop as the formation continued climbing. Blue-2, the primary Vulcan, was having problems pressurising his aircraft. Shortly afterwards, he had to declare his non-operational status and prepared to return to base. Flt Lt Martin Withers' crew had been designated as the Vulcan airborne reserve, and was now called into action to replace the unserviceable Vulcan. In the new role as Blue-2 – the primary Vulcan – Martin Withers took his place in Blue section and joined

Operation Black Buck briefing – 30 April 1982.

the ten remaining tankers. At least the weather factor at Ascension's latitude presented no problems at this stage of the mission. The skies were clear, and visibility in the star-lit night sky was unlimited. Indeed, the only problem was trying to identify which set of lights belonged to your own section leader. As White-2, and sixth in the stream, I was able to settle in echelon starboard on my leader without too much difficulty. Nevertheless, it seemed as though the whole sky was awash with flashing red beacons amidst a clutter of multi-coloured navigation lights. Before long, Red, White and Blue sections had formed up and were heading south, staggered at their respective flight levels 36, 34, and 32,000 feet. The engines settled into their familiar drone as a comfortable formation position was achieved. There was now time to relax a little after the anxieties of the less than ideal start to what was shaping up to be a night to remember.

Bracket 1 (which included the first fuel transfer) was to take place after approximately an hour and forty-five minutes, around 700 nm down track. On reaching the start of the refuelling area, the four pairs of tankers in Red and White sections paired up and prepared to refuel their respective receivers. As a routine, each receiver would stay in contact until the geographical end of the bracket so that all receiving aircraft would be full to the gunnels at the same point. The huge transfer of around 50,000 lbs left each of the fully laden Victors at their maximum all-up weight of 238,000 lbs. The depleted tankers, Red-1, Red-3, White-1 and White-3 then turned for Ascension with a 'chicken' fuel sufficient for their recovery a small reserve. Meanwhile, the remaining tanker with Martin Withers' Vulcan in Blue section had refuelled the bomber at the first bracket, and was staying with him for the time being so that a second refuelling could be made prior to sending him on his way.

Back at Ascension, the four returning aircraft were starting to arrive. There was an increasing consternation amongst the crews as all four aircraft found they had considerably less fuel than expected. There was not even time for the first landing aircraft to backtrack the length of the runway to vacate it for the following Victor. The first three aircraft were faced with no option but to land in sequence, and pull up to the end of the landing strip to leave as much room as possible for the following aircraft. By the time that Martin Todd was on finals, he was faced with the prospect of completing his landing rollout with his three colleagues stacked at the end of the runway. The potential for a major pile-up did not need to be spelled out. In the event, all was well, and the four aircraft were able to taxi back to dispersal where time was of the essence to prepare the airframes for the recovery wave. However, cracks were beginning to show in the refuelling plan.

The five-ship formation continued to the next bracket, situated 1,900 nm south of Ascension. Into the early hours of the morning, the physical exertion of upwards of twenty-five minutes in contact during the first refuelling, and over three hours of concentrated formation flying were beginning to show. At one stage, as number three to Red-2 and Red-4, Steve Biglands on my right-hand side alerted me as I slowly drifted into a dangerous roll to port – undetected by my co-pilot or me. Shaking off the momentary drowsiness, I regained my concentration, and vowed not to let my attention wander again. More changes of position took place during Bracket 2. Having refuelled Red-4, Red-2 moved across to take the lead of the formation on the starboard side where the Vulcan, Blue-2 was awaiting his third onload of fuel. At the same time, I took around 30,000 lbs from Red-4, who in turn gave a similar amount to Steve Biglands, before turning for home. Red-4, flown by Flt Lt Alan Skelton, was to face a few anxious hours during his recovery as a slow fuel leak started to eat away at his island fuel reserve. As White-2, I took over as the formation leader for the first time. Steve Biglands (White-4) joined me, followed closely behind by Martin Withers (Blue-2), and we proceeded en route to the third refuelling area.

The chances of further problems were statistically reducing with only three aircraft left. My own aircraft had behaved impeccably so far, and we had plenty of time to prepare for my planned last refuelling. This was scheduled to take place around 5 hours and 30 minutes after take-off, and approximately 2,700 nm south of Ascension Island. My nav radar Ernie Wallis and plotter John Keable assumed the navigational responsibility, and updated me with an expected time of arrival at the next refuelling area. The Carousel inertial navigation system was a great addition to John's nav kit, and on this occasion, it was working faultlessly. In order to limit all electronic transmissions for fear of alerting any possible enemy surface vessels below, all non-essential equipment, including Ernie's radar, had been left switched off. All refuelling procedures up to this point had been accomplished in complete radio silence.

The fuel transfer at Bracket 3 began without incident as we offloaded fuel for the first time. Martin Withers took on a planned 22,000 lbs prior to holding off on my starboard side. Steve Biglands in the other tanker moved astern in anticipation of his last onload. I started to lose sight of the stars for the first time that night. Unfortunately for us, and for Steve Biglands in particular as the formating receiver pilot, the ride quickly became very uncomfortable. Momentary flashes of lightning illuminated the black sky, and my nav

Nav radar's view of Vulcan in contact. (© Peter Wallis)

radar could see that our hose was starting to whip around wildly. The Vulcan closed up to maintain visual contact with the Victor pair.

Both tankers started bucking around like broncos at a rodeo. After several aborted attempts, Steve managed to make contact on my oscillating hose, and fuel started to flow. In next to no time, we encountered severe turbulence associated unquestionably with cumulonimbus cloud. As our radars had been turned off throughout the flight, we had not been able to anticipate the dreadful conditions. I was quite startled by the St Elmo's fire characterized by erratic sparks and jagged fingers of lightning dancing around my front transparencies. The aircraft started to pitch up and down quite violently, and the autopilot was beginning to respond far too aggressively for my liking. I tripped out the overworked autopilot and elected to fly the aircraft manually in an effort to smooth out the larger flight path disturbances for Steve behind. The whole crew in his tanker must have been having a nightmare in the horrific conditions. Not surprisingly, Steve was becoming increasingly unstable. With less than half the transfer complete, our receiver suddenly dropped back, and breaking radio silence, Steve called "I've broken my probe". A weak link situated just behind the probe tip is designed to break from the main probe structure when, for example, severe forces are detected. This would almost certainly have resulted from the severe whipping action of the hose while Steve attempted to stay in contact. Intended to avoid the possibility of a more serious structural catastrophe, the fail-safe design had abruptly put an end to that fuel transfer.

The whole mission was now in serious jeopardy. Firstly, White-4 had not taken enough fuel to complete the planned profile with the Vulcan. A quick solution would be for me to swap roles with Steve Biglands. However, even if I could change places and take back the fuel transferred already to Steve Biglands' aircraft, there was no assurance that my own refuelling basket was not damaged in the incident. When a probe is broken, the probe tip sometimes stays locked inside the reception coupling of the basket. In other words, even if I was able to take the fuel back from Steve Biglands, the Vulcan might not be able to achieve a latched contact on my hose. Either way, in order to have sufficient fuel to continue the mission, everything depended on my getting the fuel back that I had just offloaded. The only logical course of action, apart from the safe option of aborting the whole mission, was to change roles with White-4 and try. I had spared little thought for Blue-2, the Vulcan on my starboard wing, who had enough on his plate to keep us in visual contact.

There was no sign of the dire conditions letting up. I resigned myself to the difficult task ahead, knowing full well that if someone as experienced as Steve Biglands had lost his probe, this was not going to be a walk in the park. In an un-planned formation change, I positioned my aircraft behind Steve's while his nav radar trailed their hose. The hose was gyrating all over the place as I attempted to stabilise in the pre-contact position.

It took several approaches before I got anywhere near the basket. I recall feeling quite exhausted from the previous refuellings, and although the adrenalin was making sure I was alert, I knew that tiredness, not to mention exasperation, was really setting in. Intent on not 'chasing' the basket, I laboured for several minutes before I was finally able to make contact, and mercifully, Glyn called that we were taking on fuel. Inevitably, a

Bracket 3 at 40 degrees south – Operation Black Buck. (© Ronald Wong GAvA)

few minutes into the transfer, the hose became unstable with characteristic waves running up and down along its length. Fearing that my probe tip was just about to be swiped off in a repeat of Steve's incident, I dropped back to take a brief rest. With insufficient fuel received, it took me three to four more valuable minutes in the turbulent conditions to make a further contact, and re-establish fuel transfer. At that very moment, twinkling stars started to fill the background around the Victor's silhouette above me, and mercifully, the turbulence subsided just as quickly. Our aircraft stabilised once more, I was able to relax a little on the controls and regain some composure for the remainder of the fuel transfer.

Even though I was still in contact, my mind was racing. Paramount in my thoughts was the fact that Steve Biglands' aircraft would not be able to receive any more fuel because of his damaged probe. I therefore warned him not to go beyond that fuel state that would permit his assured recovery to Ascension Island. This would mean that I could expect to take on less than the planned original transfer. Furthermore, as both tankers had now proceeded well past the geographical end of the bracket, the situation as far as fuel was concerned was only getting worse.

As the implications of the multi-facetted problem began to compound, Steve's refuelling signal lights informed me that I had taken as much fuel as he was able to offer. I eased back on the throttles, slid out of contact, and manoeuvred to starboard so that Steve could turn left without delay and set course to Ascension. Our bomber playmate was still formating patiently on my right-hand side, no doubt wondering what the hell was going on. I re-engaged the autopilot and took a moment to consider my predicament.

We were left with two very significant legacies. Firstly, we still had the integrity of my refuelling basket to prove if we were to pass any more fuel. Secondly, as anticipated, the reduced uplift had left us woefully short of fuel. There was clearly insufficient fuel in my tanks to finish the mission detailed in the master fuel plan. There was no point in concerning ourselves unduly with the latter, as the problem might not arise if the former could not be addressed.

Ernie Wallis promptly re-trailed the hose, and I called the Vulcan astern to visually inspect my hose. In particular, I needed the basket to be looked over for signs of damage, and the reception coupling checked for signs of the detached probe tip. The two Vulcan pilots, using torches to illuminate my basket, could not categorically confirm that my basket was okay. To be certain, there was only one way of proving that we could pass fuel; so I cleared the Vulcan for a wet contact. In the restored tranquility, the bomber had no difficulty in making contact, and a nominal transfer of 5,000 lbs was successfully achieved. At least we knew our refuelling equipment was serviceable. I could continue towards the target as the probe Victor with the Vulcan for the time being.

We were well over six hours into the mission, and around 3,000 nm from our departure point. A comprehensive check of the fuel gauges revealed just how short of fuel we were. The choices available as I perceived the situation were two-fold: as formation leader, I could still call it a day right there, and call off the raid whilst my aircraft had just sufficient fuel to return to base. Alternatively, the mission could continue with my own reserves rapidly dwindling to the point where a safe recovery to Ascension would not be guaranteed.

The reality of our predicament was that, in order to refuel the Vulcan at Bracket 4 and transfer the planned fuel, my own aircraft would be left with insufficient fuel to get back to the island. A check of the gauges revealed definitively for the first time that we were about 20,000 lbs short of fuel; i.e. less than the expected fuel on board shown in the fuel plan. At this stage of Operation Corporate, and within the context of Operation Black Buck, a diversion for a tanker to the South American mainland had not really been considered. As far as I was concerned, that option was out of the question. We were not equipped with adequate aeronautical charts for a diversion, nor did we have suitable airfield approach charts.

My gut feeling was to put my trust in years of experience in the Tanker Force, or more precisely, the air commander and his ops team on Ascension Island. I felt certain that he would be only too well aware of the developing fuel crisis from the earlier returning crews. I could not let the AEO get on the HF radio to inform headquarters of our predicament for fear of jeopardising the Vulcan's position in the yet unfulfilled mission. I was strongly predisposed to pressing on, despite the risk. The ultimate consideration without doubt was the safety of my crew, and I was not about to take any course of action without giving them the chance to have their say. Without declaring my hand, I asked my crewmembers for their individual honest take on the situation. One by one, they unanimously stated that having gone that far, we might as well see it through. The single most difficult operational decision as an aircraft commander that I have ever had to make was made much easier that night with the encouragement and support of my crew.

We calculated that we could offer the Vulcan sufficient fuel to enable him to press on with the attack, bearing in mind that he'd already taken an unscheduled 5,000 lbs to check the serviceability of the hose. By the same token, I had to ensure that we had enough fuel in the tanks after Bracket 4 to stand a reasonable chance of getting close enough to Ascension to rendezvous with a rescue tanker, assuming of course that one was available.

The final transfer to Blue-2 went smoothly, up to the point where Ernie signalled the receiver that the transfer was complete. Much to our chagrin, just as we expected the Vulcan to break contact, Martin Withers surprisingly called over the radio that they had not received sufficient fuel. Having stretched ourselves beyond all reasonable limits, we were dumfounded. Irrespectively, there was absolutely no benefit in continuing further south, so we duly turned north. To our surprise, the bomber turned with us initially – away from the target. With the hose still trailed, and against my better judgement, I reluctantly asked Ernie to continue refuelling if he was prepared to take more. Fortuitously, in the next instant, the Vulcan turned away, leaving my aircraft on its own for the first time in seven hours.

A strange silence filled the cabin as I put the aircraft into a cruise climb to an altitude that would give us best range capability. Whichever way we looked at it, after checking our reserves, we could only get to within four or five hundred miles of our safe haven. There would still be a lot of South Atlantic left between that point and Mars Bay, the southerly most point on Ascension. We could not get on the blower and start calling for help as this might have prejudiced the Vulcan's impending arrival. The mood amongst my crew at that moment was one of disappointment, tinged with more than a bit of melancholy. After forty-five minutes however, Mike Beer's excited voice cut through the subdued atmosphere with the welcome announcement: "Superfuse". This was the agreed codeword for a successfully completed bombing run. The elation was immediate and unrestrained, and there was a feeling of euphoria amongst my crew. After the whooping died down, Mike immediately got on the long-range radio to send out a cry for help to HQ Strike Command and Ascension. He also informed them of the Vulcan's likely reduced fuel state, so that a modified Rio rendezvous could be planned if necessary.

Much discussion followed about the prospect of our not being able to meet up with another tanker. If this was the case, we needed to consider the options in the event of running out of fuel. Because of the design of the underside of the nose bay of the Victor, ditching was not an option. In the worse case scenario, I proposed a sequence whereby the rear crew would make a controlled bail out, followed by a sequenced ejection by the pilots. I got Mike to read through all the abandonment drills twice to familiarise everyone with their emergency actions, and then, we put the plan on the back burner. Having covered the bases, it seemed appropriate to concentrate on the more positive prospect of being rescued by another Victor.

Our situation dictated the need for us to meet a tanker at least 1,000 miles south of the island. We calculated this would give us about one hour's worth of fuel remaining: sufficient to locate our tanker; rendezvous with him, and provide a pad to manoeuvre into the refuelling position and make contact on the hose. My expectations were realised with the ultimate confirmation on the HF radio that a terminal airborne tanker was indeed on the way.

Two hours later, after eleven hours of savouring the comforts of the Mk 3 Martin Baker ejection seat, we were all ecstatic with excitement as we established radio contact with our rescue tanker. Five pairs of eyes searched anxiously around the clear blue Atlantic sky for that famous crescent wing. My boss Wg Cdr Colin Seymour, on his second sortie that day, manoeuvred his aircraft directly in front of mine after a flawless rendezvous.

His centreline hose was already trailed (as it had been for the last two hours I found out later) in anticipation of our need to make contact as soon as possible. With hundreds of prods under my belt, this was going to be the most important refuelling of my life. There was a noticeable silence and constrained expectation from my crewmembers, as I deliberately took longer than normal to stabilise astern. This was not the time to be rushed or aggressive. Nor did I feel the usual macho need to make contact in one – a necessity when in company with one's squadron colleagues looking on. The fuel remaining in the tanks as I moved up towards the basket would have kept the engines going for perhaps a little over one hour.

Flying the aircraft as smoothly as possible, I narrowly missed the basket on my first approach, albeit under total control. There was always a temptation to 'nudge' the rudder to capture the basket with the probe, to speed things up. I was not going to accept the possibility of creating the faintest side force on the probe tip during this contact, arguably the most critical that I would ever make. The stakes were too high. The second approach resulted in my probe clunking home centrally inside the reception coupling. "Contact!", as Colin Seymour's refuelling operator would have announced over their intercom for the benefit of his crew. I could almost sense my four colleagues were holding their breath

Victor's crescent wing seen from long line astern – centre hose trailed.

until the next call. I gingerly eased on a morsel of power to push the hose in a few more feet. A moment later the tanker's nav radar transmitted over the radio "fuel flows" for all to hear: that all-important corollary to the latched contact signifying a positive flow of fuel. Glyn once more confirmed fuel was indeed pouring into our empty fuel tanks. Once we had taken on board enough fuel to reach the island, the sighs of relief amongst us were clearly audible. I was now savouring the moment, but could not quite relax until a sufficient reserve existed to cater for any last-minute complications. I stayed in contact a while longer until we were happy with the total fuel on board, and I slid back to disconnect. We followed our stablemate home.

Met at the aircraft by just one of our ops officers, we clawed our way down the ladder into the dazzling afternoon sunshine after fourteen hours aloft. We were ushered to a makeshift desk where Gp Capt Jerry Price and his operations staff were assembled. We were informed that they had reservations about the fuel plan as soon as the first crews returned from Bracket 1 short of fuel. Next, Al Skelton had given them considerable cause for concern on receipt of the Mayday after his fuel leak resulting from the second series of refuellings. Until Steve Biglands' return, the near-disaster at Bracket 3 only served to confuse the ops team on Ascension. Devoid of radio transmissions to keep them in the picture, they could only surmise what might have gone so wrong as things got steadily worse. They knew that further problems had occurred at Bracket 3, but in the confusion, the ops team did not know that Steve and I had changed places until

Steve Biglands announced his arrival at Ascension. What Gp Capt Jerry Price could see was that the fuel plan had been deficient. All four K2s that returned after just four hours were desperately short of fuel. Unknown to us – although perhaps my guardian angel had whispered something in my ear once again – I had been convinced that our tanker operations team and their fuel planners from group would keep us safe. Jerry Price had indeed directed the engineers to pull out all the stops and turn around every aircraft that could be re-flown, and refuel them for use as terminal airborne tankers. In the event, two aircraft were added to the original plan; one launched for Alan Skelton's aircraft, and the other for mine.

Exhausted from the rigours of the previous seventeen hours since briefing the night before, my crew was ready to call it a day. However, with the expected arrival of the Vulcan just minutes away by now, Mike Beer and myself decided to meet the bomber crew in the only way that we knew. Temporarily 'borrowing' two push bikes from the ops complex, we hastily sped off in search of a few beers from the commissary. On arrival back at the ramp, Mike and I sat exhausted in the glorious sunshine, and drank a chilled can of lager as the Vulcan crew taxied in to their parking slot.

A rousing welcome committee of well over 100 people was anxiously awaiting their arrival. AOC No18 Group was there to pat them on the back, and armourers lingered, desperate to check for hang-ups to confirm all the bombs had left the racks. Most of the Ascension Island contingent seemed to want a piece of the action. After a while, we forced our way through the cheering crowds of well-wishers. I eventually came face to face with Martin Withers, and offered him my congratulations, and more importantly, a cold tinny. I believe he was vaguely taken aback by my offer; although we had met a couple of times before, I'm not sure he recognised me. Mike similarly dispensed a few beers amongst Martin's rear crew, and as they were whisked off for debrief, we sauntered back to our billet.

The following day, my crew was enjoying lunch in the commissary. I recall Martin and his crew appearing at our table, a case of beers slung under his arm. After debriefing, the full extent of the previous night's proceedings had been revealed to the Vulcan crew. Only then did they begin to realise the shortcomings of the fuel plan, and the predicament in which my crew had been placed at the final refuelling bracket. Needless to say, after we tucked into the beers and shared a few of the more hair-raising episodes of Black Buck 1, any ill feeling was soon lost in an atmosphere of mutual admiration for a job well done! Ironically, the single most significant reason for the extra fuel used during the mission was placed fairly on the Vulcan's doorstep. Never having been used in anger before, especially at the increased operating war load, the Vulcan's fuel consumption proved to be considerably higher than that which our fuel planners from group had calculated.

A total of eighteen tanker sorties were launched during the night of 30 April/1 May 1982 in support of the two Vulcan bombers. One of our more artistic pilots on Ascension recorded the moment that the BBC announced to the world that the RAF had bombed Port Stanley. I do recall thinking at the time this was rather premature as we were still around four hours from Ascension with about two hours worth of fuel in the tanks. Several crews were called upon to fly second sorties either in support of the inbound

THIS IS THE WORLD SERVICE OF THE BBC....
HERE IS THE NEWS....
LAST NIGHT A LONE RAF VULCAN
BOMBED PORT STANLEY AIRFIELD....
2/100
GaryW8man
8 OCT 1993

Gary Weightman's image of the Black Buck 1 effort. (© GaryW8man)

recovery wave, or as terminal airborne tankers. The participating Victor crews flew in excess of 105 hours, and five crews flew in excess of ten hours. Some twenty-three individual air-to-air refuellings took place, with a total of 635,000 lbs of fuel transferred. In my own case, our sortie duration was 14 hours and 5 minutes. In the course of no less than eight refuellings, I transferred fuel to the Vulcan during three separate transfers, passing 42,000 lbs of fuel. I was in contact for the better part of ninety minutes total whilst receiving fuel during four onloads. In the process, I took on around 120,000 lbs. The refuelling of the Vulcan in support of Operation Black Buck had demanded every bit of expertise of No 1 Group's Tanker Force. We had established a record for the longest bombing mission in the history of aerial warfare. For my part, I was awarded the Air Force Cross for gallantry, and my noble crew, the Queen's Commendation for Valuable Services in the Air.

Up to the point of the Argentine surrender, there had been seven Black Buck missions planned. My crew was stood down from the second raid, for obvious reasons of crew rest. That down time gave us the unique opportunity to watch the next operation – Black Buck 2. Armed with a case of beers, we scaled the volcano next to the runway and took grandstand seats to observe that spectacular departure from Ascension. Black Buck 3 was cancelled before it got underway. A decision was made to change from 'iron bomb' missions to missile attacks on the enemy-controlled defensive radar sites in the Falklands. This gave us a brief respite while the Vulcans were flown back to the UK to enable missile pylons to be fitted under the Vulcan's wing. On 24 May, we launched the first 'Shrike' attack: Black Buck 4. I was planned to fly as No 6 in the eight-ship formation of tankers. During one of the refuelling brackets, Badger Brooks' hose drum unit gave up the ghost

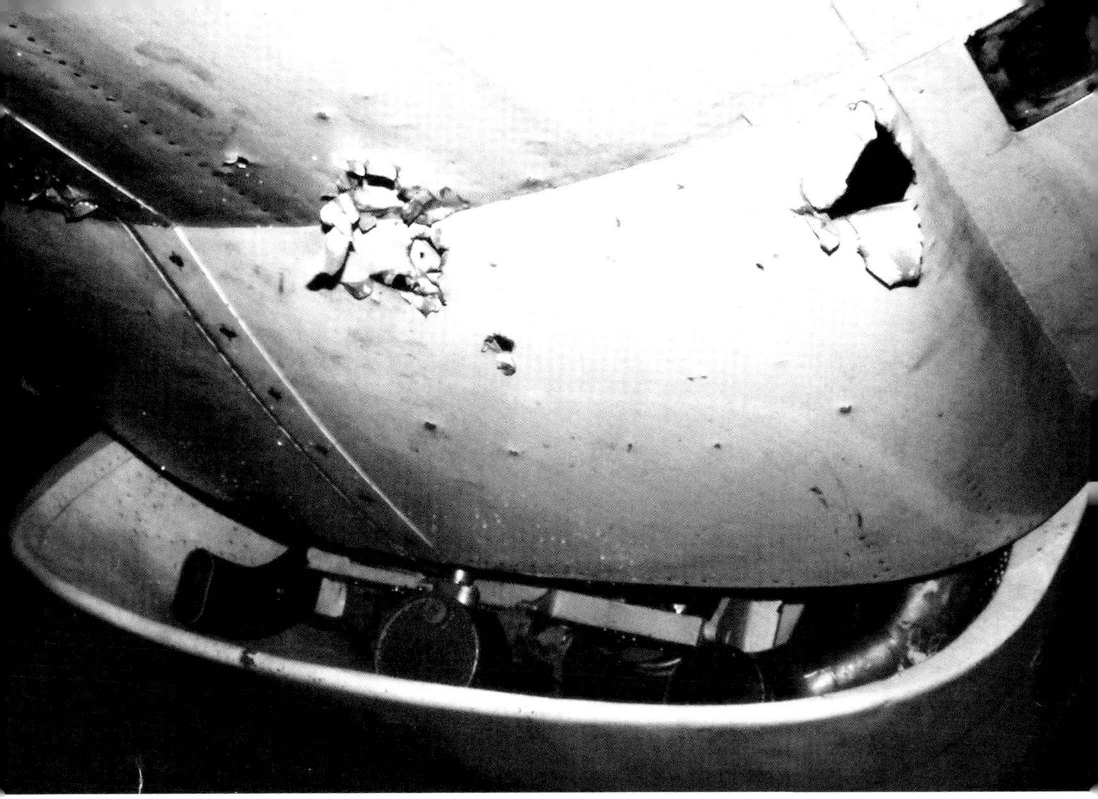

XL231's fuselage after HDU impellor disintegration – 25 May 1982.

mid transfer. The tanker in contact on his centre hose at the time was left in the dark, literally, as all the underwing lights in Badger's aircraft cut out. Fortunately, he was able to break contact and clear onto the wing without realizing the severity of the situation.

This unfortunate failure at the first refuelling bracket gave us no option but to terminate the raid. It was one of the very few Operation Corporate missions that was aborted that could be directly attributed to a fall down on the part of Marham's Victor tankers. Not until we landed back on Ascension when I saw for myself the massive damage caused by the exploding HDU impellor did I realise how close the Tanker Force had been to losing two aircraft that night. In pouring rain, I took photographs of the perforated fuselage skin. Flying pieces of hot metal had punched through the aircraft's sides, creating jagged holes as big as your fist. The rear fuselage was peppered with gaping holes around its circumference. The aft bomb bay and fuselage No 12 fuel tanks were located just ahead and to the rear of the hose drum unit's supporting frame. It seemed miraculous to me that every piece of flying metal had missed these critical tanks. Despite the fact that after the event, fuel was spewing all over the place from damaged components within the HDU, there was no fire.

During Black Buck 5 – the replanned missile attack against the Argentinian radar sites – I flew one of the long slots, which lasted over nine hours. Unlike all the iron bombs that fell from the bomb racks as advertised, not all Shrike missiles left the rails when fired. As we met the Vulcan at the Rio rendezvous after his attack, I cleared the bomber astern for his final refuelling. Ernie's usual calm voice announced with a hint of trepidation that one missile was still attached to the starboard wing pylon. The fear in this situation is, that having made all the electrical firing circuits 'live' when intending to release the missile in anger, it could become rogue later. Although all switches would have been made safe after the attack, there was always a possibility that the missile might release and fire of its own accord. Clearly, as I write this account, luck was on our side on this occasion. As my crew was due a spell of rest and recuperation, I did not participate in the last two Black Buck missions.

The next two detachments to Ascension Island during the summer and autumn of 1982 were always going to be less rewarding, although the flying demand placed on the tankers and their crews showed little sign of slowing down. In the lead up to the surrender, we had taken yet another heavy receiver into our inventory in the shape of the Nimrod MR2 reconnaissance aircraft. Several operational missions in support of the submarine hunters were undertaken to provide that much-needed intelligence to the Task Force, as the offensive to retake the Falklands intensified. Hercules C-130 transport aircraft had also been modified with refuelling probes to improve their flexibility and effectiveness.

We had supported their highly secretive long-range 'drops' and priority missions in support of Special Force units from the outset of Operation Corporate. Following the surrender on 14 June 1982, the pressure felt by the seasoned Victor tanker crews alleviated considerably. The overall military priority shifted to one of reinforcement and resupply of the new Falkland Garrison. The need to improve the operational status of the airfield at Port Stanley was imperative. Although surface shipping was better equipped to undertake the carriage and supply of heavy stores, munitions, and airfield equipment, the process was slow. High priority items were needed, and the only way of achieving their dispatch and delivery was by air. An air bridge was established straight away.

The services of the Tanker Force were clearly going to be needed for the indefinite future on Ascension Island. The operational urgency of the ongoing South Atlantic missions was diminishing, yet the frequency and workload was certainly not. Throughout the following months, the air refuelling missions south of Ascension were almost exclusively in support of the Hercules transporters carrying priority freight. These sorties had their tense moments, principally because of the differences between the fast clean Victor aircraft, and the lumbering slow propeller-driven cargo planes.

A number of techniques had to be developed to cater for these differences. In particular, the freighters had insufficient power to create the overtaking speed to make contact on the hose whilst in level flight at altitude. To overcome the problem, we would meet our playmate at the designated rendezvous altitude of around 23,000 feet, and pass him in a controlled slow descent that would enable him to 'chase' us down the hill. The process was dubbed 'tobogganing', and had the effect of reducing the excess power requirement of the turbo-prop whilst making contact. Unfortunately, it did mean that we often had to contend with the lower level cumulus clouds, which would have to be circumnavigated in order to avoid the inevitable turbulence. Many of the transport pilots were new to the air refuelling business, and they often needed longer periods of time to make contact. It was not unusual for the Victor to end up grovelling around 10,000 feet or even lower to accomplish a successful refuelling.

With my final detachment on the island coming to a close, I got the opportunity to have one last fling around Ascension. A flight of six Phantom air-defence fighters had started to assemble on Ascension. The plan was to deploy them to the Falklands mid October to establish an air-defence capability over the Falkland Islands. Having escorted the last inbound pair from the African coastline, I had arranged to link up with the four resident fighters on Ascension. I then flew across the side of Green Mountain with my six chicks as a salute to the visiting AOC 18 Group who was paying his respects at the governor's residence. We then did an impromptu display back at the airfield as a farewell for the fighters before their deployment south.

Back at Marham in early December, I flew alongside my station commander, Gp Capt Price, in my trusty airframe XL189 of Black Buck 1 fame once more. The task was in

Leading six F-4s over Wideawake Auxiliary Airfield – 8 October 1982.

support of the emerging TriStar trials being undertaken at Boscombe Down, something that I would be closely involved with in the future. The Falklands campaign had resulted in a much-increased presence on the Falkland Islands by the end of 1982, and the demands of the Garrison had spawned a new air staff requirement. In particular, a wide-body transport/tanker aircraft was needed to support the longer-term demands of the South Atlantic air bridge. Hence the sudden interest in the suitability of a future large tanker for the Royal Air Force.

By way of a swansong in late December 1982, I was given a Leopard trail, refuelling Jaguars across the pond one last time. It was a fitting farewell with which to end a remarkable and fulfilling tour on Victor K2 tankers. We trailed our two feline friends to the Azores where I announced our arrival with a fly-past at the American air base at Lages. The following day, we refuelled them onto US Naval Air Station Kindley in Bermuda. Anticipating a welcoming committee, which included local dignitaries as well as the British ambassador, I took the opportunity of leading our formation one last time across the airfield on New Year's Eve. As a final bonus, we had the pleasure of staying at a five-star hotel for our twenty-four-hour stopover. Making the best of our short stay, we hired mopeds and we took a tour around the island. My nav radar did us the honour of wrapping himself around a tree after failing to negotiate a particular bend. Fortuitously, that earned us an extra day in Bermuda before Steve could bend his strapped-up leg and squeeze it into the back end of the Victor for our transit home on 2 January 1983.

The highlight of 1982 was without doubt the occasion of my investiture at Buckingham Palace. Having missed the opportunity for Eileen to see the Queen at the garden party that we were unable to attend, I did promise her that she would get another opportunity. It was a very proud moment to have Eileen and Richard witness the Queen presenting me with the Air Force Cross. As I bowed in front of Her Majesty, she said poignantly, "I understand you were a little short of fuel".

Receiving the Air Force Cross at my investiture – December 1982.

Chapter Eleven

Learn to Test – Test to Learn

Empire Test Pilots' School
January to December 1983

Towards the end of my tour on 57 Squadron, my boss, Wg Cdr Graham Curry, was keen to write my F.1369 annual report before his impending departure. What I did not expect was a glowing recommendation for the choice of my next posting – the Empire Test Pilots' School (ETPS). In the text, he referred to our overnight trip to RAF Kinloss when we had been discussing amongst other topics the defensive measures for the unarmed Victor K2. Apparently he had been impressed with my ideas and had been very receptive to some of the crew procedures that I'd demonstrated during the flights there and back. I thought we were just going up to meet with his brother on the Kipper Fleet and have a few beers. His carefully drafted words obviously did me no harm whatsoever.

ETPS Course photo in front of Lightning T5 – January 1983.

The world's premier test pilot school was located within the Aeroplane and Armament Experimental Establishment (A&AEE) at Boscombe Down. It had not escaped my attention that two colleagues of mine with a tanker background (both ex-214 Squadron) had been accepted for test pilot training in recent years. One in particular, Sqn Ldr John Brown, came as no surprise because he was a well-respected squadron pilot who impressed us all with his analytical mind. On 214 Squadron, he was known as 'Joe 90': star of the famed science fiction TV series dating back to the 1960s. The other was Sqn Ldr Tony Banfield, who has featured earlier in this book, and was almost like a mentor to me. I had flown with him often in the Tanker Force, and had followed him to CFS and the instructing world where our paths had crossed occasionally.

Operation Corporate had raised the profile of air-to-air refuelling operations, and the pivotal importance of the tanker as a force extender. With the need to reinstate the in-flight refuelling capability in the Vulcan B2, and incorporate the same for the Hercules, the AAR qualified test pilots at Boscombe had been very busy during 1982. Clearances that would have taken months, even years in peacetime, had been rushed through within a few weeks. Not only did the same occur with the probe fit to the Nimrod MR2, but also it was decided to give that aircraft a self-defence capability in the form of Sidewinder air-to-air missiles. At the same time, some of the retiring Vulcans were being converted into tankers to supplement the over-worked Victor tankers in the air-defence role. Both John Brown and Tony Banfield had been directly involved in many of these priority trials and flight envelope clearances, not only in the lead up to Operation Corporate, but also throughout the remainder of 1982. Not surprisingly, the Queen decorated them both for their valuable services.

In the aftermath of the Falklands War, the Victor K2s were rapidly approaching their fatigue life limits, despite a number of in-service extensions. For some time, their replacement in the form of the VC10 tanker variants had been under development. This programme needed to be ramped up in the face of the increasingly fatigued Victor airframes. Looking ahead a couple of years, the next generation TriStar tanker would generate a whole raft of performance and handling trials before it could be cleared for service into the RAF. Both new acquisitions would need air-to-air refuelling envelopes cleared, not only as tankers, but also as receivers. In a nutshell, there was going to be an urgent need for AAR experienced test pilots, and sooner rather than later. Against this backdrop, my interest in ETPS took on a new perspective during the late summer of 1982. At that point, both John and Tony were on B Squadron: the heavy aircraft test squadron. I had been actively encouraged by them both to consider applying to ETPS. I finally plucked up the courage and attended the interview process at Boscombe Down. I had prepared myself as much as possible, and was pleased to make it through the interviews, despite falling a little shy of the educational requirements. The balance had been tipped in my favour by my proven experience as a receiver pilot. This particular background was seen as an absolute pre-requisite for the next heavy-aircraft test pilot student. By the end of the year, I had received confirmation that I would be joining No 42 Fixed Wing Course starting in January 1983.

The week before enrolling in the school, John Brown invited me to have a look around the heavy test squadron, and meet a few of the people with whom I would be working (hopefully) in the future. More interestingly, he offered me a spin in one of the three Hawk T1 fast-jet trainers that were a part of the ETPS fleet. Never having flown the Hawk before, I jumped at the chance with vigour. I got to put this great aircraft through its paces, rather too energetically for John's liking.

The next day, I hopped in the right-hand seat of the school's Andover C1 at the invitation of the ETPS chief instructor. The following day, I had my first experience in one of B Squadron's Harvards with my other ex-214 friend, Tony Banfield. On 20 January 1983, before my course had even started, I was offered the opportunity to fly the first conversion (convex) exercise in the Hawk with one of the school instructor test pilots. Incredibly, I finished off that same afternoon in a Gazelle helicopter with the superintendent of flying otherwise known as 'SOF'. In the week before the course had started properly, I had flown five times in four different aircraft types, none of which I had flown before. Welcome to the world of test flying.

As accommodation was available on the base, we were able to move into our fifth married quarter immediately. Although rather neglected, our new home did have a back garden that was the size of a football pitch, a great incentive for Richard. Thinking that I might get the chance to meet some of the other students, I went to happy hour on the Friday.

The mess facilities at Boscombe were somewhat quieter than those that I had frequented at my previous stations. Civilian employees rather than service personnel were used throughout the mess, and with the lack of resident squadrons, the bar was invariably empty when I turned up. The rather dour bar maid that met me on that first night did not fill me with eager expectation. However, the tempo of the evening soon took on another pace when a striking Sikh officer confidently strode into the bar. Sporting a blue turban and generous quantities of facial hair, he introduced himself as the Indian air force student. I immediately liked my new friend as we shared our first pint together.

By the time that I had established that he had flown Mig-17s and -19s, he had consumed half the contents of his glass. As he finished his beer in the time it took me to drink half of mine, he was ordering a refill. Clearly, my new colleague was going to be a challenge in the bar, although it would turn out he would prove to be a bit of a handful in the air too. Nevertheless, we had formed a strong bond by the time we said our farewells, and I was to enjoy the friendship of this likeable officer immensely over the following months.

Of the eighteen students who made up No 42 Course, only four including myself were RAF pilots, with another from the Royal Navy. Furthermore, I was the only multi-engine-rated flyer. There was a very cosmopolitan flavour to the remainder of the students, who came from countries all over the world. From North America, there was a USAF and Navy pilot, and a helicopter pilot from the Royal Canadian Air Force. Interestingly, a second Mig pilot originated from the Chilean air force.

In Europe, the air forces of Germany, France, and Italy were represented, along with an Israeli fighter pilot. To balance the cultural differences, two Aussie jocks and a New Zealander completed the pilot fraternity. Flight Test Engineering (FTE) students made up the remainder of the course: an Italian, a Frenchman and the only female from Performance Division at A&AEE. Of the pilots, four were rotary wing (RW), and eleven were fixed wing (FW) like myself. Eileen was impressed when I informed her that I was to be the course leader. However, I must add that this was purely because at thirty-three years of age, I was the most senior by some margin.

Ground school started with a bang as we revisited our school days and re-learned the disciplines of calculus and trigonometry. Although I had studied double maths and physics at A level, I was surprised to learn that the struggling RN helo pilot only possessed an O level grade in maths. With a generous teacher/student ratio however, he was afforded plenty of personalised one-on-one tutoring to get up to speed. Perhaps after all, my limited academic qualifications would not hold me back too much.

Once schooled in the art of test techniques, we started to brief for the first of the syllabus flight-test scenarios. This was to be undertaken in the Hawk. Accordingly, gaps in the ground-school programme started to appear where the fixed-wing pilots converted onto that aircraft, and the rotary-wing types got their kicks in the helicopter equivalent. The learning curve for some of the foreign pilots was steep, especially Mario from the Chilean air force. Not only did they have to contend with learning to fly a new aircraft type, but also they would need to acclimatise to the UK air traffic control environment with all the military 'lingo' that went with it. Perhaps I could demonstrate this with a short story. At this point, Mario had left his family in Chile while he settled in. As he was alone in the mess, I took him back to our quarter for a meal one evening. On being introduced to Eileen, he stood smartly to attention and bowed his head courteously. He asked Eileen in his rather limited English if we had a family. She answered, "Yes, we have one son, he's ten". Mario responded excitedly, "Ten sons – that's wonderful". Although the language skills of our Italian counterparts were quite impressive, their pronunciation could be quite comical at times. Schoolboy chuckles rippled around the classroom as the Italian FTE asked for a 'shit of paper' one day. By attempting to avoid a similar embarrassment on the next occasion that he needed stationery, he tried asking for 'a piss of paper'.

From the flying point of view, the language barrier worked very much in my favour. In the early weeks, the course instructors often asked me to fly in the back seat of the Hawk to assist those foreign student pilots whose English was not yet sufficiently fluent. We converted in turn onto the twin-turboprop Andover, which was quite a handful for the fast-jet jockeys. Needless to say, as the only multi-engine pilot, my services were in great demand for the mutual solos on this twin. I struck up a great rapport with the staff flight engineer whose job it was to keep us safe in this demanding aircraft, and I felt he was grateful to have me in the other seat to keep an eye on the fast-jet pilots. As usual, I would never refuse the opportunity to get extra hours in the air, even if it was nursemaiding the new boys.

It soon became clear that in the eleven months that we would be at ETPS, we were going to have to get checked out on all the school's fleet of aircraft with the minimum of instruction. We were not expected to fly the aircraft in question with the knowledge, skill and expertise that a squadron pilot would possess of course. However, we were expected to grasp the essentials quickly so that we could fly the aircraft as pilot-in-command and undertake the test profiles safely. After two convex instructional flights in the Hawk (not counting my flip with John Brown seven weeks before), I was sent solo. Although I had flown as the back-seater to the Indian Mig pilot the week before, I was not even afforded

ETPS Hawk T1 at the ETPS 40th Anniversary – summer 1983.

the peace of mind to have one of my pilot buddies in my back seat. This privilege (and on many subsequent occasions) was offered to Val Shaw, the female flight test engineer student who would only be permitted to fly in the company of a qualified pilot (usually me). I took it as a compliment that the staff pilots had the confidence in me to look after Val, who always seemed to enjoy her time in the air whenever we flew together.

As the first student flight tests got underway, a pattern to our training was starting to appear. Essentially, for the next few months, we would brief the test discipline in the classroom (e.g: manoeuvre stability) and discuss and plan the test points to be flown during the trial. We would then fly the test profiles over a number of sorties in the aircraft designated for that trial; and write up a comprehensive test report with all the test results, observations and recommendations as to the acceptability or otherwise of the aircraft to undertake that particular role.

We were being taught the process: 'learn to test', before as fully-fledged test pilots, we would 'test to learn'. This is the motto of ETPS that appears under the school's emblem. Much emphasis was directed at the format and style of the student reports. Not only must they be precise and factual, but also they must be written in such a language as to be understandable by those recipients for whom the trial was undertaken. I think that everyone without exception was astonished at the volume and intensity of the workload. By the time the first profiles had been flown in the Hawk, we were briefing the second phase, and putting together the sequence of test points that would make up each subsequent flight test. Airborne time was always at a premium, and there was little flex in the programme to repeat test points for whatever reason. Whilst we were undertaking the preparation for the next phase by day in ground school, we were expected to complete the report of the previous task during the evenings at home. It quickly became apparent that there were not enough hours in the day.

Another point that I would like to make about the ETPS training mentality was that we were not necessarily being prepared for future test duties on a particular group of aircraft. In other words, although I was the only multi-engine pilot, my test pilot training was not tailored towards the future testing of the RAF's heavy aircraft. As fixed-wing pilots, we were all checked out in turn on all types within the fleet, irrespective of background, and that included the sensational supersonic Lightning.

This was made no more apparent to me than at the end of March 1983. Not expecting to fly the two-seat Jaguar until much later in the course, on 28 March, I flew my first convex with the ETPS qualified flying instructor, Sqn Ldr Ron Rhodes. I always thought of all the QFI postings in the whole RAF, Ron had the best possible job. He had a very relaxed manner, but was authoritative in a way that was suited perfectly to teach such a diverse bunch of pilots. After one hour of dual-instruction sortie in the Jaguar T2 (which included shutting down one of the engines to practise its single-engine capability), I returned to the ramp pretty pleased with myself.

A fifty-minute second flight concentrated on flying in instrument conditions. The Jaguar was the most modern fast jet that I had flown at that time. It had an inertial navigation system (INS), which was first-generation equipment, and was notoriously difficult to operate whilst flying the aircraft – especially when at low level. The INS panel was located below the instrument panel and in front of the stick (control column) which made it very difficult to input changes whilst flying the aircraft. The engines, although not particularly powerful, had a reheat function which when employed, gave a significant extra thrust from afterburning fuel. The flight instruments were duplicated by the addition of a head-up display (HUD). The transparent angled glass mounted on top of the instrument coaming replicated the important information such as speed, altitude and attitude information, all displayed in such a manner that enabled the pilot to fly the aircraft 'head up'.

In a low-level role where it is imperative to keep the eyes outside the cockpit, this, piece of kit was essential. These three design features in the Jaguar were *all* new to me as a 'heavy' pilot. On the morning of 30 March, the ETPS boss checked me out on my third instructional sortie, and after forty minutes practising general handling and circuits, he cleared me to go solo. I swaggered off to the mess for some lunch, and returned excitedly to the flight line to fly the Jaguar as pilot-in-command.

I should say at this point that the school had two Jaguar T-birds (i.e. two-seaters) on its inventory up to a few months prior to my arrival. An unfortunate engine fire in one of these jets had resulted in the pilot ejecting with the loss of the aircraft. Unable to secure another T2 from the mainstream RAF, they were offered in its place a single-seat operational aircraft, the Jaguar GR1.

As I checked in at the ops desk for my solo, I asked who was scheduled to fly with me in my back seat. I expected a fellow student to accompany me on this critical first jaunt, if only to read the checks from the checklists. With a smirk on his face, the ops clerk pointed towards the green and brown camouflaged bomber – straight from the front line at RAF Lossiemouth – sitting on the ramp. Jaguar XX119 had not yet been given the ETPS 'raspberry ripple' paint job at that time. Not only would I have to fend for myself in this single-seater, but also this operational front-line aircraft carried a number of modifications and equipment changes not incorporated in the ETPS T2. Without the support of another pilot in the rear, I spent considerably longer getting the thing powered up. It took me quite a while to initialise the baffling inertial nav system, and I took a moment to get my head around the differences in the cockpit. As I pushed the throttles into the reheat detent on take-off, I recall thinking what was wrong with this picture; a tanker man about to get airborne in a current ground-attack bomber, with the grand total of 2 hours and 30 minutes on type. It was however, the best birthday present I could have expected as I blasted off the runway that day. It took quite a while before the grin was wiped off my face.

The phase of the course that required us to evaluate the Jaguar would actually come a couple of months later. I expected that part of the course to be the most demanding. Of all the students, I was probably the least familiar with the role of low-level bombing in a ground-attack aircraft: I was completely out of my comfort zone. On a positive note, (possibly a deliberate move by my mentors), I had checked out on the Jaguar much earlier than others on the course. This had given me the chance to slot in a couple of extra continuation trips, which allowed me to become more familiar with the jet.

Apart from the modern avionics already mentioned, the key to the Jaguar's strike capability was its navigation and weapon-aiming sub system (NavWASS). With a route stored in the navigation part of the system, the final positioning and timing cues were presented on the head-up display so that the pilot could keep his eyes out of the cockpit to give him the best chance of identifying the target. With seconds to go, visual displays

ETPS Jaguar T2 XX915 used for low-level bombing assessment flights.

in the HUD and audio warnings gave a countdown to the weapons release point. My job, as the student test pilot, was to assess the suitability of these visual cues and commands as displayed in the HUD, and in particular the effectiveness of their conspicuity and timeliness. I flew the Jaguar low level at 250 feet agl and 500 knots to replicate a typical squadron war mission.

During three flights in mid-June, I flew the T2 with instructors in the back seat to gain the familiarity with the NavWASS, and got my low-level flying skills up to speed once more. My relatively recent instructional tour in the Jet Provost at least had provided some currency in low-level flying, albeit at just 300 knots; i.e. five miles per minute. Navigation features go by pretty quickly at that speed. At 500 knots, I would be charging over the ground at more than eight nautical miles per minute. At this speed, the Jaguar airframe rode the terrain-hugging profile beautifully. It was relatively quiet, and seemed impervious to gusts and mechanical turbulence around the valleys and hills.

It came as no surprise to find that my one shot at this exercise would be scheduled in the GR1 single-seater. My syndicate instructor for this test phase was a former Jaguar pilot and instructor. He had openly showed me some contempt, as he did not expect me to perform well as the one ex-heavy man on the course. In the event, I got round the route without too much difficulty, and made what I thought to be a reasonable attempt at assessing the NavWASS.

I certainly enjoyed the demanding ground-attack Jaguar, and felt surprisingly comfortable assessing the jet in its operational role. It was acknowledged throughout the RAF that as a single-pilot weapons system, the Jaguar was rated as one of the more difficult aircraft to operate successfully. However, no one was more surprised than me when my tutor handed back my completed assessment with an approving smile on his face. To get his endorsement on this occasion meant a lot, and I do believe he saw me (and maybe the whole of the Tanker Force pilots subsequently) in a different light thereafter.

By way of a brief respite, another surprise that came our way was the opportunity to make a parachute jump. To avoid the possibility of any broken legs and ankles, we made the jump into water. The thought of drowning did not seem much better than a broken leg to me, but we had no choice. The danger potentially lay in getting dragged by the wind and being pulled under the surface after landing in the drink. To minimise this possibility, the Royal Navy would be on hand with their recovery craft. In particular, the group of vessels would be escorted by a large launch, which would deliberately point into wind so that we would know which way to aim our bodies on the point of impact. At least that was the theory. We were fortunate to have the parachute test facility at A&AEE, and so our para training was conveniently brief. The plan was for the whole course to fly in the ETPS Andover over Studland Bay, and make static-line jumps in sticks of four.

The fickle finger of fate was pointed at me as course leader once more. I would be the first one to jump in the first stick of four. The nearest thing that might have prepared me for this experience was a jump from a tower attached to a deployed parachute canopy on my Turkish exchange visit as an ATC cadet, sixteen years before. As the aircraft set up in the holding pattern over the drop zone, I was pretty nervous. As the senior student, I was determined not to show my fear, and kept a forced smile on my face as we stood like sardines next to the open door.

We were in the holding pattern at 3,000 feet above the bay. The red light was on as we prepared to jump, but at the last minute, the light extinguished indicating not to go. The bullish physical training instructor who was our jumpmaster yelled at us to stand slack while the aircraft described another holding pattern. The surface wind as reported by the observer on the launch below was outside the 15 knots limit prescribed for our drop. After two further aborted runs, I was starting to lose interest. As I stood by the open door, I was hanging onto the adjacent pole with white knuckles, still trying to look cool. On the fourth pass, the green light illuminated and I hesitantly leapt through the gap assisted by a helpful slap on the back from the jumpmaster. With eyes tightly shut and hands crossed across my chest (possibly in prayer), it seemed a lifetime before the static line yanked my parachute from its bag and I swung violently into the prone position.

The noise from the Andover's engines faded away as a serene calm took over. I opened my eyes and, as instructed, checked the silk above to ensure no snags, and started to enjoy the remainder of the descent from around 2,000 feet. I looked for the boat below that would give me the correct orientation for entry into the water. Adjusting the risers to face in the same direction as the pointy end of the boat, I braced myself for the dunking. As my boots hit the water, I was surprised to be pulled sideways and the left side of my body and head smacked into the choppy waves. I struggled to get on my back and adopted the star shape that would hopefully prevent me from being dragged under.

Once stabilised, I was aware that the still-inflated canopy was pulling me through the water, and I was cognisant that I needed to ditch it quickly. After giving the harness buckle a good punch, I was relieved to be stationary in the water, and watched as the canopy collapsed and settled onto the waves. A Zodiac screamed up to my side within seconds, and a couple of matelots dragged me unceremoniously into their dinghy. I was surprised at the choppy water and the strength of the gusting wind. I was hauled onto the main launch, where I was surprised to see one of my stick of jumpers already on board. Smiles and pats on the back were in order, as one of our attendant tutors handed out the beers.

Some of the wives came along to watch our exploits that day. One of the crew on the boat had also videotaped our jump, and I was lucky to get a copy of the tape later. What I had not appreciated was that the third jumper in my stick had frozen at the door, and only after some physical assistance provided by the no-nonsense despatcher was he unceremoniously pushed through the door. Reviewing the tape, I exited normally, followed by my No 2, after which there was a significant pause before the third and fourth men appeared. Interestingly, it transpired that the boat had not been correctly facing into wind. This explained why I had been pulled sideways on entering the water. The second jumper was aligned 90 degrees the other way on entry, and so actually entered the water face down. Not surprisingly, he was immediately pulled under and submarined for some time before frantically getting himself back to the surface. Considering these conditions were marginal at best, and not wishing to lose one of us, our supervisor cancelled all further planned drops. Sadly, only my stick of four students got to jump, despite another aborted attempt the next day.

During April, I was flying a mix of Hawks, Jaguars, Andovers, and latterly the school's JP 5. By 13 April however, I satisfied every RAF pilot's dream, as I got airborne in the superb Hawker Hunter. This aircraft was utilised in a manner unique to the Boscombe Down establishment. The spinning of fast jets with swept wings was regarded as a particularly dangerous activity. The RAF training system gave the student pilot a healthy awareness and respect for these hazardous departures from the normal safe flight regime. At ETPS however, the examination of these aerodynamic phenomena would be taken to another level. The JP 5 was used to give all students a reminder of the classic erect spin characteristics. Our American cousins seemed to approach this part of the syllabus with some consternation, if not fear.

After performing erect spins in the JP, we progressed onto the swept-wing Hawk. Spin behaviour in swept-wing aircraft can be unpredictable, and recovery more difficult. In the test world however, the vagaries of spinning needed to be taught and understood in depth so that the future test pilot was equipped with all the tools of his trade. With the school's Hunter, the exercise was taken yet one stage further, the dreaded inverted spinning. No other test pilot school in the world taught this aspect of flight-test techniques. This was not a test to be undertaken solo. While we would be spinning our two-seat Hunter T7, one of the experienced ETPS instructors would always occupy the adjacent seat for safety reasons. Furthermore, a third ground-based pilot monitored the aircraft and engine parameters continuously throughout the spinning manoeuvre via telemetry links.

ETPS Hunter T7 XL612 used for inverted spinning tests.

The series of test flights included erect spinning to familiarise us with the Hunter's characteristic, concluding with the last sortie when the aircraft would be deliberately pushed into an inverted spin. The scenario was designed to replicate the result of a pilot inadvertently mishandling the controls in the extreme during combat manoeuvring. In this incredibly disorientating manoeuvre, the aircraft would describe a fully developed spin, albeit in an inverted condition. The US fighter pilots were very pleased to get this stage of the course behind them. I personally revelled in the opportunity to stray into an area of the flight envelope that few pilots will ever experience, especially deliberately.

USS *John F. Kennedy* in Portsmouth Harbour – July 1983.

Talking of the American pilots, Lt Cdr Andy Mechling had flown US Naval F-14 Tomcats off carriers. By sheer coincidence, his previous ship the USS *John F. Kennedy* made a visit to Portsmouth that summer. A popular student, Andy set about arranging a visit for the ETPS staff and students to see this iconic vessel. As we were taken to a boarding ramp next to the waterline, the massive hull towered above us like a block of flats. Accompanied by our wives, no one could fail to be amazed at this truly awesome aircraft carrier. Andy was in his element as he took us through the ship. The highlight of the visit was to be able to roam around the upper deck, and walk among the ship's complement of eighty combat aircraft. The flight deck bristled with Tomcats, Prowlers and helicopters. Eileen seemed as excited and impressed as any of the ETPS students.

During the month of May, I achieved the ultimate ambition of my RAF flying career. Together with Sqn Ldr Vic Lockwood, an experienced former Lightning pilot, I took to the skies in that iconic aircraft, the supersonic English Electric Lightning. Unlike my joyride a few years before in RAF Germany, I would get to fly the whole sortie from take-off to landing. XS422 was one of the RAF's few two-seat T5s still operating in 1983. It was used on the course to investigate the characteristics of longitudinal stability at supersonic speeds.

A detailed explanation of this aspect of aircraft behaviour is beyond the scope of this book. In short, I was tasked to fly the jet along the English Channel, which offered us a narrow corridor in which we were authorised to go supersonic. Once established in level flight at around Mach 1.4 (about 1,000 miles per hour) the test included jabbing the top of the control column to trigger any inherent instability about the lateral axis (i.e. from wing tip to wing tip). The aim was to observe the response of the aircraft and its ability to damp naturally any nodding or porpoising motion: an indication of the aircraft's inherent stability in supersonic flight.

As much fun as this was, the joy of any Lightning sortie was the take-off. The first sortie was purely an enjoyable introduction to this fabulous machine. Following Vic's brief, on the runway I hit the burners promptly to get the massive Avons into reheat as quickly as possible. The acceleration was stunning. Barely a third of the way down the runway, I lifted the aircraft off the tarmac, and checked forward slightly on the stick to hold her down close to the ground. The undercarriage was selected up smartly to avoid exceeding the speed limits for the gear doors as the wheels retracted.

By the time the jet was over the airfield boundary, I pulled 3-G into a vertical climb as the speed raced through 250 knots. As the large centrally placed attitude indicator scrolled to show degrees of pitch, a star-shaped symbol appeared at the 90-degrees up position, i.e. pointing vertically. A strong check forward at this juncture was required, as the soles of my boots lay parallel with the horizon. To conclude the manoeuvre, the best way to proceed en route was to pull the jet onto its back, and roll over to get everything back to normal. There was the briefest of moments to allow the adrenalin to settle and set the jet up for the supersonic run along the corridor. On the test flights, after the supersonic run was complete, it was necessary to turn to the north-west without delay to get the aircraft pointing back towards Boscombe Down. Every flight was critical as far as fuel was concerned. The Lightning was one of the few aircraft I have flown where you can actually see the fuel gauge needles winding down as the precious fuel is used, especially while the burners were lit. The half a dozen flights in the superlative Lightning will stay emblazoned in my memory for the rest of my life.

By August, there was no let up in the workload. I can't remember how many nights I worked well past the midnight hour, struggling to meet the deadline for the submission of test reports. Personal computers were still largely a thing of the future. Just one of our fellow students, the Australian pilot, had one of the original BBC computers. It was a very basic word processor, but in terms of reducing his workload and typing final reports, it must have been a lifesaver. My hand-written paragraphs would end up in a jumbled mess, circled and arrowed to give some indication of the correct order in which they should be typed. Eileen, my valiant proofreader (even then!) and secretary, would end up typing my missives long after I'd gone to bed, in the hope I might salvage at least three or four hours sleep. Often she had no idea what the technical descriptions and aerodynamic deliberations meant.

It was not unusual for us, sitting at the dining room table, to be burning the midnight oil. On one occasion we simply ran out of time. With dawn approaching, I resorted to dictating my notes as Eileen typed. I read aloud the test results that included data concerning control forces that I had felt at the yoke, i.e. control column. As I had to salvage at least a couple of hours sleep before going to work that day, I did not even have time to scan through Eileen's typing. The submitted reports were scrutinised ruthlessly by our staff tutors, and mine were never short of red ink. On this occasion, it came back with a concluding comment; 'You really got egg on your face this time Bob'. Eileen had inadvertently referred to the forces felt at the '*yolk*' rather than yoke.

In October, we got to fly the school's largest aircraft, the Argosy. Even by my standards, this four-engine goliath was a monster. Designed as a strategic transport aircraft, it was functional, if not ungainly. Twin booms supported vertical stabilisers at the rear, which were painted in the vivid red livery of the ETPS fleet colours.

ETPS Argosy C1 XN817 used for asymmetric handling assessments.

The cavernous cargo hold could have provided floor space for half a dozen F104 Starfighters: the type that our Italian fighter pilot used to fly. This interesting character was slight in stature, and typically Mediterranean in personality. For the asymmetric trials, the 'whistling wheelbarrow', as it was affectionally known, was ideal for this part of the course. Not surprisingly, as the only one on the course who was used to handling four engines, I was deliberately crewed with him as he led me out to the waiting aircraft. Bear in mind that this Italian stallion had flown little else other than the Starfighter, and spent much of that time flying at twice the speed of sound. He was affronted to be tasked with flying a four-engine transport aircraft with a maximum speed not much greater than the take-off speed of the F-104. In the company of our staff flight engineer, as we crewed out to the aircraft, he said to me, "Bob, I do not fly aeroplanes with propellers". Somewhat bemused, he then said that I would do all the flying, and he would take the notes – the very opposite of the brief for the exercise. The flight engineer looked at me, and looked thankful that the fiery Italian would keep his hands off the controls. That was indeed how we conducted the test. On the subject of our Italian colleagues, in early October the course members were treated to another short break. Our trusty Andover was the ideal transport to ferry staff and students to the Pratica di Mare test facility near Rome. On the way, we made a brief stopover at the French air force test school at Istres in the south of France. After refuelling, we skirted the southern edge of the French Alps and flew on to Italy. After our arrival, we were treated to a splendid lunch, complete with generous quantities of wine. What happened next was somewhat unexpected.

The chief test pilot got to his feet, gave a short presentation in broken English about the airfield facilities, and then beckoned us to follow him onto the flight line. I followed a bunch of other students into a G.222 tactical transport aircraft. Taking it in turns, we each got the chance to throw this agile transporter around the sky. With something of a carefree attitude, my instructor encouraged me to shut down one of the engines to do a little single-engine flying. So much for no drinking within eight hours of flying.

Approaching the end of the course, there was one last significant hurdle remaining. Known as 'The Preview', this consisted of ten hours of assessment on an aircraft in which the pilot had not flown. For most of the fast-jet guys, this involved sending them off to various bases where they would assess the Buccaneer, Phantom, or whatever the staff at ETPS could scrounge from the Ministry of Defence. Sometimes, this meant going overseas to the USAF test pilot school at Edwards AFB or the US Navy school at Pax River in Maryland.

For me, they had wanted to get a four-engine aircraft to suit my multi-engine experience. To my great surprise, they secured the brand-new BAe 146 at RAF Brize Norton. Two airframes had just recently been delivered to Brize to form the basis of the squadron that would become the Queen's Flight. As a civilian-registered aeroplane, the BAe 146 was being flown on the civilian register, and so a handful of RAF pilots at Brize with appropriate civil licensing were gaining experience on the new type. Normally, any aircraft accepted into the MoD's inventory would require a so-called 'release to service', which of course would be undertaken by the appropriate test squadron at A&AEE. Because of the way in which these two aircraft had been procured, Boscombe Down had not assessed the type to date, and so there was considerable interest in what I might find during the course of my preview.

Normally teams of two were allocated to each preview aircraft, and in my case, my cohort was the Indian Mig pilot. In the intervening months I had flown with my Indian friend quite a few times. On one continuation flight in the Hawk, with me guesting in the back, he had rushed into the air with his usual aplomb. His fighter background shone through, in that all he ever seemed to do was raise the gear and flaps and fly balls to the wall for the remainder of the flight. The other checks did not seem to interest him. On this occasion, he was trying to impress me with his agricultural aerobatics, when he pulled energetically into a loop. Accelerating vertically downwards as he came out of the manoeuvre, the aircraft started shaking violently. With the speed racing through 300 knots, I frantically looked around for the reason behind the vibration. Instantaneously, out of the corner of my eye, I noticed the flap lever had moved towards the flaps-at-take-off position. The maximum speed for this configuration I seem to recall was 210 knots. About to exceed this limitation by some margin, I called, "I have control" and carefully

BAe 146 aircraft used for the ETPS final exercise 'The Preview'.

started a gentle pull out whilst closing the throttle to reduce speed.

I appraised my front-seater of the fact that the flap limiting speed had just been exceeded by about 100 knots, and told him not to touch anything as I turned to base. Not wishing to move the flaps any more in case they might have been damaged (or bent at least), I landed back at Boscombe with the same flap setting and taxied back to the flight line. The reason for the inadvertent flap extension was considered to be as a result of his knee nudging the adjacent flap lever, something which we subsequently learned had happened in service before. Apart from a bruised ego, my colleague faced no action. Interestingly, it was found from post-flight inspection by the airframe riggers that this sturdy fast-jet trainer suffered no damage despite the considerable over speeding.

Not particularly excited to be testing the BAe 146 as you might imagine, he reluctantly joined my team along with the student flight test engineer and my back-seater Val Shaw. Over the next ten days, we travelled up and down to Brize Norton a handful of times. As a team, we divided the test profiles evenly, and took it in turns to fly as pilot-in-command.

I did manage to convince my fighter pilot friend that I should do the asymmetric flying for obvious reasons. It was during this period that I realised how relatively poorly paid the Indian air force officers were. Although he had wanted to be independent, this proud officer could scarcely afford to buy and run a car for the duration of the course. I had taken him on the first two runs up to Oxfordshire, but on the third, he was adamant that he would drive. I had avoided getting into his decrepit Triumph Herald saloon, as it looked like a rusting death trap. However, on this occasion, I could see how important it was to my proud friend, and so reluctantly I went along as his passenger.

He drove in the same manner as he flew. There was little finesse as he swung the little car into corners with abandon, and his foot was usually flat to the floor. I remember feeling distinctly uncomfortable as he drove without fear along the winding country roads. About thirty minutes from home, we were approaching a left-hand bend when the front end sagged, and the suspension dropped onto the road surface. I vividly remember the right-hand front wheel overtaking the car and careering into the ditch ahead of us. The car ground to a halt amid a flurry of mad steering inputs from the alarmed Indian to the accompaniment of screeching metal. Fortuitously, the road was very quiet that night, and there was no oncoming traffic.

It was difficult not to laugh at our desperate predicament as we extricated ourselves from the bruised motor. In the pre-mobile phone era, I recall I had to walk to a roadside phone box and called Eileen to let her know of our awkward situation. The need to get to Brize Norton that night was overriding, as we could not risk any set backs to the carefully planned schedule of our preview test flights. Not even sure of our exact location apart from the minor B road number that we were on, I gave Eileen as much information as I had, and hoped she would be able to locate us. In the event, she sensibly called on my trusted friend John Brown who gallantly offered to accompany her on the rescue mission. Eileen left me with my car, and she returned to Boscombe Down with John. As far as I know, the Triumph Herald is still in the ditch.

At our preview presentation, there were undoubtedly more people in the audience than at any other presentation that year. The fact that no RAF test pilot had yet got his mits on the newest aircraft in the RAF bridled an intense interest amongst not only the ETPS staff and other units at Boscombe Down, but also from the British Aerospace test team at Hatfield. There was little doubt that the aircraft would be suitable for the Queen's Flight role to which it had been assigned. However, over a ten-hour assessment of every aspect of the aircraft's operation, there would be certain features and handling characteristics that we would be forced to comment upon.

Preview team – the Indian air force student test pilot and engineer Val Shaw.

Provided the over-riding deficiency did not ultimately affect the safe operation of the aircraft (or its passengers), these items could be rated as 'unsatisfactory' in test pilot parlance. This classification implied that improvement or modification could be warranted, but the inherent airworthiness was not in question. A word however that was not banded about without due consideration was 'unacceptable'. This meant that the aircraft was not suitable for the role intended, and should not be given a permit to fly without rectification.

As the team leader, the first words I uttered at our presentation were "The BAe 146 is *unacceptable* in the role of VIP passenger-carrying operations". The atmosphere in the auditorium could have been cut with a knife. Even though my words were spoken from the mouth of an unqualified test pilot, they carried some credence because of the recognised training quality that was the hallmark of the Empire Test Pilots' School.

The observation had been levelled at an external door handle indication. We had discovered that this door handle could give the impression that the passenger door was locked when in fact the handle was not quite fully at home. Any ground crew looking up at the handle from the ground could not easily see any slight misalignment, and would in all likelihood signal that all was well. The cabin crewmember on the inside looking through the door's window would get the impression that the door was shut and all indications were satisfactory. However, if the cabin crewmember tried to open the door from the inside, it would be found to be jammed, and could not be opened. In an evacuation, passengers near the door would be unable to escape via that door. I seem to recall that our finding led directly to a subsequent modification of the door handle mechanism across the BAe 146 fleet.

It had always been impressed upon us throughout the course that as a test pilot, your assessment must always be unquestionably honest. When dealing with aerospace companies, as I would find out over the next three years, there could often be intense pressure upon the test pilot who dared to suggest the aircraft being assessed might fall short of the acceptable qualification; especially where this could lead to huge financial consequences.

The final graduation celebration was held in the officers' mess. The McKenna dinner carried the name of the second commandant of the Empire Test Pilots' School, Group Captain JFX McKenna. Sadly, he was killed whilst in post in 1945. Heads of industry represented a number of aerospace companies, and the table was adorned with silver trophies and cups. The principal guest speaker was the prominent and outspoken MP, Mr Norman Tebbit.

At the time I thought this was an unusual choice for such an occasion. However, having listened to him speak I could not have been more wrong. In his twenties, Tebbit had flown the early Meteor and Vampire jets, and had more than a few hair-raising stories to tell. On leaving the RAF, he then pursued a career in civil aviation, and flew the early long-range airliners and passenger jets for BOAC. He narrated his daring exploits with an infectious humour, and everyone was spellbound. As an antidote to the sheer hard work that every student in the room had produced over the year, Norman Tebbit was a truly superb remedy. After the presentation of the various flying trophies, we were all handed our test pilot's scrolls: the graduation certificate of the Empire Test Pilots' School.

I would not recommend the course to anyone from the workload point of view. I heard it said that for every hour spent in the air, ten hours would be spent on the ground producing the onerous test reports. However, from a pilot's point of view, there cannot be a more challenging and rewarding course in the whole of the aviation world. The eleven-month course crammed in the equivalent workload of a three-year university degree, and few would disagree with that. However, the privilege of being able to apply those lower case letters 'tp' after one's name in the air force list is a reward that few have achieved, and one that carries for me, an immense pride.

The McKenna dinner and graduation certificate awards – December 1983.

Chapter Twelve

Probing the Limits

B Squadron, A&AEE, Boscombe Down
December 1983 to March 1987

After the daunting preview exercise at the end of my course, I was able to take a few days off before easing across the apron to B Squadron's hangar. By this time, Tony Banfield had assumed the flight commander's position within the Heavy Aircraft Test Squadron, an appointment referred to as the senior pilot. A small group of non-test pilot staff pilots made up the squadron strength.

Two of these chaps had been part of the furniture for some time. Flt Lts Dave Berry and Clive Osborne were like peas in a pod, and both were very likeable people. Ostensively, they were there to provide a Transport Command presence; they were very experienced Britannia, Comet and Hercules route pilots. As QFIs, they kept us (the test pilots) current on the large transport aircraft, and the smaller communications aircraft on B Squadron's inventory. The latter included our resident Beagle Basset and later on, the Navajo Chieftain.

Another two QFIs provided the training and currency in the resident Harvards, Canberras, Andover and any other type that came onto our books. Aside from the boss who was also a graduate of ETPS, one further test pilot, Flt Lt Martin Pitt, made up the complement of four test pilots on the squadron. The other aircrew to be found in the crew room were a couple of experienced navigators, an air electronics officer (primarily for the Victor and Vulcan), and two flight engineers who made up the rear crews for those larger aircraft.

Trials would be handed down to B Squadron by our masters in the Procurement Executive (PE) headquarters that was housed in a Ministry of Defence building in London at St Giles Court: referred to as MoD (PE). The resident scientists and aeronautical engineers of Performance Division, colloquially known as 'Perf Div', were all co-located within a massive three-story building across the other side of the apron at Boscombe Down. These were the boffins who would break down the Air Staff requirements from MoD (PE) into individual trials. The trials would then be directed towards the three test squadrons: A Squadron (the Fast-Jet Test Squadron), B Squadron (Heavy Aircraft Test Squadron) and D Squadron (Rotary-Wing Test Squadron). At squadron level, the senior pilot would then allocate his test pilots their respective trials together with the Perf Div directives. However, before I could become useful to Tony, I would need to get up to speed with the squadron's aircraft.

Surprisingly, my first job on B Squadron was to fly with a British Airways captain – in a

Flt Lt Dave Berry (left) and Flt Eng Ron Hendrick (centre) in Andover XS606.

TriStar. In the aftermath of the Falklands conflict, the MoD had decided to purchase six TriStar-500s to take over the air bridge role in the South Atlantic. Fortuitously, British Airways was in the process of retiring their TriStars, and the MoD had jumped at the chance to purchase them. This was the first opportunity I would get to assess the TriStar's suitability to maintain close formation whilst station keeping on another aircraft. I realised that I was being groomed from day one to play a pivotal role in the future trials of the RAF's first wide-body tanker/cargo/passenger aircraft.

The following week, Tony Banfield informed me that I was going to take over from him as the project test pilot for the Nimrod MR2. As was the case at ETPS, most conversions onto new types were conducted in-house. I would no longer have to sit through weeks of ground school, followed by a string of instructional flights to gain the qualification to act as pilot-in-command. By the end of December, I had added two more new types into my logbook. As part of my Nimrod conversion, I flew the Nimrod MR2 over the nearby Larkhill Range above Salisbury Plain, dropping sonar buoys. The proximity of the plain next door to Boscombe Down was no coincidence: flight time was kept to a minimum when transiting to and from the dropping zones for flight trials.

Next, I flew the stretched Hercules C3 with one of the staff pilots for a brief familiarity flight – another aircraft with which I would become familiar before too long. In a two-week period since graduating from ETPS, I had flown no fewer than six types: Hunter,

Hawk, JP, TriStar, Hercules and Nimrod. I knew that I was going to enjoy this tour, and the year-long graft at ETPS was already paying off.

In the new year, 1984, I was surprised to learn that I would be renewing my currency on the Victor once more. Although Martin Pitt had a V-Force background, his experience had been with the Vulcan. The task of flying the Victor therefore fell seamlessly into my lap. Once more, I got dropped off at my old hunting ground, RAF Marham. As time was always of the essence with trials flying, I learned that time wasted on surface travel was unacceptable in the test world. With a variety of suitable aircraft available to hand on B Squadron, I would always be able to ask one of the staff pilots to drop me off using the Basset or even the Canberra. In fact, it would not be long before I started to get calls from A Squadron requesting urgent transfers of their fast-jet trials pilots up and down the country.

By the following month, I was jumping in and out of the JP, Hawk or Canberra to recover stranded A Squadron test pilots to Boscombe. Although it sounds a little crass, we seemed to use the fleet aircraft like executive jets. I must qualify that comment by pointing out that the flexibility the aeroplanes gave us saved enormous amounts of otherwise wasted time travelling between the companies, stations and associated ranges. As a bonus, the ad hoc flying was particularly useful in keeping current in those types when not engaged on trials flying.

As it was a little over one year since I had last flown the Victor, I planned to use the delivery flight of our test airframe from Marham to Boscombe as my refresher. I called Badger Brooks, who was still at Marham, and coerced him into occupying the right-hand seat on the positioning flight back to Wiltshire.

In the previous year Badger had been posted as an instructor to the Victor Operational Conversion Unit. We discussed what I would need to do to get current, and we crewed out without further ado. He was rather bemused to find out that I intended to return to Boscombe Down in the K2 with only one rear-crewmember in the back. The other person riding with us that day was Phil Davies; the only qualified V-Force air electronics officer at Boscombe Down. I'm certain that No 1 Group regulations would have called for the Victor to be flown by a five-man crew. However, when flown under PE regulations, I had the flexibility to crew the aircraft and undertake the flight trials in any way that I saw fit, so long as safety was not prejudiced.

By its very nature, trials work often involved flying to the edges of the flight envelope. In this case, it made very good sense to limit the souls on board to a sensible minimum for obvious reasons. As I entered the cockpit, Badger looked on with amusement as I took out the tools of my trade: a spring balance, and a wooden dumb-bell designed to measure control forces when attached to the control column. Tickled by the simplicity of my 'fishing rod' as Badger called it, he watched me as I fired up the K2 and set off to Boscombe. I enjoyed the relaxed atmosphere as two old 'Phoenix' buddies from 57 made short shrift of the hassle-free delivery flight. On arrival, I did a couple of touch-and-goes to get back in the groove, and under the watchful eye of my apprehensive friend, landed the aircraft after a familiarisation flight that lasted less than one hour. I felt comfortable and at home once more in my trusted tanker.

Victor K2 XH672 Marham to Boscombe Down flight – 23 January 1984. Note: wooden dumb-bell stowed at lower right-hand corner of fuel tray.

The trial with the Victor involved checking the aircraft's handling after it had been modified with up-rigged ailerons. Without getting technical, this measure was designed to lengthen the remaining service life of the tanker fleet as their ever-increasing fatigue problems worsened. The flight test engineer from Perf Div was Mr John Bradley, and he had planned all the test profiles.

Although not qualified as a rear crew operator, John flew with me and coordinated the planned test flights from one of the nav seats in the back. All that John needed was confirmation that none of the Victor's handling qualities had been adversely affected by the aileron modifications. Three test flights were sufficient for me to explore the aircraft's envelope in this new configuration. It was only required that I write a brief report to confirm my findings. Bliss! I had time to type up my own report, a far cry from the intense ETPS environment. Welcome to the real world of test flying.

I would go on to fly many times with John Bradley, especially in the Victor, and I was always astonished at the trust he put in me as I would throw him around in the aged jet. Interestingly, he saw idiosyncrasies in the way I flew the aircraft, especially during air-to-air refuelling. He had witnessed John Brown and Tony Banfield's refuelling techniques from the back seat of the K2 cockpit, and he was intrigued by the differing nuances employed.

Some time later, he used the data recording equipment to trace my specific control inputs during the making and breaking of contact whilst refuelling. The sinusoidal sequence of elevator inputs captured on the printout highlighted my individual signature style. I had never before realised that I was making so many unconscious and miniscule corrections to achieve the desired aircraft response. My technique could only have resulted from spending so much time in the Victor during air-to-air refuelling operations. The difference in handling style from that of my colleagues fascinated John. We formed a mutual and strong affection for each other's professional skills as a result of working together in this unique environment.

During February 1984, I completed my brief conversion onto the Harvard, the real workhorse on B Squadron. I flew the Harvard frequently over the tenure of my tour, and it never failed to give me great satisfaction. Used extensively by the RAF throughout the Second World War for *ab initio* training, its superb slow-speed handling qualities were ideal for the photo-chase role. Like all tail draggers, it could bite the unwary pilot, but I'm pleased to say that I never had a single mishap in this great aircraft. The Harvards on B Squadron were favourites with visiting officers of air rank, who had invariably trained on this rare aircraft. Occasionally, I was asked to give familiarisation rides to the new Battle of Britain Flight pilots as a pre-curser to their conversions onto Spitfires and Hurricanes.

B Squadron Harvard T2 FT375 – photo-chase aircraft.

About the same time, our squadron QFI, Jim Cox, briefly re-qualified me in the ETPS Argosy, which B Squadron used for parachute-dropping trials. Another in-house unit on base was the parachute test team. This group of 'reprobates' sported bushy moustaches, and grew their hair considerably longer than normal service personnel (Special Forces?). Their cavalier attitude towards jumping gleefully out of perfectly serviceable aeroplanes was bordering on the reckless.

On 1 March, I took the whistling wheelbarrow across the plain no less than four times. Each time, I flew a bunch of our hairy friends equipped with parachute harnesses and spare 'chutes to the dropping zone, where they jumped with alacrity from the rear side doors. By the time I got the aircraft back to the B Squadron ramp, they were booted and spurred and ready to go and do it all over again. In fact it became a race to see whether or not we could beat them home after each drop. Bear in mind that they had to drive back by surface transport after hitting the ground.

If I was not chucking them out of the boot of the Argosy, Hercules or Andover, I was usually flying in formation with the drop aircraft in the Harvard with one of Perf Div's video photographers in my back seat. The Harvard was ideal in this photo-chase role as it was fast enough with the big radial engine to keep up, and agile enough to follow the parachutists down after they had jumped. After the parachutist had left the aircraft, it was necessary to tip the Harvard on its wing tip and pull hard to describe a tight spiral around the jumper. My photographer's task in the back was to film the parachute deployment and record any irregularities in the 'chute's behaviour during the descent. We would debrief in the test team's crew room and review the videotape footage to reveal any problems.

On one occasion, I was briefed to expect that the crazy para, having established a full canopy, was intending to cut himself free and drop a second time to test the succesful deployment of the reserve 'chute. I can only assume he had the ultimate confidence in his equipment, or was concealing a third parachute somewhere under the reserve. From my point of view as the chase pilot, this took some skilful use of the controls to stay in a good position to enable my photographer to capture a good quality continuous recording of both deployments. Mel Davies, a 'toggy' from Photographic Section enjoyed the challenge as much as I did. We developed a really good working relationship in the Harvard – to say nothing of a really close personal friendship on the ground. He was keenly interested in flying, and I would let him fly the Harvard on our return trips, and give him frequent flips in the JP on continuation flights.

My next role-change came on 13 April 1984, when I dropped my first 1,000-lb bomb over the now familiar Larkhill range. Sadly, there were no fireworks as they were inert bombs. My ride on this and many more occasions was Canberra B(I)6 WT309.

Telemetry teams on the ground were positioned at my dropping zone to record the flight characteristics of the free-falling bombs as they described their trajectory to impact point. The beauty of these trials flights lay in the fact that my job was merely to fly the profile, and drop the ordnance on the target. The rest was up to the boffins in Perf Div as they returned to their offices to number-crunch the data from their telemetry observations. I was not required to write a single word. Bliss again. As far as they were concerned, I was simply an 'airframe driver' who was being paid to be a hooligan. These were thoroughly enjoyable sorties, and they enriched the varied scope of my day-to-day test-flying activities. Over the course of the next few weeks, I dropped as many 1,000

B Squadron Canberra B(I)6 WT309 – bombing trials aircraft.

pounders as Martin Withers had during Black Buck 1, albeit with not quite the same spectacular result. To add a little more spice, in late summer, I dropped a couple of torpedoes in the Falmouth range from the Canberra: an aircraft in which I was becoming very comfortable and was starting to like immensely. In service, the Canberra had proven itself as a versatile and reliable bomber and reconnaissance aircraft; on the Heavy Aircraft Test Squadron at Boscombe Down, it was fast becoming one of my favourite rides.

Back in the realm of air-to-air refuelling, the VC10 tanker programme was progressing well. The RAF was desperate to bolster the dwindling resources of the Victor fleet, and B Squadron had been engaged in clearing the new VC10 K2 and K3 tankers into service. My first involvement with the 'Ten' came on 2 May when I flew the VC10 K2 during a trial with Tornados: the aircraft that would eventually take over the air-defence role from the Phantoms.

The VC10 'K' models used the same hose drum unit as that in the Victor, although the underwing refuelling pods were upgraded marques. Refuelling envelope clearances for the fighters were routine, and the introduction of VC10 tankers into service presented few problems. Coincidentally, around the same time, I started yet another conversion onto the squadron's other prize asset, 'Canopus'. XS235 was the last remaining Comet 4C in the world, and was a reminder of those heady days when air travel was the preserve of the rich and famous. A former Transport Command passenger jet, Canopus had been converted for use as an airborne platform from which to control navigation and avionics trials in company with other development aircraft.

Many of the aircraft's systems and features were reminiscent of the previous generation of airliners. The pilots' seats were less than supportive and comfortable for a transport aircraft, and the cockpit design was quite dated. Nevertheless, it was a sheer delight and privilege to fly this beautiful and unique aircraft. Along with the Comet, another classic aircraft in B Squadron's hangar was the Britannia. Our staff pilots jealously guarded this superbly maintained historic turbo-prop, and the test pilots were rarely offered the chance to grace her flight deck. The Brit was established so that B Squadron could undertake overseas trials independently. It could carry a large complement of spares and personnel worldwide, although I regret to say it was used rarely during my stay at Boscombe. Sadly, I never got to fly the old lady. The rear of this immaculate aircraft opened up into a wood-panelled dressing room, and the toilets would not have been out of place at The Ritz.

As the Nimrod Project pilot, I became increasingly involved with that aircraft through the autumn of 1984. As additional modifications were made to the MR2, Perf Div generated more trials for flight envelope clearances. At the end of Operation Corporate, the carriage of defensive missiles by the Nimrod had been hastily cleared into service, and now, wing tip pods and finlets had been fitted to the tailplane; necessitating a further stamp of approval. The next time I crewed up to fly the Nimrod, it was bristling with four Sidewinder air-to-air guided missiles. It looked more like an aggressive big fighter rather than the stately reconnaissance aircraft it purported to be.

In addition to the stability testing, I had to examine the stalling characteristics to ensure no adverse handling resulted from the significant airframe changes. Stalling a big heavy aircraft comes with certain reluctance – but someone has to do it – i.e. the test pilot. As no staff pilot was on hand for one of these flights, I took along another colleague who was

Nimrod MR2 XV241 Sidewinder & Finlets Trials – 8 November 1984.

fulfilling a ground tour at Boscombe Down.

I'm not sure that my stand-in co-pilot, as experienced as he was, knew what he was letting himself in for. As the Nimrod tried its best to shake itself to pieces at the point of the stall, the wing drop and subsequent severity of the full stall at heavy weight caused my colleague some consternation. It was only after he had seen me recover from a handful of these violent manoeuvres that the colour returned to his cheeks and he was able to relax a little. He was much more at home in the JP on those occasions when I was able to offer him the spare seat when available.

During August, I started to travel up to the British Aerospace factory at Woodford. Evidence of the historic A.V. Roe Company still existed in lettering above the old hangar. The company was famed of course for the manufacture of the Avro Lancaster, Shackleton and Vulcan to name but three. In my day, BAe was overseeing the newest marque of Nimrod, the Air Electronic Warfare (AEW) variant, or Mk 3.

The Nimrod AEW3 had a revolutionary radar fit which was divided between large rotating scanners housed within great bulbous mouldings at the front and rear extremities of the fuselage. I was brought into the development trials at the stage when significant problems were causing real concerns about the viability of the AEW programme. My role was to fly the trials aircraft in the capacity of a service (RAF) test pilot along side one of the company test pilots. As test pilots, we got on rather better than the two halves of the radar installation that were at the source of the problem. I was also tasked to clear this aircraft as a receiver against the in-service tankers. The aerodynamic effects of the bulbous nose fairing had a marked effect on the basket behaviour as the receiver closed up during refuelling. Although I successfully demonstrated its capability to take on fuel,

Nimrod AEW Mk 3 on B Squadron's apron – September 1984.

some of the handling characteristics were far from satisfactory. I had a considerable difference of opinion with the BAe test pilot as he tried to influence my view of the aircraft's AAR suitability. (This brought to mind my observations at the end of my ETPS preview.) Before we came to blows, the AEW3 project was cancelled, as was its successor – the Nimrod MR4. This was a bitter blow for BAe at Woodford, who had committed a great deal of effort and money into the development. I thoroughly enjoyed my trips to Woodford, and appreciated the wonderful reception I always got from the test pilots and trials teams there. In fact, the chief test pilot, Robbie Robinson, all but offered me a job on my projected leaving date should I wish to take it.

Although I was relieved from writing lengthy test reports, my working days on B Squadron were always busy. I always tried to prepare for my next trial with diligence, and this often meant working during the evenings. One saving grace, however, was that in MoD (PE), we worked a five-day week as the vast majority of supporting agencies on base were made up of civilian workers. This even included the personnel who handled and serviced our aircraft. I did therefore get to see more of Eileen and Richard than had been the case during previous tours. I supported Richard in his football interests, and even provided the odd BBQ for his mates on occasion. One rather distressing event occurred after he came home from school one day however. Richard had been asked to write a story about his pet. Problem: he didn't have a pet. As he was allergic to furry animals, we decided to purchase a budgerigar, as it was felt this would have the least impact on the household and would need the least looking after. Eileen and Richard selected a bright yellow bird, and in a nod to our yellow Harvards on the flight line, they christened it 'Harvey'. When they went back to collect him, Harvey and his mates were squawking furiously, although there was a subdued little blue budgie sitting quietly on his perch in the corner. Ever the succour for the downtrodden, Eileen scooped him up, and 'blue' Harvey became our household pet and found a niche at Netheravon. Thirteen years later, he was still gracing our living room as a free-range budgie. I don't know if Richard ever got to write about Harvey, or even submit a test report on his flying characteristics.

By the end of my first year of test flying, I had flown over 300 hours on B Squadron, well in excess of the flying rate that the average squadron pilot could expect to achieve. Also, since leaving ETPS, I had checked out on no fewer that ten new types – all but one as pilot-in-command. The expectation of a new series of flight trials on the latest VC10 K2 and K3 tankers, the Hercules C1K tanker, and the new TriStar K1 tanker meant only one thing for the Heavy Aircraft Test Squadron at Boscombe Down – a very busy year. The timing of my ETPS course had been perfect. I was about to be rewarded with a variety of air-to-air refuelling trials, the likes of which had never been seen at the A&AEE before. As Tony Banfield was nearing the end of his tour, I was set to inherit his office and take on the mantle of senior pilot. To keep up the established numbers, another new ETPS graduate from the class of '84 had just been posted in. Flt Lt Dave Carpenter came to us with a long experience in the transport world, and the Hercules C130 in particular. As we were always inundated with dropping tasks over Salisbury Plain, Dave's arrival was particularly well received.

Around this time, one of our loadmasters had sadly lost a former colleague in a tragic accident. After the funeral, he had received a request to spread his colleague's remains over Salisbury Plain. An opportunity appeared after a Hercules trial shortly afterwards. On completion of the task, we flew the Hercules around the dropping zone once more to position for one final drop: the contents of the urn. With the ramp lowered, the loadie, together with a couple of other mates, strapped on their harnesses, and eased out towards the lip of the ramp. At the pre-briefed location, the loadie reverently and with great deliberation, held out his extended arm to deposit the remains over the plain below. Before the trail of ash could be spread by the slipstream, it was picked up by eddies around the fuselage sides, and came swirling back into the cargo bay. Within a few seconds, there was a grey mist throughout the back end of the hold, and everything in sight took on a dusted covering as the air cleared. How much of the remains left the aircraft was debatable. Most of the visual evidence indicated he was still with us, if not in spirit, in body. After landing, a somewhat less than reverent clean-up operation was undertaken as the boys retold the comical series of events.

The Perf Div release-to-service trials for the VC10 tankers were progressing well. As a tanker dispensing fuel to the RAF's fighters, much of the envelope had been cleared. However, the ability to receive fuel was next on the agenda. I flew both K2 and K3 marques against the Victor K2 tanker, and each VC10 against the other in both tanker and receiver roles. When compared with the Victor, the VC10 was actually much easier to fly in close formation and to make contact on the tanker's centre hose. The cockpit was considerably quieter, the transparencies were much larger, and there was considerably less ironmongery by way of window frames. The field of vision was far superior therefore, not to mention the fact that the refuelling probe – mounted centrally on the nose cone – was directly in the pilot's line of sight when holding station behind the tanker.

Hercules dropping trials over Salisbury Plain from Harvard chase.

The VC10 was heavier on the elevators when compared with the Victor. This design feature ensured that elevator control inputs would be made more deliberately and progressively, with the result of a smoother ride for the passengers. In spite of the heavier stick forces, close formation and refuelling were straightforward and well within the remit of the 'average service pilot'. This was the yardstick against which all piloting tasks were assessed when recommending release-to-service clearances. The maximum onload in the Victor was of the order of 50,000 lbs, as we had witnessed in the South Atlantic. With the larger fuel capacity of the VC10 tanker, and therefore larger anticipated onloads, it was required that I demonstrate a 70,000-lb transfer. This I completed later in the year, and the in-service VC10 AAR clearances were issued shortly after.

During the same batch of refuelling trials, it was only a matter of time before the C130 would need to be cleared. The Hercules aircraft were still the workhorses in the South Atlantic during 1985. They were totally dependent on air-to-air refuelling to fulfil the needs of the air bridge. In order to refuel from the new VC10 tanker, B Squadron would have to complete the entire gambit of clearances for the Hercules whilst receiving fuel from both VC10 tankers. My experience in the AAR role to date had been forged entirely within the large four-jets: Victor and VC10 types. Refuelling the Hercules was a completely new ballgame. Quite familiar with the type by that time, I was delighted to find that despite the different response from the turbo-prop, close formation flying and the refuelling

Victor K2 AAR trials from VC10 K2 / K3 tankers – 24 January 1985.

task was much the same. Making contact on the VC10 centreline hose in the Hercules marques was straight forward, and the refuelling clearances were issued without much difficulty.

One disconcerting feature of the Hercules refuelling fit was the location of its probe. Due to the layout of the flight deck ceiling and associated panels and switches overhead, the probe had to be mounted on top of the cockpit but to the side above the co-pilot's station. When viewed from the captain's seat, the probe was offset laterally five or six feet to the right-hand side. This required the receiver pilot to position his aircraft to the left of the tanker's centreline to ensure the probe was in line with the trailing hose. It proved helpful therefore during refuelling for the co-pilot to give a running commentary to his captain to assist him with his line up.

Still on the subject of Hercules trials, one of the things that never ceased to amaze me was the British Army's eagerness to drop things out of aeroplanes. No sooner had we finished one trial, but another airframe had to be collected from RAF Lyneham to conduct the next. It seemed to me that they always wanted to drop increasingly heavy loads. The enhanced capability of the stretched Hercules C3 spawned the latest round of tests. I recall one sortie where the load was in excess of 30,000 lbs weight, and another where the load consisted of two 18,000-lb packs. The problem with this sort of load was not necessarily its volume and mass. For the pilot flying the aircraft, there was more concern for the effect on the centre of gravity as the load traversed the length of the fuselage inside the hold. The reinforced floor was fitted with a roller arrangement so that a normal load could be pushed to the rear often by manpower alone. The very heavy loads were mounted on pallets, and extraction parachutes would be used to pull the heavy masses out. The 'chutes would be deployed into the slipstream from the back end of the ramp, and as the canopies caught in the airflow and filled, the drag created would pull on the leashes attached to the load. There was always a possibility that a load might become snagged, and jam against the side structure with potentially catastrophic results. Guillotines had to be on hand in this event to sever the extraction parachutes.

The standard test pilot technique for achieving this sort of test point was progressive. I had done several drops by the time I approached this set of test conditions. Approaching the dropping zone with my 30,000-lb load, I gave the green light to the loadmaster, and I could feel the load starting to move rearwards. To stop the nose from pitching up, I pushed the control column fully forward with straight arms in an effort to keep the cargo floor level. About the time I feared I would lose elevator effectiveness, and potentially lose control of the aircraft, the load dropped off the back end of the ramp. With full nose down elevator applied, the aircraft response was to pitch violently nose down. I had to reverse my control input vigorously to counter the trim change. The net result was like a see-saw motion in the aircraft as full opposite control inputs were traded in quick succession. There was no option but to accept the temporary out-of-trim forces caused by the rapidly changing centre of gravity. They had to be corrected for by aggressive and coordinated inputs through the longitudinal controls. My role throughout the trial as the test pilot was to assess the piloting skills necessary to compensate for the demanding sequence of events. The guidance as always was whether the degree of difficulty was within the skill-set of the average service pilot. Only specially selected experienced pilots on the tactical transport squadrons would undertake this demanding task, and so in clearing this particular drop combination, I would qualify that release-to-service clearance accordingly.

On a lighter note, we often conducted trials that were aimed at the particular needs of our Special Forces. Earlier in the year, I had been asked to undertake an unusual trial during which I was required to drop a team of marines from the Hercules. They were planning to vacate the aircraft in company with a semi-rigid inflatable. The trial was briefed as a hi/lo drop: a jump from high level with the intent of opening the parachutes at low level. I depressurised the aircraft at the drop height of 25,000 ft amsl, and called for the red light in preparation for the jump as we approached the dropping zone. My flight engineer who was observing from the front end of the cargo bay related to me over the intercom the sequence of events. The six men, all equipped with personal oxygen sets because of the depressurised aircraft, stood either side of the dingy holding it at waist height. After receiving the go-ahead from the team leader, I cued the green light to signal them to go. Like a well-rehearsed dance troop, they set off immaculately in step and launched themselves as one out of the aircraft. In perfect harmony, they were last seen, all six firmly holding onto their boat as they fell away from view. At what height they separated from their dinghy (assuming they did of course) and at what height they chose to pull the ripcord – who knows? I was certainly not privy to the debrief, and I'm sure no one outside the Special Forces was invited to share the results of the trial either.

With such a variety of aircraft at our disposal, we were in great demand to support the various air shows during the summer months. In August 1984, I flew the Harvard with my photographer friend Mel Davies into Bournemouth Hurn airport for the TV South Air Show. Eileen, Richard and Mel's partner Liz joined us during a beautiful sunny afternoon. We sat picnicking by the wing of our canary-yellow Harvard, and mixed with the public as they poured over our classic American trainer. Two weeks later, I took Mel again, this time in our quirky Basset, to the Battle of Britain display at RAF Finningley. In July 1985, Martin and I decided to fly the Canberras to Fairford for the Royal International Air Tattoo show. I would fly the B2, and Martin the B16, and the plan was to arrive as a pair. I led the formation as we departed Boscombe, and Martin tucked in tightly in echelon as we set course for Fairford. About halfway there, I was having difficulty with my intercom, and a short time later, my radio failed completely. I signalled Martin to draw up along side as I pointed alternatively to my mask and ear giving the thumbs down signal to inform him that I could neither transmit nor receive. Pointing ahead to invite him to take the lead, he gave me the thumbs up and overtook on the right-hand side. I slid underneath him and popped up on the starboard side of my new leader. I anticipated Martin would let ATC know of my particular comms difficulties, and concentrated on keeping a tight position. He pushed up the speed to add a little panache to our run in and break. Over the middle of the runway, Martin broke with a snappy roll to port, and I gave it three seconds before doing the same. As the gear and flaps were lowered downwind, I followed my leader in loose trail and landed in sequence. We parked up and congratulated each other on a slick arrival despite the problems.

During July 1985, I commenced an interesting series of trials in the Canberra B2 WH876.

This aircraft had been extensively modified. The cockpit had been re-arranged to permit a single-pilot operation, and a brand-new Mk 10 seat replaced the old bang seat. This had to be the most comfortable Canberra in the world. A rear bulkhead was installed to seal off the modified cockpit from the compartment behind. All other equipment was removed, as were the hatches over the top, to create one spacious open bay. A plinth was mounted on the floor upon which could be placed a test ejection seat complete with telemetry dummy. Martin Baker, the ejection seat manufacturer, had a continuous development programme in place to upgrade the in-service seats. This unique B2 was tailor-made to test the latest generation of ejection seats. On the pilot's control column, there was a firing button which when operated, triggered the firing sequence of the test seat in the rear bay. Over a suitable test site, the seat could be ejected from the bay, complete with dummy.

The firing characteristics, trajectory, dummy separation and subsequent parachute deployment could be monitored and recorded on film. Martin Baker leased the former MoD airfield at Chalgrove in Oxfordshire for these trials. I would set up on a pre-planned track, and overfly the field on speed and height to enable the ground telemetry team to calibrate their equipment and tracking aids. With radio confirmation that they were ready for a live firing, I would release the safety circuit master switches, and establish the test parameters for the run in. Calling at pre-set points, I would overfly the airfield, and at the target point, fire the seat. It usually went off with a terrific bang, which left a cloud of smoke and dust in my front cockpit, and left a lingering smell of cordite to boot. A fire extinguisher bottle strapped to the rear bulkhead by a quick release strap always managed to jump from its mounting, and end up on the cockpit floor. With a brief farewell on the radio, I would make my way back to Boscombe.

Canberra B2 (Mod) WH876 – ejection seat test vehicle. (© Crown)

On one occasion, I had the misfortune of a duff firing, and the seat stayed firmly on its plinth. The danger in that situation was that one never knew if a subsequent stray electrical signal might result in an inadvertent firing. I quickly adjusted my return routing to base so that I would avoid all built-up areas and villages. On landing, I put the aircraft down as smoothly as possible to avoid jolting any mechanism, which might cause me an embarrassment on the runway. Fortunately, all was well, the seat stayed firmly on its plinth, and the armourers made it safe back in dispersal. This trials aircraft was immense fun to fly, and gave me a great excuse to rush around the Oxfordshire countryside at anything up to 450 knots, and down to 100 feet over the ground or whatever was dictated by my trials officer. On completion of the last test firing, I ran around the racetrack one final time to offer the boys on the ground a chance to see the aircraft in action one last time. At 450 knots, I flashed across the airfield, pulled up, and victory rolled the jet as I departed Chalgrove. Only as I went through the inverted position did I remember the wretched fire extinguisher, which had thrown itself to the floor as usual. Fortuitously, by keeping a slight loading on the wings, I managed to keep it from smacking me in the face or damaging the instrument panel.

One of Boscombe's less well-known units incorporated engineering apprentices who had been undertaking the restoration of a Sea Fury T20. This aircraft had been around the base for many years, and had been restored to an airworthy condition a decade earlier. The Sea Fury was one of the fastest production piston-engine fighters ever built. Developed during the Second World War, it distinguished itself in the Korean War, and was credited with several kills against the new generation Mig jet fighters. The Bristol Centaurus engine that powered this fine aircraft was an eighteen-cylinder sleeve-valve monster that developed no less than 2,500 horsepower. The laminar-flow wing incorporated the very latest aerodynamic design features, which were largely responsible for its astonishing performance. It had a maximum speed of around 400 knots (460 mph), which was typical of the very best of the piston-engine fighters. During the latter part of 1984, I had been approached and asked if I would like to take on the project to get it airworthy once more. There was some information in the squadron archives from earlier days when one of my predecessors had flown VZ345. I contacted him, and was rather surprised by his adamant suggestion that I should stay clear of it. Clearly, it had not been an experience that brought back fond memories. Fearing I would never again get the opportunity to fly such an iconic aircraft, I set about getting better acquainted with this magnificent beast.

At the time, the Royal Naval Historic Flight at Yeovilton nearby was operating a similar two-seat Fury. My plan was to visit Yeovilton, and pick the brains of the display pilot in charge of their Sea Fury, Lt Cdr Keith Patrick. Keith suggested that he visit Boscombe, and test fly our aircraft. I had completed a number of engine runs, including full power checks for which we had to lash down the rear fuselage to reduce the possibility of the big piston engine nosing the aircraft over.

On 24 September 1984, Lt Cdr Patrick flew his aircraft WG655 across to Boscombe Down. We discussed the inaugural test flight of VZ345 in detail, and I flew the sensational Sea Fury for the first time, albeit from the back seat as a familiarisation ride. Keith put the aircraft through its paces, and he seemed more than happy that it matched up to the Yeovilton bird in all respects. So confident was he that when I suggested we spin the aircraft, he was not only happy to do so, but invited me to fly the manoeuvre. I briefed a four-turn spin, and eased back the power towards the entry. It auto rotated just like

Sea Fury T20 VZ345 full power runs (note lashing) – September 1984.

the Harvard, and settled comfortably into a stable spin, which I held for four turns. I recovered using the standard spin recovery technique, and apart from a slight overspeed from the rumbling power unit, it responded in textbook fashion. I recovered the aircraft to level flight, and asked Keith how it behaved in comparison with the Yeovilton Sea Fury. His reply totally bemused me. He answered my question by saying that he could not compare the two aircraft, because he had never spun the Fury before. He then casually said that I was the test pilot, so he thought he'd leave it to me to demonstrate the Fury's spinning characteristics.

In the afternoon, Keith gave me the benefit of his experience and conducted my first conversion exercise whilst I occupied the rear cockpit of the Yeovilton Fury. The following day, I took my place in the front seat of VZ345, and with Keith in the back seat, I consolidated my introduction to the aircraft under Keith's guidance. I flew a few circuits after some general handling, at which point he said he was happy with what he had seen, and duly departed to base. This impressively large aircraft caused great interest at Boscombe each time I fired up the massive radial engine. I would continue to get familiar with the aircraft and its systems during engine and taxi runs. My dedicated ground crew meticulously monitored the progress of their baby. A few days later, I took it into the air on my own, and spent 1 hour and 15 minutes in complete awe. I devised my own test plan to monitor fuel consumption, power settings, and most importantly, took numerous recordings of the engine cylinder head temperatures and other engine parameters. It was of paramount importance to maintain the correct oil temperature and oil pressure to ensure the sleeve valves were kept lubricated. Starved of adequate lubrication, these big radials had a habit of seizing without warning. I flew this remarkable aircraft on my second solo around the local counties, making fly-pasts at five different airfields. When each controller was informed I wished to fly through their circuit at the controls of a Sea Fury, they could not clear me in quickly enough!

I flew the Fury half a dozen times over the following weeks before undertaking my last flight on 17 April 1985. The weather was fabulous as I navigated down to the Isle of Wight for a photo shoot with one of my colleagues in a Hawk. The Needles offered a stunning backdrop that sunny afternoon. I made several sweeps around the western extremity of the Isle of Wight in company with the Hawk chase aircraft.

With the pictures in the can, I set off over the New Forest and past Salisbury to return to Boscombe Down. The circuit was clear, and I practised my aerobatics above the deserted airfield. The sound of the Centaurus must have been superb as I looped, rolled and generally thoroughly enjoyed myself that sunny afternoon. I discovered afterwards that most of the people in their offices had stopped working and gone outside to watch my impromptu display. After a roller landing, I turned finals for a full-stop landing. All seemed perfectly well as I crossed the airport boundary with the gear down and flaps set for landing. As the wheels touched down, I thought I had a soft tyre on the right gear. The right wing seemed to dip down, and the aircraft started to lurch up and down in a hopping motion. At the same time, a slight swing to port developed. One of the less desirable features of these big pistons is the poor directional stability during take-off and landing.

Sea Fury T20 VZ345 over the Needles – 17 April 1985.

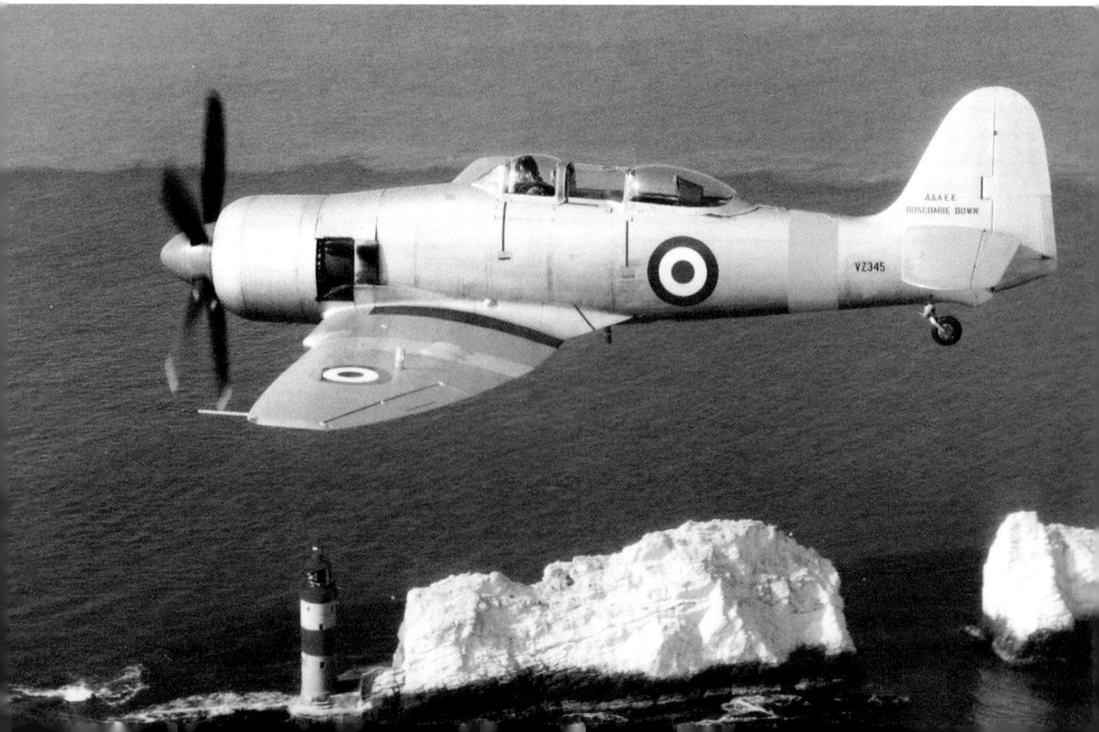

The immense power and torque effects from the engine can be controlled to some extent during take-off because the airstream from the propeller gives good rudder effectiveness, and therefore directional control. However the reverse applies on landing. As the power is pulled to idle the effect of the lack of airflow over the rudder is lost. If a swing develops, especially if there is no headwind to assist the rudder effectiveness, then the only option is to apply a little differential brake to the wheel away from the swing. At the end of this lovely afternoon, the prevailing wind had dropped to zero. I instinctively eased on a little braking to bring the swing under control, and unfortunately, the nose started to go in the other direction. This weathercocking action was the cause of many an accident in service with the heavy-piston fighters.

Things were starting to get out of control as I countered with a slight application of brake to the left wheel. Once more, the nose swung through the centreline, as I started to drift agonisingly towards the left-hand side of the runway. Although I stopped braking and resigned myself to a runway excursion, there were no obstacles on the grass to the left, which was certainly in my favour. However as I let the drift to port continue, I was aware the tail wheel was lifting. Any braking at this point would certainly encourage the aircraft to tip on its nose. I remember easing my backside off the seat, as I seemed powerless to stop the nose from lowering. In the next instant, the massive five-bladed propeller impacted the tarmac, followed by a progression of similar propeller blade contacts as the nose continued to dip. The inevitable followed as the prop dug in and the aircraft, as if in slow motion, started to tip head over heels. I remember exclaiming one unhelpful word "shit" as I went through the vertical and tumbled to earth upside down, the fin taking the brunt of the impact. I dared not touch any of the electrics for fear of sparks that might ignite the wet patches of aviation gasoline that started to appear on the ground. Weighted down by the heavy parachute pack strapped to my bottom, I found it impossible to move, let alone get out of the inverted cockpit. I waited for the emergency rescue crews to extricate me. The closed canopy was intact, although jammed as it was taking most of the aircraft's weight. I remember thinking that it would have been normal to take off and land with the canopy open in this generation of aircraft. Hindsight is a wonderful thing. Before too long, Boscombe's fire crews who had responded superbly to my predicament pulled me out.

Why had the tail continued to lift despite releasing the brake? After checking the archives, it was discovered that the pneumatic brakes on the Sea Fury had an unfortunate history of binding. VZ345 was removed to a hangar where it could be examined. The technicians were able to replicate the brake binding phenomenon, and I felt somewhat vindicated about damaging this beautifully restored historic aircraft after only ten hours of flying. I had witnessed the dangers of flying this classic piston fighter, and had, like so many of my predecessors, suffered at the hands of its deficiencies. I had walked away – unscathed – apart from a rather large dent to my pride.

As project pilot for the RAF's new TriStar tanker, I had been involved in the programme since the first modified aircraft came out of the shed at Cambridge Airport. Marshall of Cambridge Engineering (MCE) had received the contract to modify the six ex-BA aircraft and convert them into tankers at their company site. The first airframe, ZD950 was rolled out during the early winter of 1985. Boscombe Down and Marshall's test pilots would undertake the early flights together. The so-called contractor joint trials encompassed the basic handling and performance of the modified TriStar. Although the TriStar-500 had been flying on the civil register for a number of years, its maximum certificated weight was 228,000 kilogrammes. With the addition of the refuelling systems and associated equipment, not to mention additional fuel tanks, the all-up weight (AUW) of the new tanker increased to 245 metric tonnes. The aircraft would therefore require an extensive flight-test programme before it could be released for service in the Royal Air Force. Along with MCE test pilot John Blake, by late January 1986, we were assessing the aircraft's handling qualities whilst flying at the corners of the envelope. Doing this in a high performance fighter is one thing, but pulling 2½ 'G' at 435 knots in a wide-body transport-type aircraft is another. The tests were exhilarating to say the least.

The next handling characteristic to assess was engine-out performance immediately after take-off. Calm clear air was needed for these flights. The aim was to measure the two-engine climb performance at the appropriate climbing speed. For accuracy, the engine-out condition needed to be established as close as possible to the ground, and in calm conditions to ensure accurate data. Adopting the usual progressive approach, I chose to do these safety-critical test points over the English Channel during early morning. Before long, we were confidently shutting down the nominated engine, establishing the other two engines at their representative take-off thrust, and flying the test profile climbing from 2,000 to 4,000 feet above the Solent. The 50,000 lbs of thrust from the Rolls-Royce RB211-524 power units was more than sufficient to ensure an acceptable if not impressive two-engine climb capability in the event of an engine failure and continued take-off.

In order to overcome the inherent limitation of one centreline hose in the Victor and VC10 tankers, the TriStar hose drum unit, the Mk 17T, was designed with two independent hoses for flexibility and redundancy. I had the privilege of being the first test pilot to prod on the new tanker several months earlier using Canberra WH876 fitted with a dummy probe mounted on the nose. I made the preliminary assessment of both hoses on 16 July 1985, and completed fifteen successful dry contacts at speeds from 210–290 knots. In the follow-on refuelling trials during October, the hoses would need to be cleared to transfer fuel to the fighter receivers. Using their resident Phantom F-4, A Squadron test pilots started the fighter refuelling clearances on 9 October 1985.

Proving the refuelling capabilities of the larger receiver types against TriStar was less important, as the overriding priority was to clear the new wide-body for service in the South Atlantic. However, as a precursor to the later receiver trials, I was tasked to establish a limited provisional refuelling envelope to prove the TriStar K1 as receiver. I was given just two trials flights to do the job.

I arranged for a Victor K2 and VC10 K2 and K3 to rendezvous on a nearby towline, and over the two details, I was able to confirm the acceptability of the TriStar K1 to receive fuel from the three service tankers. During the second detail, I took on fuel to tanks full to demonstrate a maximum onload, taking the TriStar's weight up to the maximum

In the photo-chase Hawk filming Phantom AAR trial – 9 October 1985.

allowable in-flight AUW of 245 tonnes. Having done this, I deliberately disconnected and remade contact at that maximum weight; this proved the aircraft had sufficient excess power to remake contact in the event of an inadvertent broken contact. The TriStar was the most delightful aircraft to fly in close formation of all the aircraft I had flown in the AAR role; it was also arguably the least demanding to fly. At the conclusion of the contractor joint trials and the service handling and performance trials, the TriStar K1 was given the release to service to operate in the South Atlantic: the role for which it had been procured. Furthermore, the provisional assessments of the aircraft as a receiver in the AAR role were all positive. The Air Force Board was going to be delighted with their recent purchase.

Having cleared the fighters to take fuel from the TriStar K1, the next series of refuelling trials were directed towards the Hercules C1 as a receiver. The need for the Hercules to take fuel from the new TriStar tanker was seen as critical in the context of the continued air bridge. The Hercules refuelling speeds were considerably slower than those of the four-jets. The need to explore the lower speed handling characteristics of the Mk 17T hose/basket combinations had been anticipated in January. Problems had surfaced during these investigative flights. As a result, a number of modifications to the HDU motor settings had been introduced and a slower speed basket designed. On 13 May 1986, I collected TriStar K1 ZD950 once more from Cambridge. Through May and June, I flew the Hercules C1 no less than nine times on sorties lasting from two to six hours in duration. Over that period I made 171 refuelling contacts against the TriStar with the Hercules. During fifty of these contacts, fuel was transferred to prove the pumping capabilities of the twin HDUs. Although close formation with a turbojet aircraft behind

TriStar ZD950 refuelling trial with a VC10 K3 tanker – 10 April 1986.

another jet causes little complication as far as the engines are concerned, it is a different story with the turbo-props. The interaction between the downwash from the heavy tanker in front and the spinning propellers of the turbo-prop resulted in vibration concerns and handling difficulties in the receiver that bordered on the unacceptable in certain configurations. During one particular refuelling, my experienced flight engineer was looking down the length of the cabin to the rear of the fuselage as I maintained a close formation position. With several thousand hours on that type of aircraft, my loadmaster told me in no uncertain terms that he had never seen the rear end of the Hercules flex and twist to such a degree before. From the piloting point of view, I was gravely concerned for the structural integrity of the airframe as it was being subjected to such buffeting. Whilst exploring this phenomenon on two separate occasions, the HF aerial cables that spanned from the upper fin to the wing broke because of airframe flexing. Although I was able to demonstrate satisfactory contacts across a range of speeds and weights, it was clear that my release-to-service recommendations would carry a number of caveats for normal service operation. In one final disappointing event, I had permitted the test pilot in my right-hand seat to accomplish one particular test point. I had completed twenty-three contacts already, and the bulk of that trials flight was complete. However, as my colleague attempted the contact, the probe tip sheared, falling away fortuitously into the ocean below. This was the only time in my refuelling history that I witnessed a broken probe as a receiver whilst I was occupying one of the front seats.

With the more significant refuelling trials of the TriStar in the bag, it was time to continue with the performance and handling aspects of the basic airframe once more. Without doubt, the most enjoyable trial of my tour at Boscombe Down was about to land in my lap. On 7 July 1986, I flew the aircraft via a sub-polar route directly to the west coast of the United States. Designated as the 'hot and heavy' performance trials, we would be operating from the USAF test facility at Edwards Air Force Base, California. Accompanying me on board was a complete performance division team and engineering

Hercules C1 XV191 refuelling trial with TriStar K1 – 5 June 1986.

support of forty personnel, which would enable us to be entirely self-sufficient. As the trials project leader, I was required to clear with our American hosts a series of test flights, which would explore the TriStar's engine-out performance at maximum AUW in the hot conditions of the Mojave Desert. With the benefit of the tests undertaken in the UK already, I could afford to start this sequence of take-offs at quite a heavy weight. Perf Div's intention was to keep the duration of each test flight to a minimum, to avoid unnecessary flight hours and therefore fatigue on the airframe. The authorised maximum landing AUW for structural reasons was 180 tonnes. Any take-off appreciably above

TriStar K1 ZD950 at Edwards AFB, California – 9 July 1986.

this weight would require me to delay landing and burn fuel off to reduce weight. An alternative of course was to deliberately jettison fuel to reduce weight, which would permit a quick return to base. The day after our arrival, I met with the base commander to clear this jettison procedure, which had been provisionally approved by correspondence some weeks earlier. After giving the colonel an overview of the trials programme in the company of my colleague John Bradley, I reminded him that we would be dumping fuel to get down to landing weight on virtually every planned sortie. He seemed to be taken completely by surprise at this revelation and retorted that he would have the Sierra Committee all over his back if they knew that it was our intention to throw tons of fuel all over the mountains. When I suggested that we could alternatively use the Mojave Desert or the Pacific Ocean next door, he similarly objected because of pressure from other environmental agencies. This was a serious body blow, as it put in question the whole trials programme.

I retired with John to consider our alternative options. Landing above the 180-tonne limit was permitted only in emergency circumstances. Although physically capable of withstanding a landing right up to the maximum AUW of 245 tonnes, the landing gear and its components would almost certainly suffer structural damage. In this event, an overweight landing inspection and non-destructive testing of all components would put the aircraft out of service for weeks. However, we were in between a brick and a hard place. We mused over the possibility of landing, 'gently', at higher weights. Provided I could approach the situation progressively (the test pilot mantra), it would seem to be the only option, especially as there was little flexibility in finding an alternative test venue without incurring unacceptable delays to the programme.

I agreed with Dave Carpenter, that in order to avoid an inadvertent 'heavy' landing which would scupper the whole programme, and for the sake of continuity, I would perform all overweight landings. Fortunately, with so much at stake, Dave saw the common sense in one pilot learning from the benefit of repeated heavy landings, and this is how we proceeded. Under John's direction, the take-off weights were progressively increased, and I landed the aircraft at progressively heavier weights, starting at the normal maximum weight of 180 tonnes. By the time I had flown the twenty-two test profiles, I had taken off at the maximum authorised AUW of 245 tonnes no less than seven times. On every take-off, we had shut down one engine at the critical stage: this enabled me to examine the two-engine continued take-off performance and handling qualities of the aircraft under extreme asymmetric conditions. More importantly, I had landed the aircraft at a weight in excess of the normal maximum landing weight on sixteen separate occasions. Although the surface wind along the runway at Edwards was often quite gusty in the hot desert, I'm proud to say that on no occasion did I do a landing that merited more than a cursory inspection. John was delighted that we had covered all the test points of the hot and heavy trials plan. As an aside, we had unwittingly saved a phenomenal amount of money for MoD (PE) by bringing back a considerable quantity of fuel on every flight that we might otherwise have jettisoned (in reality, 423 tonnes of fuel saved).

The flight tests were conducted over a period of twenty-two days, during which time we flew twice on four days. This was only achievable because we had been able to keep the duration of each flight to a sensible minimum. One of the most pleasing aspects of the trial from my point of view was the remarkable serviceability of our new acquisition. Despite repeated engine shutdowns, we did not suffer any significant systems failures that dictated a premature sortie cancellation. Only on one occasion was there a failure of one of the hoses that required us to land with it in the trailed condition. Apart from an orientation flight two days after our arrival, every trials flight delivered usable and valid test data.

To provide a touch of variety, I could not waste the opportunity of doing a spot of sightseeing on one flight a week or so before our departure. After the test points were completed on 27 July, I planned an excursion for the crew and test team on board, and flew east towards Colorado. On a day when visibility was unlimited, I cancelled the flight plan for the route with the air traffic control agency, and was cleared to descend and continue visually, i.e. without the need to talk to any controller. This gave me carte blanche to fly the aircraft towards the south rim of the Grand Canyon. I flew the jet at around 4,000 feet above the gorge to keep us clear of light aircraft. I weaved a course visually following the meandering canyon all the way to Lake Mead in Arizona. Popping up to the south of Las Vegas, I called the tower at McCarran Airport at Las Vegas for permission to fly through. The ATC controller was taken aback at our sudden appearance out of the blue, and asked us to state our aircraft type. I responded, "TriStar", until I realised this would not register with him, and quickly corrected it to "Lockheed Ten-Eleven" (the American designation for a TriStar). Without hesitation, he cleared us to join the pattern, and I ran the TriStar along the length of McCarran's runway. He thanked us for the visit, and handed us back to the Edwards complex for our return to base.

Flying TriStar ZD950 above the Grand Canyon – 27 July 1986.

There had always been a strong connection between the ETPS and those test pilot schools of the USAF and Navy. I offered the USAF test pilot students at Edwards AFB the opportunity to ride along on several flights to observe the test techniques during our flight trials. They came in their droves and I filled the TriStar's flight deck on a number of occasions. I had a hidden agenda of course: to fly one of the test centre's two-stick F-16 Fighting Falcons. As we neared the end of the detachment, I was informed that a request for approval for my flight in the F-16 had gone all the way to the Pentagon. The red tape was clearly too much, and I had to settle for a consolation flight in an F-4E Phantom.

This was quite a disappointment from the flight in the latest generation F-16 fighter that I had been promised. Never wishing to pass on a new experience, I gratefully took the ride and flew in the back seat of the two-stick Phantom the day prior to our departure. The view from the instructor's rear seat in the aged jet was poor at best, but at least my pilot let me do all the flying. The flight itself was very interesting as we were providing photo-chase for a US Marine AV8B (the US Navy's version of our Harrier) engaged in engine relighting trials.

After saying our farewells to our hosts, I brought the TriStar home along a southern great circle route, and on 5 August 1986, we landed at Boscombe Down after a very successful and rewarding deployment. I flew the TriStar several more times in October, mainly with the intention of getting my boss up to speed as I was approaching my tour expiry date. For some time, there had been rumours that a position for a squadron leader 'heavy' test pilot was vacant in St Giles Court at the MoD (PE) in London. My current tour had already exceeded the normal 2½ years, and I knew the Air Secretary's Branch was on my tail again. As an ex-Cranwell cadet, I was assured a full career in the RAF until the age of fifty-five if I chose to take it. However, I had the option to leave if I so wished at what was referred to as the thirty-eight point. My 38th birthday was on 30 March 1987, barely four months away. I had deliberately tried to keep a low profile with my posting officer. To some extent, my position as senior pilot and involvement with the TriStar programme had protected me to date. I was eventually called up to Barnwood where my future career prospects would be explained to me: the occasion was known colloquially as the 'palm reading'. I should have had this appointment at least a year before my thirty-eight point, but for obvious reasons, I had been deliberately putting it off. Not sure whether I would leave or stay, I listened intently as my desk officer caressed his crystal ball. He then glibly mentioned that I had been earmarked for the MoD (PE) position in London, before nearly choking on his words. He clearly should not have made me aware of this imminent posting, as his flushed cheeks and nervous disposition attested. I was finally to be grounded in an office, and at the MoD in London. Having gone through the whole of my RAF career in nothing but flying appointments, the future looked decidedly gloomy – especially after the last wonderful four years. I saved the poor chap any further embarrassment by letting him know that his slip of the tongue had just enabled me to make the definitive decision to leave the Royal Air Force at the end of March 1987. He had done me a real favour. I suggested any further discussion was probably a waste of his time and I went back to the car to tell Eileen my news. They still got their pound of flesh, in that I would have to commute over the next couple of months to fill the appointment until they could find another candidate. I still managed to squeeze in a multi-engine training course at CSE Aviation, Oxford Kidlington Airport. This was a prerequisite to the award of an airline transport pilot's licence. The rest of the time was spent on disembarkation leave, which I used at the London Polytechnic to study for the ground school subjects. In retrospect, I graced the corridors of power at MoD (PE) in London on few occasions, as I pulled out all the stops one last time to avoid the dreaded ground tour.

I would get a final opportunity to fly with Clive Osborne on B Squadron one last time on 6 March 1987. This would be a CAA 1179 type rating on the Navajo Chieftain, in preparation for my planned venture into the very different world of civil aviation. It was wonderful to get back into my 'grow bag' one last time, and enjoy the banter with my old pal 'Ozzy'. For the time being however, there was time to share one last toast as I bade farewell to my friends and colleagues in the crew room at Boscombe Down.

Farewell drinks with OC B Squadron Wg Cdr Dennis Stangroom and the boys.

Chapter Thirteen

Breaking Contact

Initially, I thought of calling this chapter 'Closing the Hangar Doors'. On reflection however, after twenty years as a pilot in the RAF, I could not imagine doing anything else but fly. Although the thought of flying passengers in a straight line from A to B in a civilian aeroplane had never particularly appealed to me, I was certainly not ready to close the hangar doors on my flying career. A more appropriate analogy would be more like breaking contact at the end of a refuelling bracket, and positioning behind the hose for another maximum onload.

Although I have always thought of my career as a hobby, my wife Eileen has always suggested it was much more of a passion. The fact that I managed to stay in the cockpit throughout my RAF tenure, especially as an ex-Cranwellian, must be something of a record. During the 1970s, it was considered normal that after two consecutive flying tours, a ground tour would be inevitable. In my case, I had always managed to avoid flying the mahogany bomber, located in the corridors of power at Group or Command Headquarters. I left the service therefore with no animosity as the RAF had met if not exceeded all my expectations. As I approached my retirement date at the end of a remarkable test pilot tour at Boscombe Down, there could be only one career path to follow.

I used an accumulated eight weeks of leave to study for the all-important civil licenses. At the same time, I applied to a number of airlines, and to my surprise, I was offered a job with Cathay Pacific: every civil pilot's aspiration. My hopes were dashed shortly afterwards however when the offer fell through. By sheer good fortune, and within two weeks of retiring, I was contacted by Monarch Airlines and offered a first officer's position at London Gatwick. In those uncertain times, I leapt at the opportunity and within days, I was converting onto the Boeing B-757. I was fortunate to get a command within two years. In that well-respected company, I flew the modern long-range Airbus A330-200 alongside a great bunch of professional cabin crews. My travels with Monarch took me all over the world. I even operated a memorable trip to the Falkland Islands routing via Rio de Janeiro. The occasion was the 25th Anniversary of the Falklands conflict. On 6 November 2007, I ferried 250 hardened paras and marines in the back of my Airbus from Brazil to the Falklands. There were more than a few tears shed as we circled around East Falkland Island to land on the RAF's new base at Mount Pleasant. I took my young crew to the runway at Port Stanley airfield, and witnessed the scars still evident from the 1,000 pounders that the Vulcan had dropped twenty-five years earlier. When I was offered a very generous redundancy package at the age of sixty-one, the decision to hang up my boots finally was surprisingly straightforward. I would never say that I do not miss the flying and the company of like-minded aviators, but I can say that I have not dwelled on the downside of leaving the job that I cherished so dearly. After a year or so, I toyed briefly with the idea of taking up gliding again at a local airfield in East Sussex. Although I enjoyed the introductory flight, the set-up was not for me, and I quietly slipped under the radar and made a speedy departure. Perhaps this was the time to close the hangar doors after all.

About the same time however, I was to learn of an old acquaintance in the form of XM715, one of my former squadron aircraft at Bruntingthorpe Airfield in Leicester. Part of a 'Cold War Jets' collection, it and a number of other ex-service jets were, and still are, occasionally taxied down the old bomber base's runway. I visited Bruntingthorpe with no particular agenda, and have been actively involved ever since. The aircraft are in various states of preservation and restoration, and the volunteers have an enthusiasm that is infectious. I have been re-acquainted not only with the Victor, but also a Nimrod, Comet, VC10, Canberra, Hunter, and various marques of Jet Provost. I occasionally blast down the strip in these jets, putting them through their paces. I limit the fast runs to around 100 knots, before reining them back to a gentle walking pace. The temptation to ease the stick back once the wings start to generate lift can be quite strong, despite the fact that some of them last flew operationally over thirty years ago. (XM715 did get airborne inadvertently just before my involvement at Bruntingthorpe, proving that she was still capable of flight.) Little has changed when I power up the four Conways of the mighty Victor, and set off all the alarms in the cars parked next to the runway. Of all the jets, the Victor still captures everyone's imagination as she accelerates away under full power, just as she did on Ascension Island back in 1982. The glorious sight of the huge brake parachute billowing behind the decelerating jet at the end of the run never fails to delight the admiring enthusiasts.

Eileen still sees me off on these nostalgic weekends as I choose to fill my nostrils once more with the smell of old leather, oil and aviation kerosene. The only difference is that now she can safely assume that I will stay firmly on the ground, even if the wheels occasionally may see a hint of daylight between tarmac and tyre. Asked by my mother many years ago where I was that day, the uncertain Eileen replied, "It's either Scotland or Malta". Whether it was indeed Leuchars or Luqa, at least she knows now that it is only likely to be Leicester.

As far as you are concerned Richard, there must have been many times in your early years when you wondered what dad was up to during those frequent absences. I hope these recollections go some way towards filling those gaps. The one saving grace was that I always had the peace of mind in knowing that you were there to support mum each time I fled the nest. It was always a treat to get your news from home when I was stuck in some of the more remote destinations around the world. Your airmail letters from 1982 for instance – which I still have – contained snippets of your day-to-day experiences (usually football-related), imaginatively illustrated with doodles and cartoons. I would like to think you inherited your creative talent from me, but that might be stretching a point. It may well be closer to the truth to say that it came from your grandad Arthur. In his later years, he used to pencil-sketch horses in particular with a freehand style of a talented artist. It was borne out of his close relationship with the animals during his early family years and subsequent military service. He would draw a rampant stallion, his personal steed, in such detail that every muscle and sinew leapt off the paper. He told me it was his favourite mount, appropriately named 'Bob', which literally carried him through the horrors of the First World War. Your sketches showed a similar flair: one stayed attached to my clipboard for the better part of two decades. It travelled with me in my nav bag as I flew around the world. Its message urged me to 'keep my jets cool', which clearly was good advice. I'm not sure the Bart Simpson thing did my credibility much good however.

Nevertheless, it must have kept me focused in the same way as my guardian angel had watched over me during that heart-stopping incident in the Victor in October 1982. You have no idea how much I looked forward to receiving the latest sports report from home: "I played football and we won 17-0. We got to the semi finals, we lost 2-0." Often the commentary was short and punchy, and of course, there was always an update on Tottenham Hotspur's progress in the league: "On Thursday Spurs beat QPR 1 nil. It was a great match." However, along with the rest of your footballing news came those marvellous gems that only children of a certain age can deliver: "I am on holiday for a week so I can play every day. I have a mouth in my football boots so please may I have a new pear [sic] with screw in studs." Priceless!

One of Richard's doodles that accompanied me for years.

As I reflect on my time as an RAF pilot, there is no doubt that I was very fortunate to have had such a fascinating and rewarding career. It was my choice that took me into the world of air-to-air refuelling: a superb role for the pilot who wants hands-on flying. Few people could hope to serve as an exchange officer, especially in such a fabulous place as Sacramento, Northern California. The opportunity of spending three years on a USAF squadron was quite remarkable, and many long-lasting friendships were forged. It was quite an eye opener to venture into the world of instructing, and that experience brought me surprising satisfaction. My return to the Tanker Force was neither planned, nor expected. After the subsequent Argentine invasion of the Falkland Islands in 1982, I was catapulted into the South Atlantic, and witnessed a series of events that were extraordinary and memorable in equal measure. The difficult situation in which my crew and I found ourselves during the first Black Buck mission stretched my piloting skills to the extreme. Arguably, those flying experiences and the legacy of the Falklands campaign shaped my aspirations into becoming a test pilot. As arduous as the Empire Test Pilots' Course was, the three years of test flying that followed presented me with opportunities and rewards that few pilots experience. At Boscombe Down, I was incredibly lucky to be involved in the flight trials of a myriad of heavy aircraft during such a volatile era. It was thrilling to explore the corners of the envelope, and have a real part to play whilst introducing new marques of aircraft into service. As the TriStar project pilot, I was instrumental in the proving trials of the RAF's first wide-body tanker. In clearing the air-to-air refuelling envelopes of the RAF's heavy aircraft, I was fortunate to fly ten different receiver types whilst refuelling against four variants of tanker. Assessing those aircraft as a military test pilot was without doubt, the ultimate accolade for any aviator.

During a flying career that has spanned five decades, I have accumulated almost 19,000 flying hours whilst 'slipping the surly bonds of Earth'. In the process, I have been extraordinarily lucky to fly seventy different marques of military and civil aircraft. As a Royal Air Force pilot, instructor and test pilot, I was privileged to serve in six different squadrons. In the specialist role of air-to-air refuelling, I made 'contact' on no fewer than 1,085 times. Many of these contacts were undertaken during critical operational and testing circumstances, and interestingly, I never personally broke a probe. I have worn my brevet with pride, and feel blessed that I was able to fulfil a lifetime's passion and hobby.

AIRCRAFT TYPES FLOWN

Airbus A320-212 & 214
Airbus A321-231
Airbus A330-200
Armstrong Whitworth Argosy C1

BAC 1-11
BAe 146-100
BAe Hawk T1
Beagle Basset CC1 & VS
Bocian SZD-9 Sailplane
Boeing B-52H Stratofortress
Boeing B737-300
Boeing B757-200
Boeing KC-135A Stratotanker

Cessna T-37 Tweet

de Havilland Beaver DHC-2 (floatplane)
de Havilland Chipmunk T10
de Havilland Comet 4C
de Havilland Sea Heron C20

Edgley Optica
English Electric Canberra B2, B(I)6 & T4
English Electric Lightning T5

Fiat G.91
Fiat G.222

Hawker Hunter T7
Hawker Sea Fury T20
Hawker Siddeley Andover C1

Jet Provost T3/3A, T4, & T5/5A

Lockheed Hercules C1 & C3
Lockheed Tristar -500, C2 & K1
McDonnell Douglas Phantom F-4E

BAe Nimrod R1, MR2(P) & AEW3
North American Harvard IIB

Percival Pembroke C1
Piper Navajo Chieftain PA-350
Piper Pawnee

Schelicher K13 & K21 Gliders
Scottish Aviation Jetstream T1
Sedbergh T21 & Mk III Gliders
SEPECAT Jaguar GR1 & T2

Taylorcraft Auster

Vickers VC10 C1, K2 & K3
Vickers Varsity T1
Handley Page Victor B1A, BK2P, K1 & K1A
Handley Page Victor K2

Westland Gazelle HT.3
Westland Lynx AH.5X
Westland Scout AH.1
Westland Sea King HC.4X
Westland Wessex HC.2

Total All Types: 49 (70 all marques)

LOGBOOK PERIODIC SUMMARY

PERIODIC SUMMARY 1ST JULY 85-30 JUNE 86			Day Flying			Night Flying			Flight Time		Instrument Flying	
			1st Pilot	2nd Pilot	Dual	1st Pilot	2nd Pilot	Dual	Total	Captain	Sim.	Act.
Date	Occasion	Class/Type of A/C	(1)	(2)	(3)	(4)	(5)	(6)	(7)	(8)	(9)	(10)
01 JULY	ANNUAL	JET										
1986		TRISTAR K1	131-10						131-10	19-55	1-50	2·40
		NIMROD MR2	35·05			1-15			36·20	36·20	-15	1·00
		NIMROD AEW	24·30			4-10			28·40	13-40		·45
		COMET 4c	42-10						42-10	28-45	1-55	4-15
		VICTOR K2	4·50						4·50		·15	·15
		VC10 K3		13·35					13·35			
		VC10 C1		5·10					5·10			
		CANBERRA B16	5·30						5·30	5·30		1-20
		CANBERRA T4	1-10						1-10	1-10	·30	·10
		CANBERRA B2	6·25						6·25	6·25		
		BAC 1-11		3·15					3·15			
		HAWK T1	19·30			·10			19·40	18·40		2·05
		JP Mk 5	7·10						7·10	5·55	·35	·25
		TOTAL JET	277·30	22·00		5·35			305·05	136·20	5·20	12·5
		TURBO-PROP										
		HERCULES C1	69·05			2-10			71·15	62·55	·50	1-4
		HERCULES C3	8·40						8·40	8·40		·5
		ANDOVER C1	9·55						9·55	8·10	·50	·3
		TOTAL TURBO-PROP	87·40			2·10			89·50	79·45	1·40	3·1

AND ASSESSMENT OF ABILITY

SECTION 6

PERIODIC SUMMARY			Day Flying			Night Flying			Flight Time		Instrument Flying	
			1st Pilot	2nd Pilot	Dual	1st Pilot	2nd Pilot	Dual	Total	Captain	Sim.	Act.
Date	Occasion	Class/Type of A/C	(1)	(2)	(3)	(4)	(5)	(6)	(7)	(8)	(9)	(10)
		PISTON										
		HARVARD T2	22·10						22·10	22·10		
		BASSET CC1	14·25						14·25	13·40	·30	2·15
		CHIEFTAIN C1		·45	1·10				1·55			
		TOTAL PISTON	36·35	·45	1·10				38·30	35·50	·30	2·15
	GRAND TOTAL		401·45	22·45	1·10	7·45			433·25	251·55	7·30	18·20

CERTIFIED CORRECT FOR PERIOD 01 JULY 1985 TO 30 JUN 1986

Signature: [illegible]
WgCdr OC B Sqdron

UNIT: 'B' SQUADRON A&AEE BOSCOMBE DOWN

Date :- 10 July 1986

ASSESSMENT OF ABILITY:- Above the Average

REMARKS:- - An Outstanding Test Pilot in the Flight Refuelling Receiver Role.

GLOSSARY

AAR	Air-to-Air Refuelling
A&AEE	Aeroplane & Armament Experimental Establishment
AEF	Air Experience Flight
AEO	Air Electronics Officer
AFB	Air Force Base
AFTS	Advanced Flying Training School
agl	above ground level
amsl	above mean sea level
AOC	Air Officer Commanding
AREFS	Air Refuelling Squadron
ATC	Air Training Corps or Air Traffic Control
AVM	Air Vice-Marshal
Avtur	Aviation Turbine Fuel
BFTS	Basic Flying Training School
Boomer	Boom Operator
Buccex	Buccaneer Training Exercise
Buff	Slang for Boeing B-52 Stratofortress
BW	Bomb Wing
C130	Lockheed Hercules transport aircraft
CAP	Continuous Air Patrol
CB	Citizen Band (Radio)
CCTS	Combat Crew Training School
CFS	Central Flying School
CO	Commanding Officer
Convex	Conversion
ECM	Electronic Counter Measures
ETPS	Empire Test Pilots' School
F-4	McDonnell-Douglas Phantom
Fg Off	Flying Officer
Flt Lt	Flight Lieutenant
FTE	Flight Test Engineer
FW	Fixed Wing
Gp Capt	Group Captain
GVC	Girls Venture Corps
Harrex	Harrier Training Exercise
HDU	Hose Drum Unit
HF	High Frequency
HQ	Headquarters
HUD	Head-Up Display
INS	Inertial Navigation System
IP	Instructor Pilot
IPU	Instructor Pilot Upgrade
JP	Jet Provost
KC	KC-135A refuelling aircraft
Litex	Lightning Training Exercise
Loadie	Air Loadmaster
Lt Cdr	Lieutenant Commander (Royal Navy)
LZ	Landing Zone
MCE	Marshall of Cambridge Engineering
Mk	Mark/Marque
MoD	Ministry of Defence
MoD (PE)	Ministry of Defence (Procurement Executive)
MR2	Nimrod Maritime Reconnaissance Mk 2 aircraft
MRR	Maritime Radar Reconnaissance
NCO	Non-commissioned officer
nm	nautical miles
OC	Officer Commanding
OCU	Operational Conversion Unit
Ops	Operations
Perf Div	Performance Division (at A&AEE)
Phantex	Phantom Training Exercise
PR	Photographic Reconnaissance
Prodding	In AAR, making and breaking contact with the hose
QFI	Qualified Flying Instructor
RFS	Refresher Flying Squadron
RPM/rpm	Revolutions per minute
R/T	Radio Telephony
RTB	Return to base
RV	Rendezvous
RW	Rotary Wing
SAC	Strategic Air Command
SAS	Special Air Service
SBS	Special Boat Service
Sgt	Sergeant
Shrike	Anti-radiation missile
Staneval	Standardization and Evaluation
STC	Strike Command
Stn Cdr	Station Commander
TAT	Terminal Airborne Tanker
Thud	Republic F-105 Thunderchief
TLQ	Temporary Living Quarters
Toggie	Photographer
Tourex	Tour Expiry (date)
UHF	Ultra High Frequency
USAF	United States Air Force
USN	United States Navy
Wg Cdr	Wing Commander
Wingco	Wing Commander

INDEX